GODS, RITES, RITUALS AND RELIGION OF
ANCIENT EGYPT

GODS, RITES, RITUALS AND RELIGION OF
ANCIENT EGYPT

A FASCINATING EXPLORATION OF THE MYTHS AND MYTHOLOGY OF THE WORLD'S FIRST GREAT CIVILIZATION, IN 370 STUNNING PHOTOGRAPHS

LUCIA GAHLIN

LORENZ BOOKS

6th August 2008   5405000029802b

For Richard and Dexter

This edition is published by Lorenz Books,
an imprint of Anness Publishing Ltd,
Hermes House, 88–89 Blackfriars Road,
London SE1 8HA;
tel. 020 7401 2077; fax 020 7633 9499

www.lorenzbooks.com;
www.annesspublishing.com

Anness Publishing has a new picture agency
outlet for images for publishing, promotions
or advertising. Please visit our website
www.practicalpictures.com for more information.

UK agent: The Manning Partnership Ltd; tel.
01225 478444; fax 01225 478440;
sales@manning-partnership.co.uk

UK distributor: Grantham Book Services Ltd;
tel. 01476 541080; fax 01476 541061;
orders@gbs.tbs-ltd.co.uk

North American agent/distributor: National
Book Network; tel. 301 459 3366;
fax 301 429 5746; www.nbnbooks.com

Australian agent/distributor: Pan Macmillan
Australia; tel. 1300 135 113; fax 1300 135 103;
customer.service@macmillan.com.au

New Zealand agent/distributor: David Bateman
Ltd; tel. (09) 415 7664; fax (09) 415 8892

Publisher: Joanna Lorenz
Project Editor: Debra Mayhew
Designer: Jez MacBean
Illustrator: Stuart Carter
Production Manager: Steve Lang
Editorial Reader: Jonathan Marshall
Picture Researcher: Veneta Bullen

ETHICAL TRADING POLICY
Because of our ongoing ecological investment
programme, you, as our customer, can have the
pleasure and reassurance of knowing that a tree
is being cultivated on your behalf to naturally
replace the materials used to make the book you
are holding. For further information about this
scheme, go to www.annesspublishing.com/trees

© Anness Publishing Ltd 2001, 2008

A CIP catalogue record for this book is
available from the British Library.

Previously published as *Egypt: Gods, Myths
and Religion*

CONTENTS

Introduction

Though the civilization of the ancient Egyptians was arguably not the earliest to flourish, it endured longer than any other, and in its heyday it was the most spectacular on earth. It emerged about 5,000 years ago and continued to flourish for three millennia. Much of the information about this remarkable country, and the people who lived there so long ago, has lain hidden in the sands for thousands of years. Their secrets are being gradually unearthed.

It was in the fertile areas around the great rivers of the Near East and North Africa that agriculture began, and with it came the beginnings of a settled, civilized way of life which proceeded to bear rich cultural fruits. The earliest evidence of settled farming communities beside the Nile dates from c.5500 BC. These grew into a number of chiefdoms, with distinctive regional cultures, in Upper and Lower Egypt. In Upper Egypt, social stratification and craftsmanship began to evolve and the cultural developments of the south gradually penetrated Lower Egypt to the north during the Predynastic and Protodynastic Periods, leading up to the country's political consolidation as a single state in c.3100.

▲ *In this intimate scene decorating the side of Tutankhamun's small gold-plated shrine, the queen ties her husband's floral collar behind his neck. 18th Dynasty.*

Egyptian religion

When Egypt was unified under a succession of pharaohs, many local gods were admitted into the national pantheon, giving rise to a vast number of deities and a complex system of beliefs and ritual. Religion was a fundamental part of the life of every Egyptian, from the mighty pharaoh down to the most humble agricultural worker, and the annual flooding of the Nile inspired many of the myths and beliefs of ancient Egypt. The people recognized their utter dependence on the revival of their agricultural land. The arid desert in which the people of Egypt were buried also shaped their identity and inspired their religious beliefs. For us, their religion

▼ *The king was the only mortal who could be depicted face-to-face with a deity. Here Ramesses II encounters Amun. 19th Dynasty.*

is one of the most intriguing aspects of the ancient Egyptians' culture – a wealth of gods and temples, mummies, ornate tombs and fabulous treasure. Centuries of plunder by grave robbers, followed by more systematic excavations by archaeologists, have revealed an incredible quantity of artefacts, buildings, imagery and writing that provide a fascinating account of the beliefs and practices of these ancient people. The wealth of documentary information left in the form of carved inscriptions and inscribed papyrus rolls provides us with an insight into all aspects of their religion and ritual.

A vast number of graves and tombs have been excavated. They reveal that the ancient Egyptians aspired to an Afterlife that was pretty much a continuation of their existence on earth (only more fruitful and prosperous), preserving their social status, family connections and even their physical possessions. They thought of their deities, too, as leading lives very much like their own. Their tombs and temples are therefore rich in decoration, inscriptions and artefacts that offer a detailed and vibrant account of every aspect of life in ancient Egypt. ◆

Timeline of Ancient Egypt

Before c.5500 BC

Early settlers in the Nile Valley; beginning of crop farming, growing wheat and barley.

c.5500–c.3100 BC
Predynastic and Protodynastic Period

Development of craftsmanship and animal husbandry.

Beginnings of social stratification.

Boats used on the Nile.

Construction using wattle and daub and beginning of mud brick.

Early wall painting and stone carving.

c.3100–c.2686 BC
Early Dynastic Period

Unification of Egypt.

Memphis established as capital.

Development of hieroglyphs.

c.2686–2181 BC
Old Kingdom

c.2650 BC

Step pyramid built at Saqqara during reign of Djoser.

c.2615 BC

Pyramid built at Meidum.

c.2580 BC

Great Pyramid at Giza built during reign of Khufu.

c.2530 BC

Great Sphinx built at Giza.

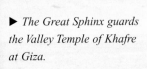

▶ *The Great Sphinx guards the Valley Temple of Khafre at Giza.*

c.2181–c.2055 BC
First Intermediate Period

Herakleopolitan and Theban dynasties control Egypt.

c.2055–c.1650 BC
Middle Kingdom

Egypt conquers Nubia, trades with Syria and Palestine.

Mudbrick pyramids built in Middle Egypt and at Dahshur.

Rock-cut tombs constructed in Middle Egypt.

c.1650–c.1550 BC
Second Intermediate Period

c.1600 BC

The horse is introduced into Egypt.

Hyksos claim control in Delta.

c.1550–c.1069 BC
New Kingdom

c.1550–c.1069 BC

Royal tombs built in the Valley of the Kings.

c.1348 BC

Akhenaten introduces worship of Aten, the sun disc, in place of established religion, and establishes a new capital, Akhetaten.

c.1336 BC

Capital moves back to Memphis.

c.1327 BC

Burial of King Tutankhamun in Valley of the Kings.

c.1250 BC

Ramesses II decorates the Hypostyle Hall at Karnak.

◀ *Nefertiti was the Chief Royal wife of the so-called "heretic" King Akhenaten. 18th Dynasty.*

c.1274 BC

Battle of Qadesh against the Hittites.

c.1209 BC

Egypt attacked by Mediterranean Sea Peoples.

c.1176 BC

Sea Peoples defeated by Ramesses III.

c.1069–c.747 BC
Third Intermediate Period

Egypt politically divided.

c.747–c.332 BC
Late Period

671 BC

Assyrians invade Egypt and reach Memphis.

525 BC

Egypt becomes part of the Persian Empire.

332 BC–AD 395
Ptolemaic and Roman Periods

332 BC

Egypt invaded by Alexander the Great, bringing it under Macedonian Greek rule. Alexandria founded.

305 BC

Ptolemy assumes power after death of Alexander.

30 BC

Egypt becomes part of the Roman Empire.

AD 324

Egypt adopts Christianity.

AD 395

End of Roman rule in Egypt.

The Land of Egypt

Ancient Egypt existed in a landscape of extremes, with vast expanses of arid desert bordering a narrow ribbon of wonderfully fertile land – and very little has changed to this day.

The Nile is Egypt's lifeblood. North of Aswan it flows for 900km (560 miles) through the Nile Valley until it reaches the Delta, which it traverses in a number of branches (five during the pharaonic period) before feeding its muddy water into the Mediterranean Sea. The silt it deposits is thick and black, inspiring the ancient Egyptians' name for their country, *Kemet* ('Black Land'). In contrast, the barren desert cliffs were seen to glow pink at dawn, so the desert was described as *Deshret* ('Red Land').

In ancient times, the Egyptian name for the summer season was *Akhet*, or Inundation. It was equivalent to the four months from July to October, when the great river overflowed its banks and flooded the Nile Valley and the Delta.

The huge volumes of water originated as rain that fell in central Sudan, raising the level of the White Nile. A few weeks later the summer monsoon rain falling over the Ethiopian highlands caused a very rapid swelling of the Blue Nile, and its tributary, the Atbara. All of these sources of water combined, reaching Egypt in a great swollen rush at the end of July.

Only in 1968 were the waters of the River Nile finally tamed, by the construction of the Aswan Dam. The Nile Valley is no longer flooded every year, and this has made a huge difference to Egypt's natural environment and way of life.

▲ *For most of the length of the Nile Valley, strips of fertile land border either side of the river, and the dividing line between desert and cultivation is clear-cut, as here at Tell el-Amarna.*

As well as providing ancient Egypt with, usually, two healthy harvests a year, the Nile was the principal means of transportation. It supplied much of the protein in the people's diet (in the form of fish and water birds). Ivory came from the tusks of the hippopotami that lived in the river, and papyrus was made from reeds that grew along its banks. Finally, the river was the source of mud, the chief ingredient of the most widely used building material – mudbricks. At the same time, the river could be treacherous: hippopotami, crocodiles, winds, currents, shallow waters and cataracts were all hazards that had to be taken seriously by the people whose lives depended on the Nile.

◀ *Scenes of agricultural life were commonly painted on the walls of private tombs. Here in their Theban tomb Sennedjem and his wife harvest their bountiful crops. c.1200 BC.*

The impregnable desert

The river was not the only place where danger lurked. The ancient Egyptians also particularly feared the desert. It was a place of searing heat by day and freezing cold by night, a waterless place of wild animals, fugitives and nomads. The desert dwellers often turned out to be marauders, and in addition there were countless demons who were supposed to live in the desert.

On the other hand, much of the greatness of the Egyptian civilization came from wealth yielded by the inhospitable desert. Its treasures included amethyst, turquoise, copper, limestone, sandstone, granite and – above all – gold. The desert lands also fulfilled another important function: they helped to make Egypt into an almost impregnable fortress. To either side of the Nile were the wastelands of the Eastern and Western, or Libyan, Deserts, to the north the Mediterranean Sea, and in the south was the first cataract of the Nile, which made the river unnavigable at that point. Egypt was protected from almost any outside threat. This resulted in an exceptionally stable society, and a strong sense of national identity flourished. A fear of the unknown resulted in a common mistrust of outsiders or foreigners (who were often described as *hesy*, meaning 'vile' or 'wretched').

▶ *The copper inlay around the eyes of this painted statue from the 5th Dynasty represents the green malachite scribes wore to protect their eyes.*

Harnessing nature

The ancient Egyptians were self-sufficient in most things, except for suitable timber for building. The agricultural cycle revolved around the Nile flood, which could usually be depended on. Measuring gauges known as Nilometers were used to record the flood levels, so that suitable precautions might be taken if necessary. Efficient irrigation was crucial to agriculture. Farmers practised basin irrigation: they built earth banks to divide up areas of the flood plain, then led water into these artificial ponds and allowed it to stand before draining it off. The system could be administered on a local level.

The major crops were emmer wheat, barley and flax. Tomb scenes and models illustrate the various stages: ploughing, sowing the seed, harvesting, winnowing, threshing, and so on. Also depicted are the production of food and drink, such as grape-picking, wine pressing, brewing and breadmaking.

The dual benefits of the Nile and the sun made the land of Egypt a flourishing place. But as with all natural elements, there had to be precautions against their dangerous aspects. As protection against the overwhelming heat of the sun, people had to wear headcoverings to guard against sunstroke, and protected their eyes by wearing green malachite (copper) or black galena (lead) eye paints. Rain is not usually associated with Egypt, but it did occur in the north, and sometimes caused floods in the desert wadis; such problems had to be coped with. It therefore becomes clear that the lives of the ancient Egyptians were very much dictated by their natural environment and the climate. ◆

The Longest River

The Nile is the longest river in the world, flowing 6,741km (4,189 miles) from its source in the East African highlands to the Delta, a fertile area of about 22,000sq km (8,500sq miles). The Delta, named by the Greeks because it resembled the shape of the fourth letter of their alphabet, lies 17m (57ft) above sea level. Here the Nile once split into several channels before emerging into the Mediterranean Sea: of these only two now remain.

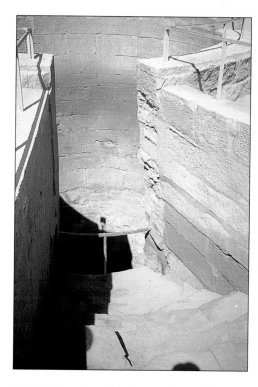

▲ *This Nilometer within the temple complex at Kom Ombo was constructed to gauge the river's rising level during the annual inundation.*

The Beginnings of Egyptian Civilization

▲ *The ceremonial limestone 'Scorpion Macehead' from Hierakonpolis, shows King Scorpion of the Protodynastic Period engaged in an activity that may be the ritual cutting of an irrigation channel, or perhaps a foundation trench for a temple.*

Ancient Egypt as people usually imagine it – as the land of the pharaohs, with great temples, cities and burial sites, beautiful art and writing in hieroglyphs – came into being with the formation of a unified and centralized state in c.3100 BC. The factors that led to this development are speculative, but the most momentous changes in Egypt's history took place around 3000 BC.

For the first few hundred-thousand years of human occupation, Egypt was home to stone-age, or palaeolithic, hunting, fishing and food-gathering communities, which lived along the river terraces of the Nile Valley. Then, from c.5500 BC, the earliest agricultural communities emerged. Over the next 2,400 years, the country came to be divided between separate, self-governing communities, which developed at different rates socially, economically, politically and culturally. These early developments can be traced mainly by examining the so-called Predynastic burials, which have been excavated at various sites throughout Egypt.

Material culture

As the local cultures developed, their craftsmanship increased in quality and sophistication. Pottery was painted and jewellery fashioned; stone-working became more elaborate, with the manufacture of palettes, mace heads, knives and vases; metal-working began with the production of copper tools; and the copper ore malachite was used in the glaze for beads.

A recognizably Egyptian style was already beginning to emerge in the items being produced, and the markets for such goods clearly became wider and more specialized. Desert resources, such as gold from the Eastern Desert, were exploited and we know contact was made with traders from outside Egypt, as lapis lazuli from Badakhshan in north-eastern Afghanistan has been found in Predynastic graves.

The evidence of such artefacts indicates that their makers would have been freed from subsistence farming and that society was becoming differentiated, with the

◀ *Celestial and bovine themes figure in what appears to be the earliest recorded religious imagery surviving from Egypt, such as on this Predynastic greywacke (slate) cosmetic palette.*

emergence of an elite who could afford luxury goods and who presumably controlled the trade routes, local irrigation systems and more elaborate building projects (especially tombs). Luxury goods may have been specially made to place in graves with the dead, and it seems that funerary customs played a major part in the increasing division of labour and the development of greater social complexity and stratification.

The exchange of goods would inevitably have been coupled with the exchange of ideas. The contact with Mesopotamia (modern Iraq) appears to have been particularly significant in the

early period of Egyptian civilization. It is likely that foreign traders would have been attracted to Egypt by the prospect of purchasing its gold.

A centralized state emerges

By c.3100 BC, Egypt was a highly efficient political state, with an administrative bureaucracy, precisely defined boundaries and elaborate kingship rites relating to a single ruler. So why did the Egyptian state emerge when it did? There have been a number of theories, reflecting various trends in thought. They relate to changes in the physical environment and climate, as well as external stimuli. It is most likely that a variety of factors coincided to create the major changes.

▲ *One of the designs most commonly found on Predynastic painted pots is that of a boat with cabins and banks of oars.*

▶ *The Protodynastic 'Two-dogs' ceremonial greywacke palette from Hierakonpolis is decorated with desert animals and two mythical long-necked beasts in the style of Mesopotamian art. The central circular area was for the grinding of pigments.*

Environmental changes are likely to have been tied in with a growth in the population, increased production, and the freeing of specialists from subsistence farming, resulting in the domination of the poor by an elite. It has been suggested that the growth in population caused the need for increased technology to meet the rising demand, which in turn resulted in the need for central organization. Other theories involve population growth leading to conflict between communities. The increasing aridity of the desert over the millennia would have led to the narrowing of the area of habitable land, thus concentrating the population, and Egypt is known to have experienced a wetter period followed by a drier period around 3300 BC. The movement of people because of climatic changes (especially northwards into the Delta region) may well have caused both alliances and conflicts, resulting in the emergence of chiefdoms. Territorial competition and the merger of local chiefdoms no doubt led to increased power in the hands of fewer people.

Outside influences

Cultural transfer, especially from Mesopotamia and Elam, is often considered to have been the catalyst for Egypt's formation as a unified state, and the simultaneous emergence of a highly developed system of writing (hieroglyphs). But the direction and impact of any contact is still highly contested. Egypt's political super-structure was very likely well under way by the time western Asiatic motifs started to appear in Egyptian art. Examples show that the Egyptians made use of foreign ideas in a very Egyptian manner and soon chose to discard them.

While the development of writing helped to consolidate the unification of the state – aiding administrative efficiency and speeding up the processes of centralization of power – there is no evidence that Egyptian hieroglyphs had their origins in a foreign writing system. The beginnings of Egyptian civilization, often referred to as the Unification of Egypt, remain hazy and speculative. ◆

Part One: State Religion

The key to Egypt's enduring stability and prosperity was the relationship between the pharaoh and the gods. The pharaoh was an absolute monarch who was believed to derive his power from the gods and who formed a link between them and the world of humankind. His mediating role was essential in maintaining the divine order that preserved the universe.

It was the pharaoh's duty to build temples and to ensure that offerings were made to the gods housed within them. In return, the gods would bestow blessings on the people, such as victory in battle, bountiful harvests and recovery from sickness. The Egyptian pantheon contained a vast number of gods and goddesses, each of whom might have several different forms or 'aspects', and the myths that concern them say much about the way in which the Egyptians perceived the divine world.

In his role as king, the pharaoh assumed divinity, but to some extent he was in fact a servant of the gods. It was the high priests who acted on behalf of the ruler in the great state temples erected throughout the country, which played a vital role in the structure of Egyptian civilization.

MEDITERRANEAN SEA

Alexandria

Buto

DELTA

Sais

Tanis

Busiris

Mendes

Leontopolis

LOWER EGYPT

Bubastis

the original obeli[sk] was sited at Heliopolis

Heliopolis

Cairo

SINAI

the mortuary temple of Ramesses II known as the Ramesseum at Abu Simbel

FAIYUM

Herakleopolis

MIDDLE EGYPT

EASTERN DESERT

LIBYAN DESERT

Beni Hasan

Hermopolis Magna

Tell el-Amarna

Assiut

the temple at Abu Simbel

Akhmim

Abydos

UPPER EGYPT

Dendera

Koptos

Qus

Naqada/Ombos

Western Thebes

Karnak

Armant

Thebes (Luxor)

mortuary temple to Queen Hatshepsut at Deir el Bahri

the late Graeco-Roman temple built at Edfu to honour the god Horus

Esna

Hierakonpolis

Elkab

Edfu

Gebel el-Silsila

Kom Ombo

● Ancient Sites

● Modern Cities and Geographical Features

Elephantine (As[wan])

Philae

1ST CATARACT

LOWER NUBIA

Main Cult Centres

The Nile river and the narrow, fertile band of arable land along its length has always supported the population of Egypt. It was along the banks of the Nile that people first settled. These settlements developed into sophisticated communities, with their own administrative centres, ruling bodies, temples, priesthoods and deities. The gods and goddesses that the local people chose to worship were initially peculiar to each location, although as society evolved and the links between the townships developed, the same gods frequently appear to have been worshipped in more than one centre. The existence of a deity helped to explain the creation of humankind, and other natural phenomena. The gods were beneficent, offering protection against war and famine in return for reverence and worship. The most well-known cult centres are indicated on the map with a red spot.

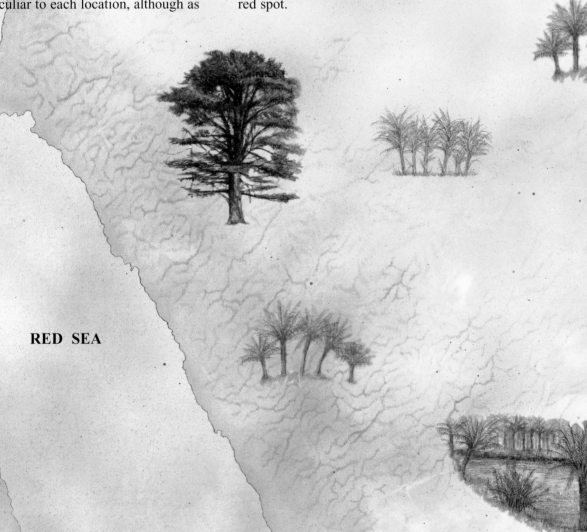

RED SEA

Gods and Goddesses

The ancient Egyptians
worshipped a multitude of
gods and goddesses, and an
understanding of these is crucial for
any enquiry into Egyptian mythology
and religion. It is, however, easy to
be baffled by the great number of
deities, the variety of forms they
take and the complexity of the
relationships between them.

The Egyptians inhabited a natural
environment that could prove
hazardous and life was unpredictable.
Much of what they encountered in
life and the world around them may
have seemed mysterious and
incomprehensible. The gods and
goddesses they conjured up were
divine personifications of all that
was important to them, particularly
in maintaining a sense of order and
well-being in this life and the next,
ensuring the survival of the next
generation and the continued fertility
of the soil. So there were, for
example, gods of the cosmos, the
afterlife, childbirth, grain, even
drunkenness and merriment. The
stories or myths that evolved around
the various gods and goddesses were
a means of explaining the unknown,
such as why it was dark at night, or
the cause of an illness.

Worship often involved making
offerings to the gods accompanied by
invocation, in order to ensure their
continued and benign presence in the
lives of the people.

◄ *Ancient Egyptian deities were represented in a
variety of forms. Here at Karnak the god Amun
appears as ram-headed sphinxes guarding the
processional way to his temple.*

Divine Forms

Religion was central to the lives of the ancient Egyptians, and central to their religion were the gods and goddesses they worshipped. They were the protagonists in the religious texts, and in the temple and tomb scenes that survive from Egypt's past. Each had their own distinctive characteristics and identities.

The ancient Egyptians appear to have had no single sacred book into which their ideas and beliefs were consolidated. Among the extant religious treatises there is no one divine explanation as to the origins of humankind and the universe, but several which seem to contradict one another. Each of the main cult centres of Egypt had its own version of the story centred around a different creator god, but it is impossible to know which one was most widely believed at any one time. The diversity of these creation myths serves to emphasize the interconnected and yet seemingly contradictory system of beliefs referred to as

▶ *Bastet was often represented as a cat, but could also appear as a woman with a feline head. Her statues are often adorned with jewellery. The bronze 'Gayer Anderson cat' has silver inlays and gold earrings and nose ring. 30 BC.*

ancient Egyptian religion. Various sources reveal the extreme complexity of the representations and interrelationships of the gods and goddesses.

Thoth, for example, was a lunar deity; he was also the god of wisdom and of scribes. He was often represented as a man with the head of an ibis, or entirely in the form of this bird, but he could also be depicted as a baboon. Horus, on the other hand, is always found in partial or complete falcon configuration (not to be confused with the Theban god of warfare Montu, who was also depicted in this way) but on some occasions his mother is said to be the goddess Hathor, whereas at other times she is said to be the goddess Isis. Seemingly distinct deities may actually be incarnations of the same one; for example, Bastet, the mother goddess in cat form, appears to be the more gentle embodiment of the aggressive Sekhmet, the lioness goddess whose name translates as 'the powerful one'.

So we see that in the imaginations of the Egyptians, the gods fused human and animal elements. Greater

◀ *This scribe from the ancient city of Akhetaten sits cross-legged before Thoth, represented here as a baboon. The god's headdress bears both the full and the crescent moon, indicating his lunar association. 18th Dynasty.*

accessibility might have been achieved by representing deities in male and female human form, but a sense of mystery was instilled by the combination with animal form. It is interesting, however, that divine personifications of the environment or the cosmos, such as Geb, the god of the earth, or Hapy, god of the Nile inundation, tend to be given human form. Even when deities are represented partially or totally as animals, they exhibit human behaviour and express human emotions, haranguing each other in court for example, or getting drunk and falling asleep.

Gods in animal form

The attributes and behaviour of an animal clearly determined its selection as the representation of a deity. For example, the fierce goddess Sekhmet takes the form of a ferocious lioness and Khepri, god of the sun and creation, is represented as a dung beetle, which has

▶ *Taweret's sagging breasts and large rounded stomach identified her with pregnant women and mothers.*

the habit of rolling its eggs in a ball of dung. Another consideration appears to have been that, by depicting a deity in the form of a dangerous animal such as a snake (for example, the fertility goddess Renenutet or Mertseger, the patron deity of the west Theban peak), and then by worshipping that deity, the animal in question might in turn be placated and the hazard allayed.

Sometimes the form particular deities were given must also have been apotropaic (able to ward off harm). Take, for example, the protective goddess of childbirth, Taweret, who is portrayed as a hippopotamus with additional characteristics of a crocodile and a lion. The idea was that such a potentially threatening combination would keep harm away from mother and child.

The concept of a composite animal is most clearly exemplified by the demon deity, Ammit, who was responsible for devouring the hearts of those who had done wrong during their lifetime, thereby denying them a life after death. She was represented as part crocodile, part lion or panther, and part hippopotamus. The ancient Egyptians clearly dreamt up strange combinations of animals in order to represent the more menacing of divine forces.

All the animals in the collective visualization of the divine world were indigenous to the Nile Valley, the marshy Delta region and the desert fringes. Though the giraffe was known to exist, because it had been brought into Egypt as an example of exotica from sub-Saharan Africa; it was never chosen to represent a deity. There is, however, one god whose animal form remains a mystery, and that is Seth. Perhaps due to his association with chaos and infertility, he was depicted as an animal with a forked tail, a greyhound-like body, a long snout and squared-off ears. Either such a beast did not actually exist, or it is long extinct.

The significance of names

Perhaps by visualizing and verbalizing the divine world in terms of customary animals and routine human behaviour, the intention was to demystify and make explicable what was by definition mysterious and incomprehensible. Nevertheless, divinity can never be fully understood and must instil a sense of wonder in the non-divine. In the myth of *Isis and the Sun God's Secret Name*, it is the one unknown name of Re that is the source of his power; the hidden essence is crucial. The names of the deities were decidedly as important as their particular characteristics and the means by which they were represented. Offerings and prayers could be made only to a divine force that had its own name.

Myths served to explain the origins, personalities and relationships of the deities, but it is impossible to know for certain how and when the identities of the gods and goddesses of ancient Egypt evolved. All we can do is identify the earliest known occurrence of the deity in each instance (whether a representation or textual reference). It is likely that the priesthood formulated and developed the various theological ideas associated with the gods and goddesses. ◆

▼ *Hapy, the god of the Nile inundation, was portrayed with rolls of fat and heavy breasts, emphasizing his connection with fecundity. This image, symbolizing the Unification of Egypt exemplifies the ancient Egyptians' love of symmetry in art.*

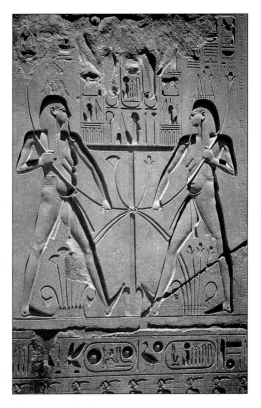

Deities and Cult Centres

During the Dynastic Period of Egyptian history, from the formation of the state of Egypt in c.3100 BC through to the conquest of Egypt by Alexander the Great in 332 BC, Egypt was divided into administrative districts, called nomes, each with its own capital. There were 22 nomes in the Nile Valley (Upper Egypt) and twenty in the Delta region (Lower Egypt). They probably reflected the composition of the separate chiefdoms of the Predynastic Period, before the unification of Egypt under one king. Each nome had its own cult centre, with a priesthood to service the needs of the local deity (or *njwty*, from the ancient Egyptian *niwt* meaning city), and a temple with a shrine for the residence of the god or goddess.

In fact, each cult centre tended to house not a sole deity but a whole divine family or triad, such as Ptah, Sekhmet and Nefertem at Memphis, or Osiris, Isis and Horus at Abydos. Sometimes, an extended family tree of gods and goddesses can be traced, such as that connected with the cult centre of Heliopolis (see *Creation Myths*). There might also be a mythological link between deities associated with

temples some distance apart. For example Hathor of Dendera and Horus of Edfu were united on certain festival days, when Hathor was said to make an annual voyage to Edfu to be united with Horus.

A division of deities into more manageable genealogies would have been necessary for the ordering of such a multitude of divine beings. A survey of these groupings, however, soon reveals overlaps; Amun ('the Hidden One'), for example, occurs in both the triad of Thebes and the Ogdoad (eight gods) of Hermopolis. This does not appear to have troubled the ancient Egyptians. Theirs was an add-on religion, from

Egyptian economy

The administrators of Egypt's forty-two nomes were responsible for the collection of taxes on behalf of the central government. Most people were subsistence farmers and much of the local economy was based on bartering. Taxes were collected in the form of grain, meat, minerals and other goods. The tax system was the responsibility of the king's vizier, or chief minister.

The agrarian system also came under the supervision of the nome administrators, who registered landowners. The total yield of grain in any one year largely depended on the amount of land that could be cultivated as a result of the annual inundation. Irrigation systems were developed to extend this area as far as possible, and it was in the interests of the authorities to see that they were kept in good condition.

◀ *This statue of Horus stands at the entrance to the Hypostyle Hall in the temple of Edfu. As the god of kingship, the falcon deity wears the Double Crown of Upper and Lower Egypt.*

which ideas were never discarded in favour of new ones; instead a cumulative effect can be seen, and in fact the antiquity of any religious element heightened its sacredness.

Politics

The development of the state religion was heavily influenced by political factors. A local deity might rise to national importance because he or she shared a home town with a new ruling family, such as the Eleventh and Eighteenth Dynasties, whose capital was Thebes. Their conquests and claiming of the throne resulted in the prominence of the gods Montu and Amun.

Political motives might also be responsible for the fusion of two deities into one (a process known as syncretism). An example is Amun-Re, head of the pantheon during the New Kingdom (c.1550–c.1069 BC). He was a combination of Amun the patron deity of Thebes, by then the religious capital of the whole of Egypt, and the ancient sun god Re, whose cult at Heliopolis was one of the oldest and whose priesthood had always had particular influence. This union was probably the result of a political alliance.

The degree to which politics and religious belief could interact became

◄ *Amun can often be identified by his double-plumed headdress. Here he sits behind a figure of Tutankhamun. 18th Dynasty.*

▲ *Akhenaten attempted to abolish the traditional polytheistic religion. Here he is shown offering lotus flowers to his sole god, Aten, represented as the sun's disc. 18th Dynasty.*

even more apparent during the reign of the Eighteenth-Dynasty king Akhenaten (c.1352–c.1336 BC), when he abandoned Thebes to found a new capital, Akhetaten. Here he tried to establish a new religion, erasing the inscriptions to Amun and the other traditional gods and recognizing only one deity, the Aten. Akhenaten's actions may have been an attempt to curb the political power of Amun's priests, but his reforms failed, possibly because they were not welcomed by most Egyptians, who clung to the rich complexity of strongly personalized deities to whom they could relate directly. ◆

Deification of Mortals

It was rare but not unheard of for the ancient Egyptians to deify eminent individuals from the past. The king himself was considered a god to some extent, particularly after his death, but occasionally a local cult might grow up around a ruler in addition to his official funerary cult, and he would be worshipped as a patron deity in a more unusual way. The most popular was Amenhotep I (c.1525–c.1504 BC), the second ruler of the Eighteenth Dynasty. Together with his mother, Ahmose-Nefertari, he was worshipped as a protective deity and founder of Deir el-Medina, the west Theban village of tomb builders. He was treated like the patron saint of this small workmen's community. There was a shrine dedicated to him, festivals were

Imhotep's Pyramid

The Step Pyramid at Saqqara was built c.2650 for the burial of the Third-Dynasty king Djoser. The building began as a mastaba tomb (a superstructure named from the Arabic word for 'bench'). This was then extended in size and three further levels were erected over it to form a four-step pyramid. Finally, it was enlarged again and two further steps were added.

The base of the pyramid measures 140 x 118m (459 x 387ft) and it is 60m (197ft) high. At the time of its construction it was by far the largest monument in Egypt, and was also the first to be built from blocks of limestone rather than mudbrick. It was surrounded by a funerary complex for the king, containing mortuary temples and a statue chamber within a walled enclosure.

celebrated in his honour, and sometimes his statue was carried by priests so that his oracle might be consulted.

The best-known non-royal figures who were posthumously honoured with deification were Imhotep and Amenhotep son of Hapu, but from the New Kingdom onwards (c.1550 BC) victims of drowning began to be deified. The River Nile was the lifeline of the ancient Egyptian people and much religious belief surrounded it. By the Late Period a person who had drowned in it might sometimes have a cult established in their honour.

Imhotep

The great vizier, or chief minister, of the Third-Dynasty king Djoser (c.2667–c.2648 BC), Imhotep was the architect of Egypt's earliest monumental stone structure, the Step Pyramid Complex of Djoser at Saqqara, the chief

◀ *Amenhotep son of Hapu is shown here with his scribal palette hanging over his shoulder, loaded with two circular cakes of red and black ink. 18th Dynasty.*

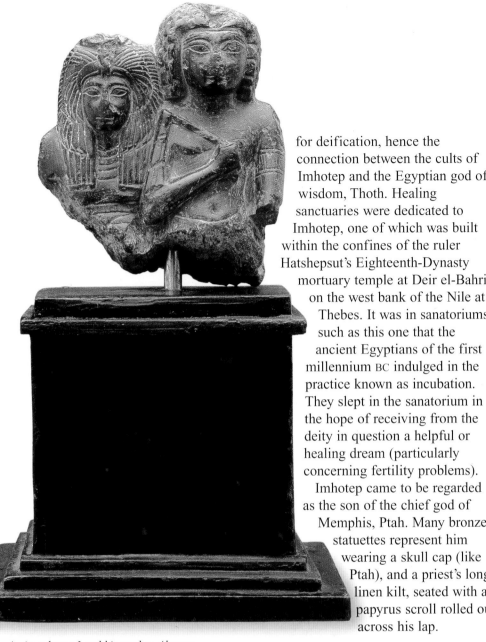

▲ *Amenhotep I and his mother, Ahmose Nefertari, were worshipped as patron deities of Deir el-Medina long after their deaths. 18th Dynasty.*

for deification, hence the connection between the cults of Imhotep and the Egyptian god of wisdom, Thoth. Healing sanctuaries were dedicated to Imhotep, one of which was built within the confines of the ruler Hatshepsut's Eighteenth-Dynasty mortuary temple at Deir el-Bahri on the west bank of the Nile at Thebes. It was in sanatoriums such as this one that the ancient Egyptians of the first millennium BC indulged in the practice known as incubation. They slept in the sanatorium in the hope of receiving from the deity in question a helpful or healing dream (particularly concerning fertility problems).

Imhotep came to be regarded as the son of the chief god of Memphis, Ptah. Many bronze statuettes represent him wearing a skull cap (like Ptah), and a priest's long linen kilt, seated with a papyrus scroll rolled out across his lap.

Amenhotep son of Hapu

The Deir el-Bahri sanctuary was also dedicated to another god of healing, the second deified sage, Amenhotep son of Hapu, who had been an important official during the reign of the Eighteenth-Dynasty king Amenhotep III (c.1390–c.1352 BC). Like Imhotep he was remembered for his wisdom, and as Director of Royal Works he was also responsible for building a great funerary structure for

his king. This was the west Theban mortuary temple of Amenhotep III at Kom el-Heiten. Amenhotep son of Hapu was granted the unique royal favour of his own mortuary temple among those of the kings at Thebes, and statues of him were set up in the largest and most influential temple of the time, that of Amun at Karnak on the east bank at Thebes. ◆

burial site at the time for the capital at Memphis. An inscription on a statue of the king honours his vizier as a master carpenter and sculptor, while carvings on stone vessels say that he was a priest.

Imhotep was obviously remembered throughout pharaonic history, but he was not actually deified until the Late Period, some 2,000 years after his death. In fact he was particularly acknowledged during the Ptolemaic Period (332–30 BC), when he was identified with the Greek Asklepios as a god of wisdom and medicine. A reputation for great wisdom does appear to have been a prerequisite

▶ *Imhotep was a favourite subject for bronze figurines during the Late and Graeco-Roman Periods. He sits here with a papyrus scroll stretched across his lap.*

The Deities

The ancient Egyptian gods and goddesses could take many different human and animal forms; Thoth, for example, could be depicted as a baboon, an ibis; or a man with the head of an ibis. Many of the deities would have been worshipped in temples and shrines throughout Egypt, but only their cult centres best known today are listed below. All aspects of life in the human world were reflected in the divine world and the range of associations held by the deities and goddesses listed below show this.

▶ *Hathor was depicted as a cow leaving the desert to come to the papyrus marshes. 19th Dynasty.*

GOD/GODDESS	APPEARANCE	MAIN CULT CENTRE(S)	ASSOCIATION(S)/ROLE
Aker (god)	Two lions back-to-back; tract of land with lion or human heads at either end		Earth; east & west horizons in Underworld
Amaunet (goddess)	Snake-headed	Hermopolis Magna	Primeval; hidden power
Amenhotep Son of Hapu (god)	Man	Thebes	Healing
Ammit (goddess)	Head of crocodile; front part of panther or lion; rear of hippopotamus	Thebes	Devourer of heart at Judgement
Amun (god)	Man with double-plumed headdress; ram or ram-headed; goose; frog-headed	Thebes; Hermopolis Magna	'King of gods'; primeval; hidden power
Anat (goddess)	Woman with lance, axe & shield		War; Syria-Palestinian
Anubis (god)	Jackal or jackal-headed		Cemeteries; embalming
Anuket/Anukis (goddess)	Woman with tall plumed headdress & papyrus sceptre	Elephantine	Cataracts; huntress
Apis (god)	Bull	Memphis	Manifestation of Ptah
Apophis (god)	Snake		Underworld; chaos; enemy of sun god
Arensnuphis (god)	Man with plumed crown	includ. Philae	Nubian
Astarte (goddess)	Naked woman with *Atef*-crown or bull's horns, riding horse		War; Syrian
Aten (god)	Sun disc	Akhetaten	Solar
Atum (god)	Man with *Nemes* headdress or Double Crown; snake	Heliopolis	'Totality'; creator; solar
Baal (god)	Man with pointed beard & horned helmet, holding a cedar tree, club or spear		Sky; storms; Syrian (Ugaritic)
Baba (god)	Baboon		Aggression; virility; penis = bolt of heaven's doors or mast of Underworld boat

GOD/GODDESS	APPEARANCE	MAIN CULT CENTRE(S)	ASSOCIATION(S)/ROLE
Banebdjedet (god)	Ram	Mendes	Virility; sky
Bastet (goddess)	Cat or cat-headed	Bubastis	Daughter; 'Eye of Re'
Bat (goddess)	Human head with cow's ears & horns, & body in shape of necklace counterpoise	Upper Egypt	Celestial; fertility
Benu (god)	Heron	Heliopolis	Solar; rebirth
Bes (god)	Leonine dwarf		Household; childbirth
Buchis (god)	Bull	Armant	Manifestation of Re & Osiris
Duamutef (god)	Jackal-headed		Canopic; stomach & upper intestines; east
Geb (god)	Man (smtms ithyphallic), smtms with goose on head or Red Crown	Heliopolis	Earth; fertility
Hapy (god)	Man with pendulous breasts & aquatic plants headdress	Gebel el-Silsila; Aswan	Nile inundation
Hapy (god)	Baboon-headed		Canopic; lungs; north
Hathor (goddess)	Cow; woman with cow ears, or horns and sun disc on head, or falcon on perch on head	Dendera; Deir el-Bahri	Mother (esp. of king); love; fertility; sexuality; music; dance; alcohol; sky; Byblos; turquoise; faience
Hatmehyt (goddess)	Lepidotus fish	Mendes	
Hauhet (goddess)	Snake-headed	Hermopolis Magna	Primeval; formlessness; flood force
Heket (goddess)	Frog or frog-headed	Qus	Childbirth
Herishef (god)	Long-horned ram with Atef-crown & sun-disc headdress	Herakleopolis	Primeval force; creator; solar
Horus (god)	Falcon or falcon-headed	Edfu; Hierakonpolis; Behdet	Sky; kingship
Hu (god)	Man		Divine utterance; authority
Huh/Heh (god)	Frog-headed; man holding notched palm-rib	Hermopolis Magna	Primeval; formlessness; flood force; infinity
Ihy (god)	Child	Dendera	Sistrum (rattle)
Imhotep (god)	Seated man with skull cap & papyrus roll	Memphis; Thebes	Wisdom; medicine
Ipy/Ipet (goddess)	Hippopotamus	Thebes	Magical protection
Ishtar (goddess)	Woman		Astral; 'lady of battle'; sexuality; fertility; healing; Assyrian
Isis (goddess)	Woman with throne headdress	includ. Philae	Mother (of king); magic
Imsety (god)	Human-headed		Canopic; liver; south
Kauket (goddess)	Snake-headed	Hermopolis Magna	Primeval; darkness
Khepri (god)	Scarab beetle or man with scarab beetle for head		Creator; solar
Khnum (god)	Ram or ram-headed	Elephantine; Esna	Creator; potter; cataract; fertile soil
Khons(u) (god)	Child with headdress of full and crescent moon	Thebes	Moon
Kuk (god)	Frog-headed	Hermopolis Magna	Primeval; darkness
Maat (goddess)	Woman with single feather headdress		Order, truth, justice
Mafdet (goddess)	Woman; panther		Protector against snakes & scorpions
Mandulis (god)	Man with headdress of ram horns, plumes, sun-discs & cobras	Kalabsha; Philae	Solar; Lower Nubian
Mehen (god)	Coiled serpent		Protector of sun god

GOD/GODDESS	APPEARANCE	MAIN CULT CENTRE(S)	ASSOCIATION(S)/ROLE
Mehet-Weret (goddess)	Cow		Sky; primordial waters; 'great flood'
Mer(e)tseger (goddess)	Cobra	Western Thebes	'Peak of the West'; 'she who loves silence'
Meskhen(e)t (goddess)	Brick with human head; woman with bicornate uterus headdress		Childbirth; destiny
Mihos (god)	Lion	Leontopolis; Bubastis	
Min (god)	Man with erect phallus, & double-plumed headdress	Koptos; Akhmim	Fertility; mining regions in Eastern Desert
Mnevis (god)	Bull	Heliopolis	Sacred bull of sun god; oracles
Montu (god)	Falcon or falcon-headed, with sun disc & double-plumed headdress	Thebes	War
Mut (goddess)	Vulture	Thebes	Motherhood
Naunet (goddess)	Snake-headed	Hermopolis Magna	Primordial waters
Nefertem (god)	Man with lotus headdress; lion-headed	Memphis; Buto	Primeval lotus blossom
Neith (goddess)	Woman with Red Crown of Lower Egypt holding shield & crossed arrows	Sais	Creator-goddess; warfare; weaving
Nekhbet (goddess)	Vulture	el-Kab	Tutelary goddess of Upper Egypt
Neper (god)	Man		Grain
Nephthys (goddess)	Woman with headdress of a basket & enclosure		Funerary; protective
Nun (god)	Man; holding solar barque above head; frog-headed; baboon	Heliopolis; Hermopolis Magna	Primordial waters
Nut (goddess)	Woman; cow	Heliopolis	Sky; sarcophagus
Onuris (god)	Man; beard; four plume headdress;	This	Warrior/hunter carrying spear
Osiris (god)	Mummified man with *Atef*-crown, holding crook & flail	Abydos; Busiris	Death; Afterlife; rebirth; fertility; agriculture
Pakhet (goddess)	Lioness	Includ. entrance to wadi in E. desert nr Beni Hasan	
Ptah (god)	Semi-mummified man with skull cap and *was-djed-ankh* sceptre	Memphis	Creator; craftsmen
Qadesh (goddess)	Naked woman standing on lion		Sacred ecstasy; sexual pleasure; Middle Eastern
Qebehsenuef (god)	Falcon-headed		Canopic; lower intestines; west
Re/Ra (god)	Ram- or falcon-headed with sun disc & cobra headdress	Heliopolis	Creator; solar
Renenutet (goddess)	Cobra	Faiyum	Harvest; nursing
Reshef/Reshep (god)	Man with beard & White Crown with gazelle head at front & ribbon behind		War; Syrian (Amorite)
Sah (god)	Man		Orion
Satet/Satis (goddess)	Woman with White Crown & antelope horns	Elephantine	Protectoress of southern border; fertility
Sekhmet (goddess)	Lioness or lioness-headed	Memphis	'Powerful'; daughter of Re; healing
Selket/Serket (goddess)	Woman with scorpion headdress		Funerary; protective
Seshat (goddess)	Woman with panther-skin robe, & seven-pointed star on head		Writing

GOD/GODDESS	APPEARANCE	MAIN CULT CENTRE(S)	ASSOCIATION(S)/ROLE
Seth (god)	Unidentified quadruped or 'Seth-animal' headed	Ombos Naqada	Chaos; infertility; desert; storm
Shay (god)	Man		Destiny
Shezmu (god)	Man	Faiyum	Underworld demon; wine & unguent-oil presses
Shu (god)	Man with feather on head; lion-headed	Heliopolis; Leontopolis	Air; 'Eye of Re'
Sia (god)	Man		Divine knowledge; intellectual achievement
Sobek (god)	Crocodile or crocodile-headed	Kom Ombo; Faiyum	Pharaonic might
Sokar (god)	Mummified man with crown of horns, cobras, *atef*, & sun disc; hawk-headed	Memphis	Funerary
Sopdet/Sothis (goddess)	Woman with star on head		'Dog star' Sirius
Tatenen (god)	Man with double-plumed crown & ram's horns	Memphis	Emerging Nile silt from receding flood waters; vegetation
Taweret (goddess)	Hippopotamus (with lion & crocodile parts)		Household; childbirth
Tayet (goddess)	Woman		Weaving
Tefnut (goddess)	Woman; lioness-headed; cobra	Heliopolis; Leontopolis	Moisture; 'Eye of Re'; *uraeus*
Thoth/Djehuty (god)	Baboon; ibis or ibis-headed	Hermopolis Magna	Moon; knowledge; scribes
Wadjet/Edjo (goddess)	Cobra; lioness	Buto	Tutelary goddess of Lower Egypt; *uraeus*
Wepwawet (god)	Jackal or jackal-headed	Assiut	'Opener of the Ways'

▲ *The goddess Neith was associated with warfare. 25th Dynasty.*

▲ *The goddess Nut continued to be represented inside coffins well into the Roman period in Egypt. Early 2nd century AD.*

▲ *The goddess Maat, the divine personification of truth, order and justice, wore an ostrich feather on her head. 19th Dynasty.*

27

Headdresses and Crowns

An incredible variety of crowns and headdresses are represented in the art of ancient Egypt. For those who are unable to read the hieroglyphic inscriptions which often accompany the depictions of gods and goddesses, the headdress can be crucial for identifying a particular deity. Some of the characteristics of divine headdresses include: feathers; horns, lunar and solar discs; various birds, insects and other creatures; stars; a notched palm frond; a pot; a lotus flower; a shield with crossed arrows; a throne; and so on. The king might be depicted wearing one of several different crowns, although he was often shown wearing the simple linen *nemes* (headcloth). Various deities could also be portrayed wearing a royal headdress, for example Osiris who often sported the *Atef*-crown. The Blue Crown was especially associated with warfare.

White Crown of Upper Egypt (*hedjet*)

Red Crown of Lower Egypt (*deshret*)

Double Crown of Upper and Lower Egypt (*pschent*)

Atef crown

Blue Crown (*khepresh*)

Tatenen

Wadjet/Edjo

Thoth

Isis

Nephthys

Re

Neith

Buchis

Nefertem

Neith

Meskhent

Bes

Heh

Nut

Renenutet

▲ *Identification of this Nile deity by Itis head-dress is especiallly useful when late period bronze figurines such as this one are uninscribed.*

Selket/Serket

Khepri

Montu

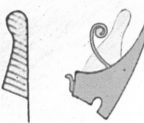
Maat, Shu   Atum, Horus

▲ *The elongated headdress is characteristic of 'Amarna Art'. Here Akhenaten's headdress is surmounted by ram's horns, a sun disc, and the tall plumes. 18th Dynasty.*

Osiris

Neith

Nekhbet, Mut, Isis

Hathor, Isis, Ipy/Ipet

Mandulis

Seshat

Khnum

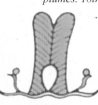
Sobek

Re-Horakhty, Sekhmet, Sokar

▲ *Osorkon II as Osiris, flanked by Horus and Isis, wear characteristic headdresses. Isis is also often shown with a throne on her head. 22nd Dynasty.*

Geb

Hathor

Khons

Satet/Satis

Reshef/Reshep

Amun, Horus, Min

Onuris   Anuket/Anukis   Sopdet/Sothis

Geb

Gods and Goddesses

The Egyptian pantheon included hundreds of deities: many originated as local gods who became the focus of important cults, while some were borrowed from other cultures. Some deities were merged, or 'syncretized' with each other, blending their attributes, sometimes allowing a lesser god to take on the distinction and importance of a greater one. Most of the major, or universal, deities represented cosmic forces, such as the sun or the flood, or were associated with the mysteries of human life, such as birth and death.

Aker

The earth god Aker was the divine personification of the eastern and western horizons, which signified the entrance and exit into and out of the Netherworld, Aker was important in funerary texts and imagery. He was represented as two lions sitting back to back, or as a piece of land with a lion or a human head at each end (one facing east and one facing west).

Amun

By the New Kingdom (c.1550–c.1069 BC) Amun had achieved the position of head of the state pantheon. His national significance was due to the emergence of local Theban rulers who were successful in reuniting and ruling the whole of Egypt after a period of disruption. An early Twelfth-Dynasty inscription in the jubilee chapel of King Senusret I (c.1965–c.1920 BC) at Karnak describes Amun as 'the king of the gods'. His pre-eminence also had much to do with his amalgamation with Re, the ancient sun god of Heliopolis, to create the deity Amun-Re. He was also combined with the fertility god Min, to form the god Amun-Min or Amun Kamutef ('Bull of his Mother').

Amun's name means 'the Hidden One' and one of his epithets was 'mysterious of form', although he was usually

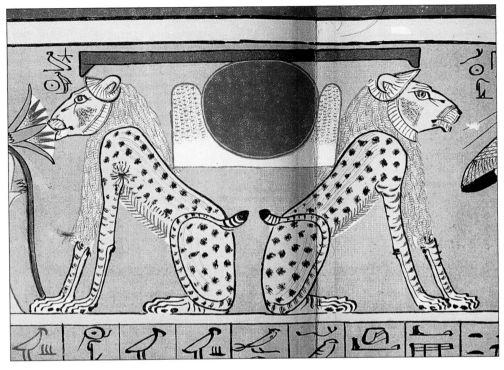

represented in human form wearing a tall double-plumed headdress. He could also be envisaged as a ram – *Ovis platyra* – with horns curving inwards close to the head. In a hymn on Papyrus Leiden 1,350, he is described as the 'Great Honker' – a primeval goose.

From at least as early as the Eleventh Dynasty (c.2055 – c.1985 BC) Amun's chief cult centre was the temple at Karnak in Thebes, where he was worshipped with his consort, the vulture mother-goddess Mut, and their child the lunar deity Khonsu. As early as the Fifth Dynasty (c.2350–c.2345 BC) he appeared in the Pyramid Texts accompanied by a consort named as Amaunet.

Anat

As a goddess of war, Anat was believed to protect the king in battle. Thus she was often depicted with a lance, axe and shield. She also wore a tall crown surmounted by feathers.

Anat is an excellent example of the Egyptian acceptance of foreign deities into their pantheon of gods, because she actually originated in Syria-Palestine as

▲ *Above the backs of the two lions representing Aker, the artist of this papyrus Book of the Dead of Ani has painted the hieroglyphic signs for 'horizon' (*akhet*) and 'sky' (*pet*).*

▼ *In reliefs at Luxor the supreme god Amun takes an ithyphallic form as Amun Kamutef.*

▲ *These ram-headed sphinxes (criosphinxes) originally formed part of the avenue between the temples of Luxor and Karnak. Both were dedicated to the god Amun, who was sometimes represented as a ram.*

a deity of the Canaanites and Phoenicians. She was said to be the sister, or sometimes the consort, of Baal. There is evidence of a cult dedicated to her in Egypt from at least the late Middle Kingdom (c.1800 BC).

Like other more benign goddesses, Anat held the titles 'Mother of All the Gods' and 'Mistress of the Sky'. At various times she was regarded as the consort of Seth or the fertility god Min.

Anubis

The god of embalming and cemeteries, Anubis was an ancient deity to whom prayers for the survival of the deceased in the Afterlife were addressed during the early Old Kingdom before Osiris rose to prominence as the god of the dead. Anubis continued to assist in the judgement of the dead and accompanied the deceased to the throne of Osiris for the ritual of the Weighing of the Heart. He was also the patron of embalmers. Anubis had several epithets including 'foremost of the westerners' (i.e the dead buried on the west bank of the Nile); 'he who is upon his mountain' (i.e the desert cliffs overlooking the

cemeteries); 'Lord of the Sacred land' (i.e the desert in which the burials were located); 'the one presiding over the god's pavillion' (i.e the place where embalming took place, or the burial chamber); and 'he who is in the place of embalming'.

Anubis was depicted as a jackal or as a man with the head of a jackal. Priests who prepared bodies for burial and conducted burial ceremonies are thought to have impersonated the god by wearing jackal masks. Since jackals were common scavengers in Egyptian burial sites, the honouring of Anubis in this guise may have represented a way of protecting the dead from molestation.

Astarte

This goddess appears to have been almost interchangeable with Anat. She was also associated with war (particularly with horses and chariots), and was thought to protect the king in battle. She was of Syrian origin, and there is no evidence for her cult in Egypt before the Eighteenth Dynasty (c.1150–c.1295 BC).

She was usually represented as a naked woman riding a horse and wearing the *atef*-crown or bull's horns on her head. She was variously regarded as the daughter of Re or of Ptah, and was thought to be one of Seth's consorts.

Atum

Atum ('the All') was the self-engendered creator god who arose from the primordial waters of chaos, Nun, in order to form the primeval mound and to bring the elements of the cosmos into being. As the head of the so-called Ennead (or nine gods), he held the title 'Lord to the Limits of the Sky'. His cult

▲ *As a funerary deity, Atum's presence is significant on the walls of non-royal Theban tombs of the New Kingdom (c.1550–c.1069 BC) such as that of Sennedjem. C.1300 BC.*

centre was at Heliopolis, and he was regarded very much as a solar deity (at some stage he was syncretized with the pre-eminent sun god, Re, in order to form the combined deity Re-Atum).

Atum was very much associated with kingship, and was believed to lift the dead king from his pyramid to the stars. Later, as a result of the gradual democratization of funerary religion, he came to be regarded as the

▶ *Relative size is used to denote importance in Egyptian art, as shown by this diorite statue of Horemheb kneeling before the seated figure of Atum. c.1300 BC.*

protector not only of the king but of all dead people on their way into the Afterlife.

Atum was usually represented as a man wearing the Double Crown of Upper and Lower Egypt, although he could also be portrayed as a snake. Additional animals were deemed sacred to him, including the lion, bull, mongoose, lizard and dung beetle.

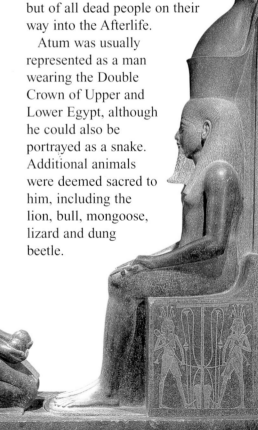

Baba

At his most dangerous, Baba was believed to murder humans and feed on their entrails. He was associated with aggression and virility – especially those of the king. Sometimes his penis was said to be the bolt on the doors of heaven, and at other times it was the mast on the ferry in the Netherworld. He was believed to be able to ward off snakes and to control darkness and turbulent waters. He was represented as a baboon.

Eye of Re

According to this strange concept, the eye of the sun god was in fact separate from him and could act independently. In the myth of *The Destruction of Humankind* it manifested itself first as Hathor and then as the more ferocious divine female force, Sekhmet.

The Eye was also identified with the cobra goddess Wadjet, one of the protective female deities of kingship, who appears rearing up at the front of the royal headdress, ready to spit poison at the king's enemies. This rearing snake is known as the uraeus.

Geb

As the divine personification of the earth, Geb was a god of fertility. For this reason, he was sometimes coloured green and was visualized with plants growing out of him. He was often depicted reclining beneath the arched body of

◄ The influence of the Near Eastern goddess Astarte was widespread in the ancient world. This pectoral plaque depicting the goddess was found in the Camirus cemetery on Rhodes. Early Greek.

◄ The sistrum was shaken like a rattle by priestesses of Hathor. Late Period.

his sister-consort, the sky goddess Nut. In *The Creation Myth of Heliopolis*, Geb and Nut, were the two children of Shu and Tefnut. They were lovers, but were forcibly separated by their father Shu, the god of air.

Geb was always represented in human form, sometimes with an erect penis. He occasionally wore the Red Crown of Lower Egypt, but more often had a white-fronted goose on his head. Thus, his daughter Isis could be described as the 'Egg of the Goose'. Like his father Shu, he had a dark side to him, which was expressed in funerary religion: he was considered able to trap the dead in his body. Earthquakes were described as the 'laughter of Geb'.

Hathor

A mother goddess, Hathor was associated with love, fertility, sexuality, music, dance and alcohol. She was sometimes represented entirely anthropomorphically, in the form of a cow, or as a woman with cow's ears. When in human form, her headdress could be one of cow's horns with a solar disc, or a falcon on a perch. She was also a sky goddess, and was regarded as a vast cow who straddled the heavens, with her four legs marking the four cardinal points.

◀ The cow-goddess Hathor was often depicted with a human face but with cow's ears on column capitals, such as this one at Dendera, site of the most famous of her temples. Hathor's representation as a cow identified her as the great mother, symbolizing fertility, motherhood and nurture.

▼ The favourable support and protection bestowed on the king by the whole of the divine world is epitomized by the image of the cow goddess Hathor suckling the adult ruler (in this case Amenhotep II). 18th Dynasty.

In various contexts she was honoured as 'Lady of the West' or 'Lady of the Western Mountain', 'Lady of Byblos', 'Lady of Turquoise' and 'Lady of Faience'. The 'west' or 'western mountain' refers to the place of the setting sun and thus, by analogy, the realm of the dead. Byblos was a port on the Lebanese coast, important for Egyptian trade and particularly in the importing of cedar wood, since Egypt had no native timber for the construction of boats or large buildings. Egypt exploited turquoise mines from Predynastic times, especially in the Sinai Peninsula (a temple to Hathor has been found at the mining site of Serabit el-Khadim). Faience was a much-used glazed ceramic material composed primarily of crushed quartz or quartz sand, and usually a blue or green colour (perhaps a cheap imitation of turquoise).

Like Isis, Hathor was considered to be the mother of the falcon deity Horus, and thus of the king (who was closely identified with Horus). Her name means 'the House of Horus'. However, inscriptions on the temple of Horus at Edfu refer to Hathor marrying this deity. The king was sometimes depicted being suckled by the goddess in cow form, as shown by a wonderful statue in the Cairo Museum from Deir el-Bahri of the Eighteenth-Dynasty pharaoh Amenhotep II (c.1427– c.1400 BC) enjoying just such sustenance. Although she was sometimes identified with the Eye of Re, she appeared on other occasions as the sun god's daughter.

From the Old Kingdom (c.2686– c.2181 BC) Hathor's chief cult centre was at Dendera. Her festivities appear to have been suitably debauched. An emblem of her cult was the sistrum (or rattle), which would have been shaken as part of the ritual proceedings. The existing temple on this site dates to the Graeco-Roman Period, and is dedicated to the triad Hathor, Horus and Ihy, Hathor's son, who played the sistrum in her honour.

Horus

The king of Egypt was closely identified with Horus from the beginning of Dynastic history (c.3100 BC). The god was represented as a falcon, or with the head of a falcon, and one of his most ubiquitous symbols was the 'Eye of Horus' (the *udjat*- or *wadjat*-eye). In one version of the myth of *The Contendings of Horus and Seth*, Horus had both his eyes gouged out. In other versions he lost (and then regained) only his left eye. As the weaker of the two, it came to be associated with the moon while the right eye was associated with the sun. Because in both instances his eyesight was eventually cured, his eye came to symbolize healing (*udjat* literally means 'sound'). It was used as a

◄ *As the god of kingship, Horus was often shown wearing the combined Red and White Crowns of Lower and Upper Egypt, as on this column at the temple of Kom Ombo.*

▲ *The 'Eye of Horus' is a ubiquitous emblem in ancient Egyptian art. It symbolized healing, wholeness, strength and perfection. New Kingdom.*

protective amulet, symbolizing strength and perfection, and also represented the waxing and waning moon.

Horus's name means 'He Who is Above', and is probably linked to his status as a god of the sky and to the high soaring of the falcon. As 'Horus in the Horizon' he was called a Horemakhet and in this capacity he was amalgamated with the solar deity Re to become Re-Horakhty.

From the Late Period (c.747 BC) he appeared in his child form, Hor-pa-khered (whom the Greeks called Harpocrates) on a form of stela known as a *cippus* of Horus. He was usually depicted treading crocodiles underfoot and grasping snakes, scorpions and other such dangerous creatures. It is always clear that he was intended to be a child because he was pictured naked, sporting a particular hairstyle known as the 'side-lock of youth'. The idea behind

this aspect of the god was that since Horus as a young boy had managed to survive certain dangers, a ritual could be performed using his image to protect children from similar threats (or perhaps to cure snake bites and scorpion stings). Water was poured over the *cippi* (which were covered in spells), causing the liquid to be imbued with their magical potency, so it could be ritually imbibed or applied.

Horus was honoured as an element of the divine triad at the cult centre of Abydos, but he is most associated with the temple at Edfu (ancient Mesen), where he was worshipped as part of a triad with his consort Hathor and their child Harsomtus. He was also closely associated with Hierakonpolis ('Town of the Hawk', ancient Nekhen) in the south and a town called Behdet in the Delta. As 'Horus of Behdet' he was represented as a winged sun disc.

▲ *On the back of one of Tutankhamun's thrones, the god Heh kneels on the hieroglyphic sign for gold, and clutches notched palm branches, symbolizing the passing of time. 18th Dynasty.*

▼ *Khepri is depicted here in the tomb of Seti I on a boat on the waters of Nun. The wish is expressed in the early royal funerary texts that the sun should come into being in its name of Khepri. 19th Dynasty.*

Huh/Heh

The frog-headed god Huh was the personification of formlessness and infinity. His consort was the snake-headed goddess Hauhet. He was often represented anthropomorphically holding in each hand a palm-rib (the hieroglyph for 'year').

Isis

Like Hathor, Isis was a mother goddess and was identified more specifically as the mother of Horus, and thus of the king. The image of her suckling Horus (especially found in the form of numerous bronze figurines dating to the Late and Graeco-Roman Periods) is reminiscent of the Christian mother-and-child icon.

Isis tended to be represented as a woman with a throne, or solar disc between cow's horns, on her head. She was sometimes regarded as the personification of the throne: the hieroglyph for her name is the image of a throne, and her lap came to be seen as the throne of Egypt. She was also frequently depicted with huge, sheltering wings. She was part of the Ennead of Heliopolis, and as consort to Osiris and mother of Horus, she appeared in the triad of deities worshipped at Abydos. Her best-known cult centre was on the island of Philae, on the southern border of Egypt, near Aswan. She was particularly closely associated with magic. Her ability to heal and to transform herself into any guise she desired are evident in the myths about her. Two important manifestations of this goddess were the 'Great White Sow of Heliopolis' and the Isis-cow which gave birth to the sacred Apis Bull of Memphis. Her following eventually spread beyond Egypt, to Syria, Palestine, Greece and throughout the whole Roman Empire, and she was worshipped until well into Christian times.

▶ *Several species of dung beetle are found in Egypt, but the large sacred scarab,* Scarabeus sacer, *is the one most commonly represented in ancient Egyptian art.*

Khepri

The god Khepri (which literally means 'He who is Coming into Being') was a creator and solar deity. He was represented as a scarab or dung beetle, or as a beetle-headed man. The choice of a dung beetle to portray a creator god and the manifestation of the rising sun is significant because of the activities of such a beetle. It was observed to roll its eggs in a ball of dung along the ground, and the ball was identified with the sun. The baby beetles were seen to emerge from the dung, as if life was emerging from the primeval mound, and so dung beetles were thought capable of spontaneous creation.

From the Middle Kingdom (c.2055–c.1650 BC) onwards the scarab-form amulet was very popular, and was worn in bracelets and necklaces. Scarabs were used as funerary talismans, and were placed over the heart of the deceased to keep it from confessing sins during its interrogation.

Khnum

Khnum was an ancient deity represented as a man with the head of a ram, or in entirely ram form. The type of ram used to portray him was the earliest one to be domesticated in Egypt – the *Ovis longipes* – which had curly horns extending horizontally from the head. The ancient Egyptian for 'ram' was *ba*, which was also the word for a concept akin to our 'personality' (possibly those non-physical attributes which make any one human being unique, or perhaps the moral essence of a person's motivation and movement). It may well then have been thanks to the ancient Egyptian love of puns that Khnum came to be

regarded as the *ba* of the Sun god Re, and so this deity was represented with a ram's head while passing through the Netherworld in his solar barque. Certainly the *ba* of the dead appeared to be more mobile than their *ka* ('spirit').

Connected with Khnum's capacity as a creator god was his role as patron deity

▼ *The ram was a symbol of fertility and male virility. It was used to represent the creator god Khnum, who fashioned the universe out of clay.*

of potters, and his association with the fertile soil, the annual inundation and the Nile cataracts. His chief cult centre was situated on the island of Elephantine, at the first cataract at the southern border of Egypt. Another important temple to Khnum was located at Esna. Here his consort was the lioness-goddess Menhyt. And it was here that the Festival of the Potter's Wheel was celebrated each year.

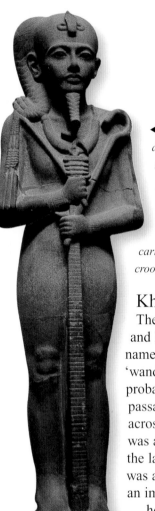

◄ *Khonsu was depicted as a young man usually wrapped in the bandages of a mummy or other tight-fitting garment and carrying the royal crook, flail and sceptre.*

Khonsu

The son of Amun and Mut, Khonsu's name means 'wanderer', which probably refers to the passage of the moon across the sky, as he was a lunar deity. In the late period, he was also considered an important god of healing. His chief cult centre was at Thebes.

Kuk

The frog-headed god Kuk was the personification of darkness. His consort was the snake-headed Kauket.

Min

As a god of fertility, Min was represented in semi-mummified human form, his left hand holding his erect phallus and his right arm raised. The key feature of his headdress was two tall plumes. The emblems of his cult were the lettuce and an unidentified shape which could possibly be a door-bolt, a barbed arrow, a lightning bolt or a pair of fossil shells. He was a particularly

▶ *Ramesses I is depicted on the wall of his tomb face to face with Nefertem, the divine personification of the lotus blossom.*

ancient deity, and was also regarded as a protector of the mining regions in the Eastern Desert.

His main cult centres were at Koptos and Akhmim (which the Greeks called Panopolis because they identified their god Pan with Min). He was sometimes described as the son of Isis, but on other occasions he was said to be her consort, with Horus as their son. By the New Kingdom (c.1550–c.1069 BC) he had merged with the Theban deity Amun.

Nefertem

This deity was associated with the lotus blossom, and was represented in male human form with the blue lotus (*Nymphaea caerulea*) on his head (see *Plants and Flowers in Mythology*). His headdress sometimes also incorporated two plumes and two necklace counterpoises.

The *Creation Myth of Hermopolis Magna* states that the sun rose from the primeval lotus flower, and Nefertem was

with her consort Seth and their child Sobek, the crocodile god. As a mother goddess she was given the epithet 'Great Cow' (as were the goddesses Nut and Hathor). She was also considered a creator goddess and as such was equated with the primordial waters of chaos, Nun.

Together with Isis, Nephthys and the scorpion goddess, Selket, she was a funerary goddess: they each protected one of the 'Four Sons of Horus' who in turn looked after the internal organs of the deceased. Neith was specifically associated with the jackal-headed Duamutef who protected the stomach and upper intestines. She was also linked with the linen mummy bandages because she was believed to have invented weaving.

Nephthys

In later mythology, Nephthys was regarded as the mother of the jackal-headed god of embalming, Anubis, as a result of a union with Osiris. She was the sister of Isis, Osiris and Seth (of whom she was also thought to be a consort). She appears to have been an aide to her better-known sister Isis. Like her, Nephthys was usually depicted in human form, but could also be represented as a kite. Her name means 'Lady of the Mansion', and her headdress consisted of the hieroglyphs for this epithet (a basket on top of the enclosure wall of a grand house).

Nephthys was associated with the head of the deceased or the coffin (in collaboration with Isis at the foot). She was also one of the protective canopic deities: she protected the baboon-headed son of Horus, Hapy, who in turn guarded the lungs of the deceased.

closely linked with the sun god. The Pyramid Texts of the Old Kingdom refer to Nefertem as 'the lotus blossom which is before the nose of Re' (Utterance 266). His universal importance is expressed in his title 'Protector of the Two Lands' (*khener tawy*), referring to Upper and Lower Egypt.

Nefertem was worshipped at Memphis as the son of god Ptah and the lioness-goddess Sekhmet, so he was sometimes depicted as lion-headed. He was also occasionally referred to as the son of the cat-goddess Bastet or, to complicate matters further, as the son of the cobra-goddess Wadjet at Buto.

Neith

A particularly ancient goddess whose main cult centre was at Sais in the Delta, Neith rose to particular prominence during the Twenty-sixth Dynasty (664–525 BC), when Sais was the home of the ruling family and the capital of Egypt. Her emblem was a shield with crossed arrows, emphasizing her association with warfare (the Greeks later identified her with their goddess Athena). This symbol has been found on objects dating all the way back to the First Dynasty (c.3100–c.2890 BC). She is usually depicted wearing the Red Crown of Lower Egypt. Neith formed a triad

▲ *In the Pyramid Texts of the Old Kingdom (c.2686–c.2181 BC), the sky goddess Nut, painted inside this coffin of Seti I, is variously described as the king's coffin, sarcophagus and tomb. 19th Dynasty.*

▼ *In illustrations of the Heliopolitan creation myth, as here on the papyrus of Nespakashuty, Nut arches naked over her consort Geb, the earth god.*

Nun

Nun was the divine personification of the primordial waters of chaos, which preceded creation. He was described as the 'eldest father' and 'maker of humankind'. After creation had taken place, chaos was believed to continue to exist beyond the edges of the universe, and in the Netherworld, and was the place of social outcasts and demons.

The mudbrick enclosure walls of temples were sometimes constructed in curved courses (pan bedding), which resulted in a wavy effect. This was possibly meant to imitate the waters of Nun, the temple itself symbolizing the universe (see *Temple Architecture*). Nun was also thought to be present within the context of the temple, in the form of the sacred lake.

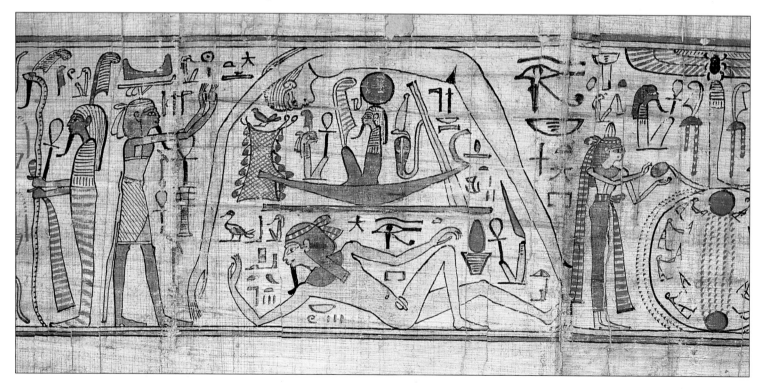

Nun could be represented as a baboon, or with a frog's head, or in an entirely human form, with a beard. In the latter guise he was often depicted holding the solar barque aloft. His consort was the snake-headed goddess Naunet.

Nut

The goddess Nut was the divine personification of the sky. According to the Heliopolitan creation myth, she was one of the children of Shu and Tefnut, and the sister and consort of Geb, the earth god. The darkness at night was explained by the belief that Nut swallowed the sun in the evening and gave birth to it at dawn, so it spent the night hours travelling through her body. This image was often depicted on the ceilings of tombs and on the undersides of sarcophagus lids, expressing the belief that Nut divinely personified the coffin and burial chamber. Because the

▼ *Ani's Book of the Dead shows the dead man being led by Horus to the enthroned Osiris, who is attended by his sisters Isis and Nephthys.*

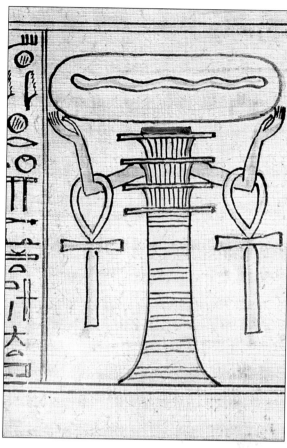

▶ *In the papyrus Book of the Dead of the priest of Amun-Re, Chensumose, the djed-pillar, considered to be the embodiment of Osiris's backbone, is semi-personified:* ankhs *hang from its arms and it holds aloft an encircled snake. 21st Dynasty.*

sun was said to be born from her each morning, the deceased might be reborn from her into the Afterlife.

She was usually shown as a woman arching over the earth, but could also be represented as a cow. The 'Divine Cow' was believed to carry Re, the sun god, on her back each morning.

Osiris

God of the dead and the Afterlife (as well as of rebirth and fertility), Osiris was represented in a mummified anthropomorphic form, often holding a crook and flail, and with the *atef*-crown (described as 'sky piercing') on his head. His skin could be green or black (signifying fertility or the thick black Nile silt), or white (the colour of the linen mummy bandages). One of his emblems was the *djed*-pillar, a symbol of stability, which was equated with his backbone and was particularly revered at his cult centre of Busiris (ancient Djedu) in the Delta.

The chief cult centre of Osiris was his legendary burial place (and consequently an important pilgrims' destination) Abydos (ancient Abdjw), where he was worshipped together with his sister-consort Isis and their son Horus, and where an annual festival was held in his honour. He was a member of the important Ennead (nine gods) of Heliopolis (see *Creation Myths*), a genealogy that appears for the first time in the Pyramid Texts of the Fifth Dynasty. These were found – as the name implies – on the interior walls of certain pyramids. Epithets applied to Osiris included 'eternally good' and 'foremost of the westerners' (that is the dead, who were thought, like the sun, to enter the Netherworld in the west). He was assimilated with two

Memphite deities, the creator god Ptah, and the hawk-headed funerary deity Sokar, forming the syncretized funerary god Ptah-Sokar-Osiris.

The deceased king of Egypt was identified with Osiris from at least the Fifth Dynasty (c.2494–c.2345 BC). By about 2000 BC, a democratization of funerary religion had begun to take place, and dead people other than the king were also identified with Osiris.

Ptah

Recognized as the chief deity of the city of Memphis, Ptah was worshipped as part of a triad with his consort the lioness-goddess Sekhmet and the lotus-god Nefertem. At a later stage, Imhotep, the deified architect of Djoser's Step Pyramid Complex at Saqqara, was regarded as a son of Ptah (see

◄ *Wooden figures of Ptah-Sokar-Osiris were part of a wealthy Egyptian's funerary equipment. Miniature rolls of papyrus might be deposited in a compartment in the base. Late Period.*

▲ *The Theban tomb-builders' village of Deir el-Medina, located in the desert about 2km (1 mile) west of the Nile Valley, consists of about 70 limestone and mudbrick houses of uniform size.*

Deification of Mortals). As chief creator god, Ptah was regarded as the patron deity of craftsmen, and so was an important figure at Deir el-Medina, the village of craftsmen who were responsible for the tombs in the Valley of the Kings. At Memphis, the High Priest of his cult held the title 'Great Over-seer of Craftsmen' (*wer kherep hemw*).

Ptah was represented in human, semi-mummified form, wearing a skullcap and holding a staff which combined the *was*-sceptre of power, the *djed*-pillar of stability and the *ankh*-sign for life. From the Middle Kingdom (c.2055–c.1650 BC) onwards he was depicted with a straight beard.

During the Old Kingdom (c.2686–c.2181 BC) Ptah was merged with the Memphite hawk-headed funerary deity Sokar, creating the god Ptah-Sokar. This composite deity went on to become Ptah-Sokar-Osiris in the Late Period. Wooden, mummiform, hawk-headed figures of this god were often placed in tombs as part of the funerary equipment.

Re

With good reason, the ancient Egyptians considered the sun to be a potent life force; together with the annual inundation of the Nile, it was responsible for their successful harvests. Re was the pre-eminent solar deity.

His cult centre was at Heliopolis (called Iunu by the ancient Egyptians and now a suburb of modern Cairo) where an extremely powerful priesthood officiated. From the Fourth-Dynasty reign of Djedefre (c.2566–c.2558 BC) onwards, one of the king's five names was introduced with the epithet 'Son of Re', emphasizing the association of the king with the god. The focal point of Re's cult was the obelisk, or *benben* stone (deriving from the verb *weben* 'to shine forth').

In the myth of the Destruction of Humankind, Re is described as having the bones, flesh and hair of an old man, but his divinity is evident because they are of silver, gold and lapis lazuli (the last was considered especially valuable by the ancient Egyptians because it had to be imported from as far away as Badakhshan in north-eastern Afghanistan). This description may be that of a cult statue, such as would be found in the *naos* or shrine of each temple, housing the very essence or potency of the deity in question. The myth also states that he was self-created, coming into being in Nun, the primordial waters.

Re was frequently represented anthropomorphically, but with the head of a ram or a hawk wearing a sun-disc headdress. As the sun god, he was thought to voyage across the sky in a boat during the twelve hours of daylight, and through the Netherworld during the hours of darkness. In another version of the myth of his nightly journey, he was swallowed by Nut, the sky goddess, and

▼ *The royal title 'Son of Re' is written with the hieroglyphic signs of a duck (meaning 'son') and a solar disc. Karnak.*

travelled through her body to be reborn each morning.

The sun god was ubiquitous and powerful. By the process of syncretism, Re was amalgamated with other deities such as Amun, becoming Amun-Re, and Horus, becoming Re-Horakhty ('Horus of the Two Horizons'). Or he might be identified with other gods; one of the texts inscribed on the walls of some tombs in the Valley of the Kings during the New Kingdom (c.1550– c.1069 BC) is the 'Litany of Re', in which Re is identified with Osiris, god of the dead.

Sekhmet

The goddess Sekhmet was the ferocious aspect of female divinity, whether of Hathor, Bastet (the cat goddess of Bubastis in the Delta) or the mother goddess Mut whose temple at Karnak was filled with statues of Sekhmet by the Eighteenth-Dynasty king Amenhotep III (c.1390–1352 BC): it is thought that there was one for each day of the year. She was associated with war and battle, and helped the king to vanquish his enemies. Her name literally means 'the Powerful One', and she was visualized, appropriately, as a lioness, or at least as a woman with the head of a lioness. She wore a sun disc identifying her as the daughter of Re.

Sekhmet played an important role in the capital city of Memphis, as the consort of the creator god Ptah and the mother of Nefertem.

Seth

Seth was Osiris's 'wicked' brother and, as such, was a member of the Heliopolitan family of gods and goddesses. He was associated with chaos, infertility and the desert, but in certain geographical areas (such as the north-eastern Delta) and at certain times in Egyptian history, he was highly honoured. There were kings of the Nineteenth and Twentieth Dynasties, for example, whose names derived from his, such as Seti and Sethnakhte. His worship recognized that chaos had to be acknowledged before order could be seen to exist, and though the desert was an arid and dangerous place it was also of enormous value to the Egyptians (particularly for its natural resources such as gold, amethyst and turquoise). The god had an important cult centre at Naqada in Upper Egypt. Tradition maintained this had been the place of his violent birth from the sky goddess Nut.

Seth was represented in the form of an animal that cannot be conclusively identified: it had a long curved snout, pricked, flat-topped ears, a canine body and a forked tail. He was sometimes shown as a man with this animal's head. It is possible that this animal may have

▲ *The bizarre Seth animal, with its long snout and pricked, blunt-ended ears, often appeared on magical objects, such as wands designed to protect against harm.*

belonged to a species that is now extinct, but it is more likely to have been fabricated to produce a disconcerting appearance for a deity associated with trouble and barrenness. Seth could also be represented as a pig, a donkey or a hippopotamus (see *The Contendings of Horus and Seth*).

Shu

The divine personification of air as well as sunlight, Shu's name probably means 'He who Rises Up'. Although he was thought to bring the sun to life each morning and to protect it against the serpent demon Apophis in the Netherworld, he was also often associated with the lunar deities Thoth and Khonsu. Perhaps improbably, he was additionally thought to be the leader of a

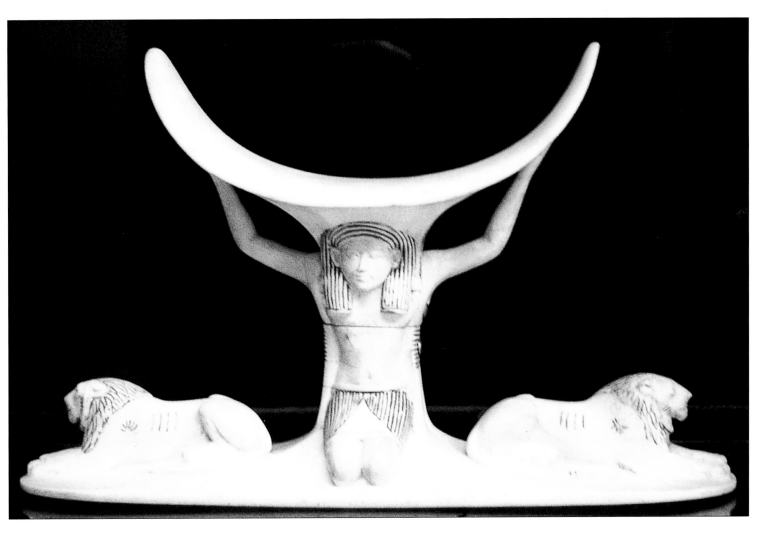

pack of demons that threatened to torture the deceased.

He was represented in human form with a feather on his head, and was often depicted standing between his offspring, Geb (the earth god) and Nut (the sky goddess), supporting the latter. He could also be visualized with the head of a lion, and it was in this guise that he was referred to as an 'Eye of Re', and was worshipped at Leontopolis (Tell el-Muqdam) in the Delta.

Sobek

The crocodile god was represented either as the reptile itself or as a man with the head of a crocodile. Sobek was worshipped in the Faiyum and at the temple of Kom Ombo. Sobek was associated with the might of the Pharaoh, and in the form of Sobek-Re he was worshipped as a manifestation of the Solar diety. His consort was Hathor and Khonsu, elsewhere said to be the son of Amun and Mut, was regarded as their child.

▲ *Incorporated into the design of this ivory headrest found in the tomb of Tutankhamun is Shu, the god of air, who here supports the head of the sleeper rather than his usual load, his daughter Nut, the sky goddess.*

▼ *The ancient Egyptians worshipped Sobek in the form of a crocodile, or with the head of a crocodile, in the hope that this would help to protect them from the hidden dangers of the River Nile. Kom Ombo.*

Sokar

This god was associated with the earth and fertility, but particularly with death and the cemetery of the capital city of Memphis. His funerary association led him to be syncretized with Osiris, and his Memphite importance resulted in his syncretism with the chief deity there, Ptah – hence the invention of the god Ptah-Sokar-Osiris. Sokar's association with Ptah also meant they shared the same consort, the lioness goddess Sekhmet.

▶ *In his role as scribe and messenger of the gods, Thoth was usually represented as a man with the head of an ibis. 19th Dynasty. Valley of the Kings.*

▼ *One of two colossal granite statues of Thoth, the god of wisdom and writing, represented as a baboon. They are all that remains of the once great temple at Hermopolis Magna. 18th Dynasty.*

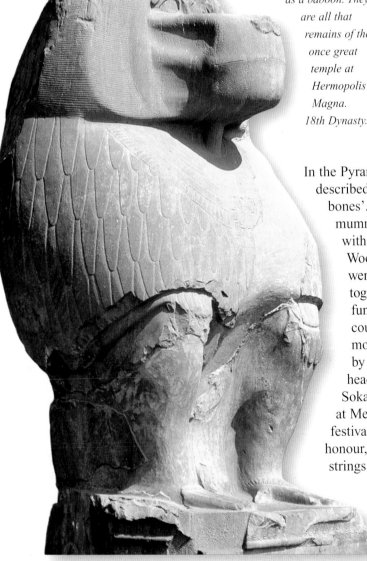

In the Pyramid Texts, Sokar is described as the maker of 'royal bones'. He was represented as a mummified man, sometimes with the head of a hawk. Wooden statuettes of him were placed in tombs together with a host of other funerary equipment. He could also be portrayed as a mound of earth surmounted by a boat containing the head of a hawk.

Sokar's chief cult centre was at Memphis. During the festival held there in his honour, his devotees wore strings of onions around their necks. Onions were certainly used in the embalming process – their skins or whole bulbs were placed over the eyes or stuffed into the ears or the body cavity. Today onion is used to disguise nasty smells, and in folklore it is believed to combat infection.

Tefnut

As one of the cosmic deities of the Ennead, Tefnut was the divine personification of moisture. To tie in with the imagery of symmetrical pairs, when her brother-consort Shu was associated with sunlight, Tefnut was associated with the moon.

Like Shu, Tefnut could be regarded as an 'Eye of Re', and as such was represented with a lioness head (and was worshipped at Leontopolis). She also appeared in the form of a rearing cobra, in which case she was identified with the *uraeus* on the front of the royal headdress. When depicted in human form, she wore a sun disc encircled by a cobra on her head.

Thoth

The god of wisdom and the scribal profession, Thoth manifested himself as a baboon, an ibis or a man with the head of an ibis. He was frequently represented recording important proceedings, such as at the 'Weighing of the Heart' ceremony which was believed to take place after death. He was also closely associated with the moon, so was often depicted wearing a lunar disc and crescent on his head.

His chief cult centre was that of Hermopolis Magna (ancient Khmun; modern el-Ashmunein) in Middle Egypt, where all that remains today are two huge statues of baboons erected by the Eighteenth-Dynasty king Amenhotep III (c.1390–c.1352 BC). These statues are extremely impressive; they are sculpted from great blocks of quartzite, are about 4.5m (15ft) tall (excluding the bases), and weigh about 35 tons each.

During the Ptolemaic Period (332–30 BC) Thoth was identified with the Greek god Hermes; for this reason the city of Khmun became known as Hermopolis ('the city of Hermes').

Wadjet

The ancient goddess Wadjet was nearly always portrayed in the form of a cobra wearing the Red Crown of Lower Egypt. The Egyptians regarded the cobra as a symbol of sovereignty. Wadjet had her cult centre at Buto in the Delta. Her name means 'the Green One' or 'She of the Papyrus'. Together with the vulture goddess Nekhbet (whose cult was based at El-Kab in Upper Egypt) she was believed to protect the king. One of the ruler's five names was his *nebty* or 'two ladies' name, referring to these two particular goddesses. Wadjet appeared as the *uraeus* ('she who rears up') on the king's forehead, poised to spit venom at an unsuspecting enemy. She was also sometimes represented as a lioness. ◆

▲ *The vulture head and cobra on the brow of Tutankhamun's solid-gold mummy mask are decorated with glass and faience, with quartz, carnelian, lapis lazuli and obsidian inlay. The uraeus, or rearing snake, was poised to protect the king from attack by his enemies.*

▼ *The Eye of Horus, flanked by Nekhbet, the vulture goddess of Upper Egypt, and Wadjet, the cobra goddess of Lower Egypt, adorns this pectoral pendant found wrapped under the twelfth layer of linen bandages on Tutankhamun's mummy.*

Myths and their Settings

Stories or myths evolved in all cultures in order to provide a divine explanation for the fundamentals of human existence. In ancient Egypt the realm of the gods was clearly envisaged to reflect that of mortals, as a means of bringing the divine world to life and furnishing the gods and goddesses with a certain accessibility.

Surprisingly few myths actually survive considering the vast time-span of the Egyptian culture and the huge number of its deities, as well as the cult centres with accompanying priesthoods that might have been expected to generate such literature. It is likely that there was a strong oral tradition and that many stories have been lost, but those to which we do still have access were inscribed in hieroglyphs on the walls of temples and tombs, or written on papyrus in the more cursive hieratic and demotic scripts.

The myths that follow have been selected to show how the Egyptians assimilated the mysteries of creation, life and death into their world-view, and to illustrate the recognizably human characters of the major deities, their displays of emotion and the relationships between them. Each myth is accompanied by explanatory details which help to set it in a historical and sociological context.

◀ *The creation myth of Heliopolis envisaged the sky and earth as anthropomorphic deities: Nut the sky goddess and Geb the god of the earth.*

Creation Myths

Several explanations as to how the universe came into being survive from ancient Egypt. Each major centre of religious belief had its own version of the myth of creation, with a different main creator deity who was self-engendered and who went on to generate the other gods and goddesses before creating humankind. The particular deities mentioned in each of the stories relate to the geographical areas where the myths originated. It is impossible to say which of the myths was the most widely accepted at any one time.

The Creation Myth of Memphis

Ptah was the self-engendered creator god who was referred to as the 'father of the gods from whom all life emerged'. He brought the universe into being by conceiving all aspects of it in his heart, then speaking his thoughts out loud. First he created the other deities, and then towns with shrines in which to house them. He provided wood, clay and stone statues to act as bodies for the spirits or divine power (*ka*) of the deities, and offerings to be made to them forever. All things, including all people and animals, were brought into being by Ptah declaring their names.

▲ *Ptah's role as a creator god made him the ideal candidate for patron deity of craftsmen. His high priest was given the title of 'Lord of the Master Craftsmen'. Kom Ombo.*

The Creation Myth of Elephantine

The creator god of this cult centre was the ram-headed deity of the southern cataract region, Khnum. He created the universe by modelling the other gods, as well as humankind (both Egyptians and all those who spoke other languages), animals, birds, fish, reptiles and plants out of clay on his potter's wheel. He paid particular attention to the moulding of the human body, getting the blood to flow over the bones and stretching the skin carefully over the body. He took special care with the installation of the respiratory and digestive systems, the vertebrae, and the reproductive organs. Afterwards, he ensured the continuation of the human race by watching over conception and labour.

The Creation Myth of Hermopolis Magna

This myth begins by concentrating on the elements that were necessary for creation to take place. The fundamental factors were arranged in four male-female pairs: primordial water (Nun and Naunet); air or hidden power (Amun and Amaunet); darkness (Kuk and Kauket); and formlessness or infinity, otherwise interpreted as flood force (Huh and Hauhet). These divine personifications

◄ Thoth had several guises, including that of a man with the head of an ibis, as shown here in a wooden figure with a bronze head dating to the Late Period.

▼ This papyrus scene, from the Third Intermediate Period Book of the Dead of Tameniu, shows the sky goddess Nut arching over her prostrate consort, the earth deity Geb. The fertility of the earth is clearly indicated, and as was usual, the cosmological deities are represented in entirely human form.

of the basic elements of the cosmos are referred to as the Ogdoad (Greek for 'group of eight'; in Egyptian, *khmun*). The four male gods were all frog-headed, and the four goddesses were snake-headed. At some point the eight elements interacted to create a burst of energy, allowing creation to take place.

There are two versions of the events that followed in this creation myth. In one version a primeval mound of earth described as the Isle of Flame rose up out of the primordial water. The god Thoth, in the form of an ibis, placed a cosmic egg on the mound of earth. The egg cracked, hatching the sun, which immediately rose up into the sky.

According to the alternative version, a lotus flower (divinely personified as the deity Nefertem) was bobbing on the surface of the primordial waters when the petals opened and the sun rose out of it. On this occasion the sun was identified as Horus.

The Creation Myth of Heliopolis

Before anything existed or creation had taken place, there was darkness and endless, lifeless water, divinely personified as Nun. A mound of fertile silt emerged from this watery chaos. The self-engendered solar creator god Atum ('the All' or 'the Complete One') appeared upon the mound. By masturbating (or sneezing, according to other versions of the myth) he was able to spit out the deities Shu (the divine personification of air) and Tefnut (moisture). Now that a male-female pair existed, they were able to procreate more conventionally. The results of their sexual union were Geb (the earth) and Nut (the sky). These two were forcibly separated by their father Shu, who lifted Nut up to her place above the earth.

The so-called Ennead (Greek for 'group of nine'; in Egyptian *pesedjet*) of Heliopolis includes these deities: Atum ('the Bull of the Ennead'), Shu, Tefnut, Geb and Nut, and is completed by the offspring of the latter two gods – Osiris, Isis, Seth and Nephthys.   ◆

The Creation Myths in Context

The principle underlying all the different creation myths is that of order being established out of chaos. A state of primordial wateriness is used to represent chaos, out of which emerges a mound, and on it a solar deity. This mythological chain of events clearly reflects the annual flooding of the Nile and the subsiding of the water to reveal deposits of thick black silt, which were incredibly fertile but which required the sun for growth to take place.

All the explanations tend to hinge on the fertility of the land (thanks to the Nile inundation) and the heat of the sun. However, at Memphis the priests devised a myth centred around their supreme deity Ptah, which was decidedly less earthy and rather more metaphysical. Instead of relying on solar energy for creation to take place, the Memphite explanation depended upon the harnessing of three abstract catalysts: *heka* (magic or divine energy), *sia* (divine knowledge) and *hu* (divine utterance). This is similar to the 'logos' doctrine of the biblical New Testament, according to which the word of God became incarnate in the body of Jesus, the second person of the trinity.

The Background to the Creation Myth of Memphis

Memphis (ancient Men-nefer) is about 24km (15 miles) south of modern Cairo in the area of the modern village of Mit Rahina. It was founded as the administrative capital of Egypt at the beginning of the First Dynasty (c.3100 BC), but very little of this ancient capital survives today, mainly because its ruins were quarried during the medieval period for stone to use in the building of Cairo's churches and mosques.

The Memphis creation myth has survived inscribed on a rectangular slab of black granite measuring 92 x 137cm

▲ *The Shabaqo Stone bears a hieroglyphic inscription which is partially obscured by the slab's subsequent use as a mill stone.*

▼ *From the Middle Kingdom Period, the god Ptah was portrayed wearing a strap-on beard like that of the living king.*

◀ *The water table is so high in the region of Memphis that the ancient administrative capital is all but submerged. Preservation of this great city is extremely poor.*

During the embalming process the brain was removed through the nose and discarded as if a waste product, while the heart was always left safely inside the body. The belief was that the dead person required his or her body and – even more importantly – heart in order to be reborn into the Afterlife. The dead person was judged by weighing his or her heart in a balance against the feather of Maat, the goddess of truth.

Order and chaos

The Egyptians had a high regard for order, as is evident from their carefully regulated social structure and intricately documented ritual procedures. Yet their lives were governed by a natural phenomenon which was beyond their control and was not entirely predictable – the inundation of the Nile. This was an event that tended not to be depicted: pictures of the landscape invariably showed the orderly state of the countryside once the river had returned to its normal course.

The creation myths envisaged the beginning of the world as the imposition of order on primeval chaos. The primordial waters of Nun symbolized chaos, while a sense of order was associated with the agricultural cycle and the passage of the sun. Maat, the goddess of truth and justice, also represented social and religious order, which maintained the equilibrium of the Egyptian world.

(36 x 54in) now in the British Museum in London. The inscription was commissioned by the Twenty-fifth Dynasty king Shabaqo (c.716–c.702 BC), who ordered it to be set up in the temple of Ptah at Memphis.

The introduction explains that the king ordered the story to be copied on to stone because the original was written on a material which was becoming very worm-eaten (presumably papyrus or leather), and thus difficult to read.

It was once thought that the language used in the inscription was typical of the Old Kingdom (c.2686–c.2181 BC), and that the original must date to this period. It is now agreed that the original was probably of the late Ramesside Period (c.1100 BC), or possibly even later, although Ptah was clearly regarded as a creator god as early as the Old Kingdom. In the Coffin Texts of the Middle Kingdom (c.2055–c.1650 BC), as well as in later Ramesside texts (c.1200 BC), he is deemed responsible for fashioning the gods and the sun, and for ripening the crops.

The thinking heart

In this myth it is clear that the heart is regarded as the organ for thinking. The ancient Egyptians were not aware of the function of the brain, and instead believed the heart to be the seat of both wisdom and emotion (the idea of thinking with the heart appears frequently). The fact that the brain was considered to be mere stuffing in the head is particularly well exemplified by ancient Egyptian funerary practices.

◄ *Horus performs the Opening of the Mouth ceremony on the mummified body, restoring Sennedjem's senses and enabling him to be reborn into the Afterlife. From the tomb of Sennedjem, Deir el-Medina, 13th century BC.*

last rite before emtombment, various ritual instruments were held up to the mouth and nose of the statue or dead body in order to ignite the senses and breathe life into the vessels for the *kas*. Ptah, the creator god of Memphis, was credited with having invented this particular ritual.

The modern name 'Egypt' derives from the Greek word for the country, *Aiguptos*, and it has been suggested that this in turn derived from the name of one of Ptah's temples at Memphis, *Hwt-ka-Ptah* (which means 'The Mansion for the *ka* of Ptah').

▼ *Figures of bound captives were used in execration rituals. The potency of the magic was heightened by inscribing the name of the enemy (potential or actual) on the figurine. It is unusual for an execration figure to be female.*

The potency of names

The idea of naming something in order to give it a life force is apparent here, as elsewhere in ancient Egyptian thought. The belief that the name was the essence of a deity's potency is clearly illustrated in the myth of *Isis and the Sun God's Secret Name*. In the world of mortals, 'Execration Texts' show that if the ancient Egyptians knew an enemy's name they believed that they could magically destroy him by writing it in a curse on a clay bowl or figurine in the form of a bound captive, which could be smashed as part of an execration ritual.

In the Memphite creation myth the initial concept of a god coupled with the uttering of his or her name caused his or her vital force (*ka*) to come into being; this then required a vessel in which to reside. Most usefully the vessel would be a statue, because this could then act as the icon or focus of the cult.

Human beings were each believed to have their own *ka* which was represented in art as a person's double. On death it was thought necessary to preserve the body so that the *ka* (often translated as 'spirit') could survive. A similar ritual was performed on statues of gods and kings destined for the shrines and temples as was performed on mummified bodies before burial. In the 'Opening of the Mouth' ceremony, the

▲ *The cataract region of Aswan looks idyllic, but the granite rocks over which the river flows here can make navigation treacherous.*

The Background to the Creation Myth of Elephantine

Elephantine is an island in the centre of the River Nile opposite the modern town of Aswan, in the area of the first cataract at the southern border of Egypt. Archaeological excavations since the 1970s have established that it was the site of a large urban settlement, by at least the Roman period.

The city of Elephantine was the chief cult centre of Khnum, the ram-headed god. Here he was worshipped as part of a triad with his consort Satet (usually depicted as a woman wearing the white crown of Upper Egypt with antelope horns on each side) and their daughter Anuket (normally represented as a woman wearing a tall plumed crown and holding a papyrus sceptre), who was the goddess of the first cataract. Khnum's female counterpart was the frog goddess Heket, who was regarded chiefly as a goddess of childbirth, acting as a divine midwife at royal births. Just as Khnum fashioned the first humans on his potter's wheel, so Heket gave life to the unborn child by fashioning it inside the mother.

The Elephantine version of the creation myth appears on the walls of the Graeco-Roman temple at Esna in Upper Egypt. This temple survives only in the form of one hypostyle hall. Hymns dedicated to Khnum by his priests relay the premiss of the myth. The same theme can be found in the myth of the divine birth of the ruler, in which Khnum fashions the ruler and his or her *ka* from clay on his potter's wheel (see The Divine Birth of the Egyptian King).

Deities of the Nile

The creative force of the Nile was acknowledged in the worship of deities associated with the river. While Khnum was revered at Elephantine as a creator god, his consort Satet was associated with the annual flood, and daughter Anuket with the cataracts. Goddesses of fertility and childbirth were portrayed as Nile creatures, such as Heket, the frog-goddess and Taweret, the hippopotamus goddess. The chief deity of the Nile inundation was Hapy who was thought to live in the caverns of the cataract presided over by Khnum. Hapy was depicted as a man with a paunch and pendulous breasts. He often wore aquatic plants on his head.

The Background to the Creation Myth of Hermopolis Magna

Hermopolis Magna (modern el-Ashmunein; ancient Khmun) is situated on the west bank of the Nile in Middle Egypt, close to the modern town of Mallawi. It was the chief cult centre of the god Thoth, identified by the Greeks with their god Hermes.

The earliest known version of this myth dates to the Middle Kingdom (c.2055–c.1650 BC). It offers a perfect example of the way a local deity associated with a specific theology could rise to national prominence when the centre of his cult grew in importance. In this case the god was Amun, who occurs in this myth as Amun Kematef ('he who has completed his moment'). At Thebes, Amun came to be considered as the supreme creator god, and his priesthood was able to surpass the king in power in that region (see *The High Priests*).

Elsewhere, in representations of the sun god coming into being, the eight primordial deities mentioned in this myth are sometimes depicted as baboons in the posture of greeting the rising sun. This is a fine example of the way in which the ancient Egyptians made observations of the natural world and then incorporated them into the iconography of their religious beliefs. At dawn, baboons have a habit of sitting up on their hind legs with their front paws raised, in order to warm their undersides in the morning rays of the sun. This upright posture, with arms and hands raised in front of the face, was adopted as the posture of adoration by humans before the gods.

The numbers four and eight were considered magically significant by the ancient Egyptians. Both numbers were associated with totality, and so the creation of eight deities, in four pairs, makes sense within the context of the Hermopolitan idea of the cosmos.

▲ *The sacred lake in a temple complex such as Karnak would have been the source of water for libations and purification rituals.*

The city of Thoth

Thoth, the god of wisdom and writing, was the scribe to the gods and also their messenger. Because of this latter role, the Greeks identified him with Hermes. His city, Khmun, was therefore renamed Hermopolis ('City of Hermes') during the Graeco-Roman period.

Thoth was worshipped in this period under the name of Hermes Trismegistos ('Thrice-great Hermes'). He was believed to command 'the sacred books in the house of life', i.e papyrus rolls housed in temple libraries, inscribed with medical treatise, mathematical problems, etc.

The Background to the Creation Myth of Heliopolis

Heliopolis is a Greek name meaning 'City of the Sun'. The ancient Egyptians called the city Yunu or On; it is now known as Tell Hisn. It lies a short distance north of the ancient capital at Memphis, and today the site is built over as the area forms part of the north-eastern suburbs of Cairo.

The Ennead (nine gods) of the Heliopolitan myth occur for the first time in the Pyramid Texts of the Old Kingdom (c.2350 BC). Elsewhere the word ennead sometimes serves as a collective noun for gods. In the Pyramid Texts for example, all the gods of the Egyptian pantheon are described as the 'Two Enneads'.

The idea of the primeval mound emerging from the watery chaos is quite clearly an image borrowed from the natural environment – that of the

floodwaters subsiding to reveal the deposits of fertile Nile silt. The ancient Egyptians built their settlements on the highest possible ground in order to avoid the damaging inundation. When the Greek historian Strabo (c.63 BC– c.AD 21) visited Egypt during the reign of the Roman emperor Augustus (30 BC–AD 14), he commented that as a result of the annual flooding of the Nile, 'the whole country is under water and becomes a lake, except the settlements, and those are situated on natural hills or on artificial mounds and contain cities of considerable size and villages which, even when viewed from afar, resemble islands' (*Geography* 17.1.4).

Once Atum has sparked off the process of creation, the myth hinges on the existence of male-female partnerships, and sexual intercourse is the catalyst for continued creation. It is interesting that the divine personification of earth (Geb) is male whereas in most other cultures earth is considered to be female. It is

▲ *When David Roberts drew the Colossi of Memnon in the 1838, the Nile still flooded annually, as it had done in ancient times. These two giant statues of Amenhotep III originally flanked the gateway to his mortuary temple in western Thebes.*

also noteworthy that all the procreative couples have brother-sister relationships, thereby providing divine stereotypes for childbearing marriages within the royal family, especially in the case of Osiris and Isis who were regarded as the archetypal royal couple. However, this incestuous arrangement seems to have been confined to royal couples, stressing their divinity and separating them from ordinary people: when non-royal husbands and wives (both lovers and married couples) referred to each other as 'brother' and 'sister', they appear to have been using these terms as expressions of affection rather than describing actual familial relationships. ◆

The Death of Osiris

During a time beset by turmoil, the birth of the god Osiris was heralded by an array of good omens and positive signs. Before his appearance, war and cannibalism appear to have been the order of the day – the people were said to be barbarians. Osiris became king of the Delta town of Busiris, but it was not long before he was made king of all Egypt. His skill lay in his ability to teach the unruly population to farm the land successfully and to lead law-abiding lives and worship the gods. Order had quite clearly been restored to the country when Osiris decided to go away on a journey and his wicked brother Seth seized the opportunity to gather together 72 conspirators. They hatched a treacherous plot.

On Osiris's return they threw a party and, following an enormous banquet, Seth suggested that the revellers should play a game (devised by him of course). A chest was laid out in the great hall and the game was to see who could fit inside it. When Osiris's turn came, he climbed into the chest, and – not surprisingly – it was the perfect-sized coffin for him.

One of the conspirators leapt forward and slammed down the lid, trapping Osiris inside. Unable to free himself, Osiris died and thus became ruler of the dead in the Afterlife.

This is by no means the end of the myth, however, because Osiris's dead body, still inside the chest, was disposed of in the Tanitic branch of the Nile. Its journey had only just begun, for instead of sinking to the murky depths as Seth had hoped, it floated with the current northwards towards the coast, and then out into the Mediterranean Sea. As if that was not far enough, it proceeded to bob all the way to the busy Lebanese port of Byblos, and finally came to rest in the entangled roots of a tree. Engulfed by the tree, the chest became part of its

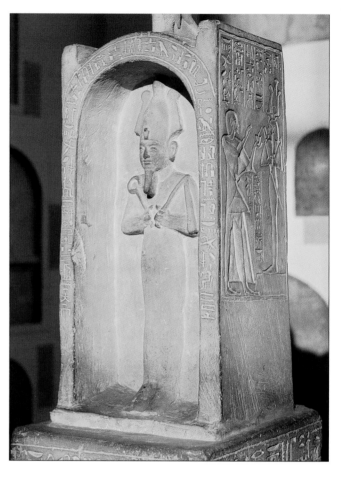

▲ *It is appropriate that this shrine of Osiris should resemble a coffin, as he was god of the dead and the Afterlife. In his myth he dies when he is confined in a chest by his brother Seth.*

trunk. In due course the tree was cut down and turned into a pillar. Soon, Osiris's body was helping to support the roof of the palace of Byblos's ruler.

The quest of Isis

Meanwhile, Osiris's sister and consort Isis had set her heart on retrieving the body of her husband, in order to give it a proper burial in accordance with Egyptian customs. To make her searching easier, and fearful of her brother Seth's intentions, she hid her young child Horus in the Delta marshes, under the watchful eye of the protective cobra-form goddess Wadjet, who had her cult centre at Buto (ancient Pe).

Isis followed a tip-off to Byblos, where she befriended a group of the queen's maids and thereby gained access to the

▼ *In the funerary art, Isis (here on the left) and her sister Nephthys are often shown as kites.*

◀ *In addition to faience examples such as this one, an enormous number of bronze figures of Isis suckling the infant Horus have survived from the Late Period of ancient Egyptian history.*

▲ *This papyrus illustration from the Book of the Dead of Lady Cheritwebeshet shows Seth protecting the sun god from the threat of the serpent-demon Apophis. 21st Dynasty.*

temple. Her magical powers (including turning herself into a swallow, and performing rituals to make the dead Osiris immortal) became known to the king and queen, who offered the goddess anything they might be able to give her. They presumably hid their surprise when she requested a certain column in the royal house.

Osiris's burial

Thus in possession of the chest, Isis returned to Egypt with it, and hid it in the marshy Delta while she went to collect her son. This proved to be unwise, because Seth happened to be out hunting that night in that particular vicinity, and no doubt could not believe his luck when he happened upon the chest. He proceeded gleefully to hack Osiris's body into 14 pieces (or more, according to inscriptions at the temples of Dendera and Edfu), scattering them far and wide.

It seemed as though Osiris's body was destined not to receive the burial it deserved, but Isis refused to give up and began her search for the strewn pieces. At each place that she found a missing piece, she conducted a burial ceremony (thus explaining the claim made by several of the ancient Egyptian temples that they housed the tomb of Osiris). Only one part of his body was never found, and that was his penis, which had been swallowed by a fish. In order to ensure the correct burial of Osiris's entire body, his dutiful wife made him an artificial penis.

So Isis was able to work her magic, not to bring her husband back from the dead, but finally to bury his dismembered remains. Meanwhile Osiris had taken up the position of king of the dead in the Afterlife. ◆

Osiris's gifts to humankind

As the son of Geb, the earth, and Nut, the sky, Osiris probably originated as a fertility god of earth and underworld. During his reign as king of Egypt, he taught his subjects how to make bread and wine, and oversaw the building of the first temples and statues to the gods. He built towns and set just and fair laws. Having civilized Egypt, Osiris embarked on a journey to repeat the process in neighbouring countries.

The Death of Osiris in Context

This version of the myth of Osiris is the one recorded by the Greek writer Plutarch (c.AD 46–c.126). He visited Egypt and was inspired to write an account of this age-old story (albeit with a Greek slant). He called it *Peri Isidos kai Osiridos*. There is no doubt that Plutarch was relating a truly Egyptian tale, but a survey of the various accounts of Osiris's death reveals a number of variations.

The legend of Osiris's rule over Predynastic Egypt was being written down from as early as the Fifth Dynasty (c.2494–c.2345 BC), but those references that survive in the Pyramid Texts really give very little detail. The king dies 'falling on his side' on the riverbank at Abydos (or Nedjet) but no cause of death is given. Early accounts do not mention the dismemberment of Osiris's body but they do tell us that Isis has to search for the body and, finding it, she 'gathers up his flesh' so that it can be embalmed at Abydos. The mention of this temple site is significant because throughout pharaonic history it was believed to be the burial place of Osiris.

The Coffin Texts of the Middle Kingdom (c.2055–c.1650 BC) inscribed, as the name implies, on coffins of this period embellish the story. They say that it was indeed Seth who killed Osiris at Nedjet, and Isis (together with her sister Nephthys) is said to have mummified the dead body.

Osiris's penis

A major variation on Plutarch's telling of the myth can be found in the Chapel of Sokar, in the temple built by the Nineteenth-Dynasty king Seti I (c.1294–c.1279 BC) at Abydos. It contains reliefs indicating that Horus

▶ *Osiris's false curled beard, as illustrated here in the tomb of Nefertari in the Valley of the Queens, is distinct from the false straight beards worn by the living pharaohs. 19th Dynasty.*

▲ *This Roman period gilt coffin shows Isis and Nephthys mourning the death of Osiris. Isis is also portrayed as a kite hovering over the mummified body.*

had not been born before Osiris's death. In one scene Osiris is lying on an embalming table manually stimulating his penis. The relief on the opposite wall displays Isis in the guise of a sparrow-hawk hovering over Osiris's erect penis so as to be impregnated by him. Unlike Plutarch's version, in the pharaonic

▼ *The fish motif, used in this glass vessel from Amarna, was common in ancient Egyptian art. 18th Dynasty.*

tradition Osiris's penis was not swallowed by a fish, but was laid to rest in the capital of Memphis (close to modern-day Cairo).

The idea of Horus as a young boy being hidden away in the marshes is evident in the pharaonic tradition because he is thought to have survived a scorpion sting while hiding. The ancient Egyptians believed that if children were stung by a scorpion they must identify them in spells with the child Horus, and this, it was hoped, would cure them.

Mummification

In the myth of Osiris, the belief, is evident that the gods ruled over the Egyptian people before the advent of the mortal dynasties.

This myth is, however, particularly important because it provides a divine prototype for the practice of mummification, and for the concept of rebirth into the Afterlife. It was believed that Osiris's body was the first to be mummified, and the lengths to which Isis went in order to retrieve the various parts of Osiris's body and to give them a proper burial, weaving lengths of linen for the wrapping of the body, reflects the ancient Egyptian fear of dying in the desert or abroad in case this meant that they would not be buried in accordance with traditional funerary rituals.

The ancient Egyptians believed that in order to be granted a place in the Afterlife a person needed his or her body to be buried intact and should also have a suitable funeral, including all the correct spells and rituals. So this myth provides a model for ancient Egyptian funerary beliefs as well as for the concept of the deceased king of Egypt being identified with the god Osiris. It is also the prototype for brother-sister marriages within the royal family. ◆

Dying and rising gods

Osiris's death and the story of his grieving consort Isis contain elements common to myths about dying and rising gods in other cultures. All were associated with vegetation, fertility and the harvest, offering reassurance that their worshippers could rely on bountiful crops. They underlined the regenerative powers of nature, suggesting the continuance of future generations and, above all, the annual rebirth of the natural world.

Isis and the Seven Scorpions

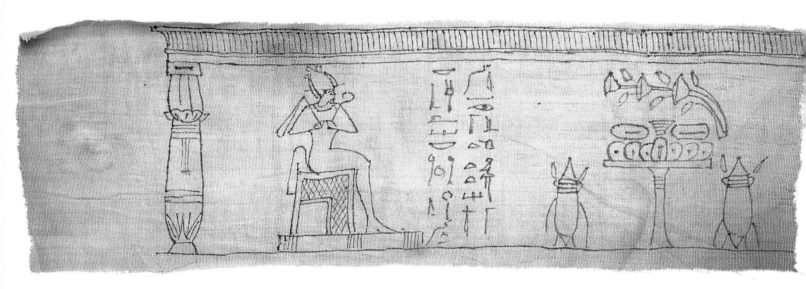

The tale begins with Isis busily weaving the linen mummy wrappings for the body of her dead husband Osiris, who had been murdered by their brother Seth. She was interrupted by the god of wisdom and writing, Thoth, who advised her to take her young son Horus into hiding, in order to protect him from his uncle Seth.

Isis took heed of Thoth's words, and that evening she set off with an escort of seven scorpions. In order that Seth should not learn of their absence, Isis instructed the scorpions to be vigilant, and on no account to talk to any strangers on the way. Travelling through the Delta, they arrived at a place called the Town of the Two Sisters. There, rather than being welcomed by the local prosperous family, they had the front door slammed in their faces by the lady of the house. The scorpions were riled and vowed to wreak revenge. Six of them added their own personal supplies of poison to the sting of the seventh, who crawled under the rich woman's door and stung her young son almost to death. Beside herself, the woman rushed around the town desperately seeking help, but nobody responded to her cries.

▲ It has been calculated that a mummy might be wrapped in up to 375sq m (450sq yd) of linen bandaging. This bandage bears a vignette from the 'Book of the Dead'.

A happy ending

Just as the boy was about to die, Isis intervened. She had been given lodgings by a peasant girl, and would not tolerate the death of this innocent child. To cure him, she held him and uttered a magic spell that involved naming each of the scorpions in turn, thus allowing her to control them. The event was to be life-changing for the boy's mother, who offered Isis and the peasant girl all her worldly possessions.

◄ Egypt is home to two types of scorpion, the darker, relatively harmless Scorpioniae, and the paler, more poisonous Buthridae. The goddess Selket, shown here, took the form of a scorpion, and guarded the canopic jar containing the intestines.

Isis and the Seven Scorpions in Context

This story about the magical powers of Isis offered a means of curing, or protecting against the possibility of, scorpion stings. The same purpose is served by the myth of *Isis and the Sun God's Secret Name*.

The myth of Isis and the Seven Scorpions is found inscribed on the Metternich Stela, which is now in the Metropolitan Museum of Art in New York. This stone stela is a *cippus*, which means that it resembles a gravestone in shape, and has a central image of Horus as a child standing on a crocodile, clutching scorpions, snakes and other threatening creatures. Within this particular vignette the child Horus (Hor-pa-khered) is protected not only by the presence of the spirit deity Bes, but also by other deities and *udjat*-eyes, since the Eye of Horus was used as a protective amulet. A number of spells are also inscribed on the *cippus*, for use in a ritual in which water became imbued with magical potency when it was poured over the *cippus*. The liquid could then be ritually drunk or applied.

The recitation of the spell used by Isis in this myth was to be accompanied by a prescription of barley-bread, garlic and salt. Cereals, bread and salt are still used in Egyptian rituals today to appease and ward off evil influences. A poultice of barley-bread is also still used to draw out the poison when someone has been stung by a scorpion. The idea of sympathetic magic is very much apparent on the Metternich Stela: by identifying any child suffering from a scorpion sting with the young boy in the myth, they too could be healed.

Knowledge is power

As in the myth of *Isis and the Sun God's Secret Name*, the belief in the knowledge of a name giving control is an extremely important element. Isis can exert power over the scorpions only by naming them in her spell. The fact that there are seven scorpions is also significant, because the number seven was deemed to be magically potent and was used in various spells, particularly one involving the ritual tying and untying of seven knots.

Although healing spells derived from myths like this one often dealt with the most commonplace of problems, some of the most important of the Egyptian deities were involved in their solutions and remedies. So even the most superior of the gods and goddesses might play a part in the daily lives of the Egyptians, indicating how closely state and popular religion were interwoven. ◆

Horus and the scorpion

Although Isis's magic was effective in counteracting the poison of the seven scorpions, she seems not to have had the power to cure her own small son, Horus. Having hidden him in the marshes at Khemmis in the Delta while she went to find food for herself, she returned to find that he had been stung. Her screams reached the ears of the sun god, Re, and caused him to bring his solar boat to a halt so that the earth was plunged into darkness.

Thoth left Re's boat and uttered a spell to cure Horus, threatening that the earth would remain dark until the poison left him. Horus was restored to health and Thoth charged the people of Khemmis with his care. Then he returned to Re's boat, which set sail again.

▶ *The magical potency of a Cippus of Horus was no doubt strengthened if it was held by a statue of a priest.*

The Contendings of Horus and Seth

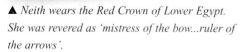

The myth opens with a courtroom scene and plunges straight into the deliberations of a trial that had already been dragging on for 80 years. This was, of course, no ordinary courtroom, but that of the gods, presided over by the sun god Re, and centre stage were Horus and Seth, who were there to contest the rightful claim to the throne of Egypt.

This long episode follows the death of the reigning king Osiris. The murder of this god, who had been maintaining a stable and prosperous rule over Egypt, was clearly the first step in a plan by his brother Seth to usurp the throne, but Osiris had died leaving a son and heir, Horus, who, it might be assumed, would have inherited the throne.

▲ *Neith wears the Red Crown of Lower Egypt. She was revered as 'mistress of the bow...ruler of the arrows'.*

▲ *Kharga is the southernmost and largest of the major Egyptian oases in the Western Desert.*

The indecision of the jury

The gods presiding in the court were by no means unanimous in their opinion. Some considered Horus too young to rule, and they believed Seth's strength would make him a more successful ruler. They were swayed by the fact that Seth travelled in Re's boat and repulsed the sun god's enemies, especially the serpent demon Apophis (see *The Journey of the Sun through the Netherworld*).

The divine court decided to turn to the advice and wisdom of the ancient goddess of warfare, Neith, who resided at Sais in the Delta. She was adamantly in favour of Horus, but was a fair arbiter and believed that Seth should be compensated with treasure and two Syrian goddesses, Anat and Astarte (described as Re's daughters). Her decision was coupled with a threat not to be taken lightly: if Horus were not allowed to succeed to the throne, the sky would fall down on the Egyptian people.

The gods appeared not to take this threat seriously because they still refused to agree on a final outcome. The argument was starting to get heated, especially when the deity Baba dared to insult Re by telling him his shrine was empty. The great sun god left sulking and returned only when he had been cheered up by his daughter Hathor, who made him laugh by exposing her genitalia to him.

A change of scene

The gods were beginning to get bored by the proceedings, so they decided on a change of scene. They relocated to an island, but Horus's mother Isis, who was particularly concerned that her son should inherit his father's throne, was believed to have a biased view, so the ferryman Nemty was forbidden to take her across the water from the mainland. But this goddess was a mistress of disguise and, transforming herself into an old hag, she fooled the ferryman into transporting her to the island. Once there she turned herself into a beautiful young woman and proceeded to seduce the unsuspecting Seth. She claimed to have been married to a cattle herder who had died, leaving her with a young son. She spun the piteous yarn further by telling him that a stranger had turned up and

Courts of law

The administration of justice was not dealt with by specialized lawyers, but by general tribunals, consisting of local officials and respected citizens, which met when the need arose. The site of Deir el-Medina has yielded information on these courts. From the time of the New Kingdom (c.1550–c.1069 BC), oracles were sometimes consulted to help settle legal arguments.

Punishments for crimes included beatings and enforced labour, and the death penalty was used in serious cases such as treason.

▶ *The hippopotamus hunt depicted on the wall of the tomb of Mereruka at Saqqara symbolizes the victory of good, or order, over evil, or chaos, epitomized by the triumph of Horus over Seth. Old Kingdom.*

had tried to steal their cattle and throw her son out of their house. As Isis had hoped, Seth condemned the behaviour of this stranger, and in so doing, passed judgement on himself for his attempt to confiscate Horus's inheritance.

Horus was awarded the throne, but just as the matter seemed to have been decided, the proceedings became still more complicated and ambiguous.

Seth appealed and challenged Horus to an underwater contest, with both gods taking the form of hippopotami: if either of them was to surface before the end of three months he would lose his claim to the throne. Isis of course wanted to help her son as much as possible, so she decided to kill Seth and hurled a copper harpoon into the water. But the result was not as planned, for it accidentally embedded itself in Horus's flesh. Isis panicked, but was able to withdraw the weapon using magic, and threw it again. This time it hit Seth, but Seth reminded Isis that he was her brother and a pang of guilt caused her to withdraw the harpoon a second time.

Events grew stranger still when Horus rose out of the water, and in a fit of rage cut off his mother's head. She turned into a flint statue and he realized that he had overreacted. Fearing punishment he fled with his mother's head to the area of the Kharga and Dakhla oases in the Western Desert. But Seth was out to avenge his sister's decapitation. He tracked down his nephew lying under a tree, and gouged out his eyes (which, when buried, grew back as lotus flowers). It was left to the cow goddess Hathor to cure Horus's sight, which she did using gazelle milk.

The gods realized that things were getting out of control, so they summoned Horus and Seth back to court. But nobody could have predicted what would happen next.

A banquet was thrown during which Seth sexually assaulted Horus in order to humiliate him publicly,

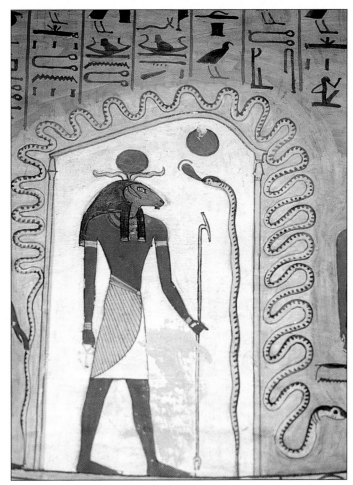

▶ *Re, the sun god, was often depicted in his solar boat with a ram's head, wearing a sun disc on his head.*

and to display his own strength and superiority. The incident did not go as Seth had planned, however, because Horus managed to catch Seth's semen in his carefully positioned hands before it could enter him. He went running to his mother (whose head had been magically restored) with the rogue ejaculate. Shocked, she cut off her son's hand, disposing of it (and thus the semen) in the marshes. She realized that to foil Seth's plan completely he must now be tricked into ingesting Horus's semen, so Horus obliged (having had his hand magically replaced by Isis) and she spread some on Seth's favourite food, lettuce. Seth duly tucked into his doctored snack.

Back in the courtroom, the semen of the two gods was asked to speak out in order to ascertain its whereabouts and prove Seth's story about the assault. But instead of speaking from inside Horus, Seth's semen spoke out from the marshes, while Horus's identified itself inside Seth and emerged as a gold sun disc (indicating its divine origins) from the top of his head.

The final outcome

Seth was, of course, livid and challenged Horus to a boat race. Extraordinarily (although by now little should surprise us), it was decided that the boats must be made of stone. Horus craftily built his using pine painted to look like stone; Seth's (which was made out of a mountain peak) sank. Enraged, Seth turned himself into a hippopotamus and smashed up Horus's boat.

Enough was enough. Osiris sent a threatening message from the Netherworld and Horus was at last confirmed as the rightful heir to the throne. Seth's strength was not to be overlooked, however; he was employed by the sun god to thunder in the sky and to keep evil at bay.

Egyptian morality

The episode of Seth's homosexual assault on Horus seems to show him in a bad light, yet he had planned the whole episode to expose Horus by proclaiming the act himself before the gods' tribunal to help him win his case. The story would have been understood by the Egyptians in terms of the humiliating treatment of a defeated enemy.

Thus, when Horus's semen spoke from inside Seth, the general mockery was turned on him and he was seen as the defeated adversary. The New Kingdom Book of the Dead implies that homosexuality was condemned, but earlier texts suggest that homosexual relations were not considered morally wrong so long as there was mutual consent.

▼ *Wooden model boats were commonly placed in tombs of the Middle Kingdom Period. They might have oarsmen for heading north with the current, or sails when their journey was southwards with the wind.*

The Contendings of Horus and Seth in Context

This detailed version of the myth is found on a papyrus roll that has come to be known as Papyrus Chester Beatty number one (now in the Dublin Museum). It covers almost sixteen pages, and is written in hieratic script (the cursive form of hieroglyphs) by a scribe who had very fine handwriting. It comes from Thebes and dates to the Twentieth-Dynasty reign of Ramesses V (c.1147– c.1143 BC).

The Edfu reliefs

A more combative version of the myth appears on the walls of the Ptolemaic temple at Edfu, which is dedicated to Horus. In this series of text and relief it was Horus who, in the form of a winged disc, accompanied the sun god Re in his solar boat, and protected the sun against its enemies (which appear mainly as hippopotami and crocodiles, two animals that regularly threatened the safety of the ancient Egyptians).

In this version Seth was the leader of the pack of enemies, so he and Horus repeatedly came up against each other, taking various forms; for example, Seth was a cheetah or a snake while Horus was a lion. In the final showdown, Seth turned himself into a red hippopotamus. The battle took place at Elephantine, at the southern boundary of Egypt, and is said to have happened during a wild storm which churned up the river. In this way, an explanation is provided for the cataract at Elephantine – a granite outcrop under the water that turns that particular stretch of the river into a series of unnegotiable rapids. Horus triumphed by killing Seth with his harpoon. As Seth was dismembered, Isis decided that his bones should be fed to the cats and his fat to the worms.

The principal point made in this myth is that the son of the king should inherit the throne. The story provided a model for the smooth succession of the royal line. The aim was to protect the son and

▲ *The gods in the reliefs in the temple at Edfu, as elsewhere, were considered pagan by the Christians and were vigorously excised. Graeco-Roman Period.*

heir by providing a divine prototype – the living king would be identified with Horus, and the deceased king with Osiris. Seth played the possible usurper, who in reality may or may not have been a member of the royal family. The royal office was especially vulnerable when the son and heir was a minor on his father's death, as in the case of Horus, and when the alternative claimant was supported by a powerful court faction.

▶ *On the walls of the temple at Edfu, Horus wears the double crown of the pharaoh and harpoons Seth as a hippopotamus. Graeco-Roman Period.*

▲ *Temple reliefs and religious texts make clear the divine or magical properties believed to be held by breast milk.*

Courts of justice

The ancient Egyptians clearly believed that the divine world reflected that of mortals, and gods and goddesses behaved in much the same way as humans, for example in taking their disputes to court.

The important role of the court in ancient Egyptian society is well documented, particularly at the site of Deir el-Medina, the village on the west bank at Thebes inhabited during the New Kingdom (c.1550–c.1069 BC) by the tomb builders and their families. The local court was called the *kenbet* and its members were respected villagers joined by government officials connected with the community, such as a scribe from the

vizier's office, which was based across the river in the main city of Thebes. The *kenbet* was mainly concerned with civil disputes between private individuals, especially over property and arising from economic transactions.

The vizier, who was the king's chief minister, presided over the 'Great Kenbet' or 'Supreme Court'. This was not a permanent assembly, but a selection of between eight and fourteen Theban VIPs who gathered when necessary to preside over the prosecution of particularly serious crimes, such as the tomb robberies of the late Ramesside Period (c.1100 BC).

Milk and lettuce

Both milk and lettuce have an interesting significance in this myth: Horus's eyes are said to be cured by the application of gazelle's milk, and it is

said that Seth's favourite food, which is consequently drizzled with Horus's semen, is lettuce.

The milk used in the myth is that of a gazelle, but it is also true that human breast milk was considered an effective ingredient in medical prescriptions and magical rituals (although distinct in modern minds, the two were closely related according to the ancient Egyptian magico-medical texts). The milk of a mother who had given birth to a male child was considered especially useful for remedying colds, burns and eye diseases.

Similar cures continued to appear in the work of Hippocrates and of other classical writers such as Pliny and Dioscorides, as well as in Coptic medical texts and in European medical treatises up until the seventeenth

Sons and heirs

The throne of Egypt, having been granted to Horus, was thereafter known as the Horus Throne. Each successive king was identified with Horus while he lived and with Osiris, perceived as Horus's dead father, after his death.

The act of burying his predecessor, reflecting the service performed by Horus for Osiris, was enough to fulfil the new king's role as Horus and legitimize his position as son and heir to the throne. This could hold true even if the old king had not actually been his real father. If a king died without having produced a son, a successor – who might not necessarily be of royal blood – could validate his claim to the throne by burying the dead king. According to ritual, seventy days should elapse between the king's death and his burial, to allow for the funeral preparations.

◄ *The tall lettuces behind the ancient god Min, on this fragment of relief from Koptos, were symbols of his cult and of fertility and sexuality.*

pot holds just over 100ml (4fl oz), roughly equivalent to the amount of milk produced by one breast at one feed. Perhaps the ancient Egyptians believed that when they put an animal's milk in such a pot, it magically became (or at least took on the therapeutic properties of) a woman's milk.

Lactating women were obviously considered in some way special in religious terms, because they were credited with *heka* or magic. A wet nurse might bear the title *Sau*, implying that she had a protective, safeguarding role, as *sa* was the word for 'protection' and also for 'amulet'.

The type of lettuce referred to in the myth is *Lactuca sativa longifolia*, which grew tall and straight like a modern cos lettuce and emitted a milky-white liquid when pressed. This fluid was presumably thought to resemble semen because the lettuce was closely associated with the fertility god Min, and the Egyptians considered it to be an aphrodisiac. Thus the choice of this particular vegetable in the context of this myth becomes more understandable.

In Egyptian folklore today, the lettuce is still considered an aphrodisiac. But classical writers had very different views on the effect the lettuce might have. Athenaeus stated that lettuce caused impotence; Pliny wrote that one particular sort of lettuce was called 'the anti-aphrodisiac' or 'the eunuch's lettuce' because it was 'an extremely potent check to amorous propensities' (instead, he recommended leeks as a sexual stimulant). Lettuce must have had a similar reputation in the seventeenth century as it was 'commended for Monkes, Nunnes, and the like sort of people to eate'. ◆

century. Even today, in Britain and other Western countries, mothers are commonly advised to treat their babies' eye infections with breast milk.

Some ancient Egyptian pots have been discovered that may well have been designed to hold breast milk. They are modelled in the shape of a breast-feeding woman or Taweret, the hippopotamus goddess of pregnancy and childbirth. Occasionally the pot has a hole in place of one of the nipples, which would presumably have acted as a spout. It has been calculated that each

The Destruction of Humankind

he events of this myth took place when the sun god Re was king of both the divine and the mortal worlds. He is described as elderly, with bones made of silver, flesh of gold, and hair of lapis lazuli.

The king learnt that humankind was plotting a rebellion against him. His immediate reaction was to destroy the race, but he felt he ought first to seek advice. He summoned his followers and ordered them to bring a number of deities to his court. Among them were to be Shu, Tefnut, Geb, Nut, Nun and, most crucially, a goddess he referred to as his 'Eye': this turned out to be Hathor in her peaceful manifestation, turning into Sekhmet when she became savage. The gods had to arrive secretly so that the human beings would not discover that their plot was being foiled.

The Eye of Re

The gods arrived at the palace and bowed before the king, who asked for their opinion on the matter in hand. Their unanimous suggestion was that he should send his Eye to slaughter the humans as they tried to escape into the desert. Re adopted their recommendation and the goddess readily obliged. However, after a day of massacre, Re was compassionate and felt that enough had been done to show humankind who was in charge. But the Eye of Re, as Sekhmet, was bloodthirsty and out of control: she was ready to wipe out the human race.

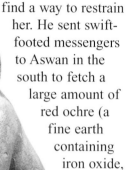

Now that the malevolent force of the goddess had been unleashed, Re had to find a way to restrain her. He sent swift-footed messengers to Aswan in the south to fetch a large amount of red ochre (a fine earth containing iron oxide,

▲ *This gold statuette of Amun-Re holds an ankh, symbolizing the giving of life, in one hand, and the scimitar, a symbol of strength, power and foreign conquest, in the other.*

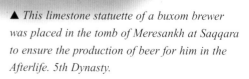

▲ *This limestone statuette of a buxom brewer was placed in the tomb of Meresankh at Saqqara to ensure the production of beer for him in the Afterlife. 5th Dynasty.*

◄ One of the black granite statues of Sekhmet placed by Amenhotep III in the temple of Mut at Karnak. 18th Dynasty.

or haematite) and take it to his temple at Heliopolis, where the high priest was instructed to grind up the haematite. Maid servants were ordered to crush enough barley to make 7,000 jars of beer. This was to be no ordinary beer, but was to have the red ochre mixed in with it, so that it looked like blood. Work began immediately and continued throughout the night.

Could the human race be saved? Re rose early and ordered the fields where Sekhmet was due to resume her massacre to be flooded with the red beer. The goddess was ecstatic when she saw it, thinking she had happened upon a sea of human blood, and she gulped it down greedily. This had the desired result, and in her drunken state she did not even notice the people of Egypt, let alone continue to kill them off.

▲ Hathor's customary headdress was a sun disc sitting between cow's horns, but she was also shown wearing a falcon on a perch, as in this painted relief in the tomb of Horemheb in the Valley of the Kings, Thebes.

Re's abdication

Re had saved his people, and the frenzied goddess was once again peaceful. But the experience had been too much for the king. He decided he had had enough and abdicated, leaving the responsibilities of government to Thoth, the god of wisdom and writing. Re left Thoth to teach humankind the skill of literacy, and ascended into the sky on the back of the Divine Cow for a spell of peace and quiet.

The Destruction of Humankind in Context

Sections of this myth have been found in five of the tombs in the Valley of the Kings, on the west bank at Thebes. This particular royal burial site was employed by rulers of the New Kingdom (c.1550–c.1069 BC). The earliest example of the myth occurs on the interior of the outermost of the four gilded shrines that were found by Howard Carter in 1922 over the sarcophagus of the Eighteenth-Dynasty king Tutankhamun, (c.1336–c.1327 BC). The contents of this tomb are now in the Cairo Museum. There is a longer version of the text in a side-room off the burial chamber of the tomb of the Nineteenth-Dynasty ruler Seti I (c.1294–c.1279 BC), as well as variations of the text in the tombs of his successor

▲ *The sky goddess could also be represented as a sow. A comparison was being made between a sow eating her young and Nut swallowing the sun and stars.*

Ramesses II (c.1279–c.1213 BC), and two of the Twentieth-Dynasty kings, Ramesses III (c.1184–c.1153 BC) and VI (c.1143–c.1136 BC). Although all the known copies of the myth date to this particular period of Egyptian history, the style of writing is in fact that of the Middle Kingdom (c.2055–c.1650 BC), and so it is likely that it was originally written down at that time.

The myth is actually part of a longer religious text known as 'The Book of the Divine Cow', incorporating spells to protect the body of

◀ *The cobra goddess Mertseger ('she who loves silence') was known as the Goddess of the Peak. She commanded fear and respect among the villagers of Deir el-Medina, especially as she was believed able to cause blindness and venomous stings.*

the king and to ensure his safe ascension to the heavens. This was done by identifying him with the sun god, who rises successfully into the sky at the end of the myth.

The wrath of the gods

The main theme of the myth is, of course, the divine punishment of the human race, a theme which also occurs in the Mesopotamian and Biblical stories of the Flood. The significance of the image of a flood for the ancient Egyptians cannot be underestimated, but in this myth they are saved by it; their lives would have revolved around, and even depended upon, the annual flooding of the Nile that took place between July and October.

It is known from other sources that the ancient Egyptian gods were believed capable of meting out punishment to

◄ *The original obelisk was the sacred* benben *stone at Heliopolis on which the first rays of the sun were said to have shone.*

past. In the early third century BC an Egyptian priest named Manetho was commissioned to write a history of Egypt by the Ptolemaic ruler of Egypt Ptolemy II (285–246 BC). Although he wrote his *Aegyptiaca* in Greek, he would presumably have had access to earlier Egyptian lists of kings, temple archives, and popular tales. Before dividing the rulers up into thirty-one dynasties, beginning with a king named Menes and ending with Alexander the Great, he described a period when gods had ruled over the Egyptian people. ◆

Flood myths

A limitless ocean featured in the creation myths of many cultures as the primeval state of the world. A flood of global proportions was also a common theme, in which an inundation was sent to wipe out sinful humankind and restore the world to its pristine original state. The Egyptians believed that Re might well one day tire of humanity and that he had the capacity to return the world to the watery abyss of Nun.

Myths about overwhelming floods reflected the ambiguous nature of humanity's relationship with water, which was vital to life but also carried the threat of violence and devastation. In Mesopotamia, the Rivers Tigris and Euphrates flooded unpredictably, and their fearsome character was expressed in several versions of a flood myth which eventually found its way into the Hebraic tradition as the story of Noah's ark.

individuals for wrongdoings. The offences might be against specific deities (as witnessed by various penitential hymns found inscribed on stelae from Deir el-Medina), or they might be more general offences, such as the long list of wrongdoings that the dead had to be able to swear they had not committed in order to be granted a place in the Afterlife.

Born of the gods

But the gods were quite clearly merciful because it was perceived that their own existence was ultimately dependent upon the existence of mortals. The gods required the ancient Egyptian people to tend to them, provide them offerings of food, and build temples for them. A marked interdependence was evident – the gods were worshipped in exchange for their benefice.

Another reason why Re might well have had a change of heart when it came to wiping out all human beings was the fact that humankind had emanated from the sun god himself, that is to say from his tears, when he created the world. The ancient Egyptian love of wordplay and punning is conspicuous here, considering the similarity between the ancient Egyptian words for people (*remetch*) and tear (*remyt*). The magical association of similar-sounding words also occurs in the texts known as Dream Papyri. These were collections of dream scenarios that were thought useful for predicting the future.

The idea of the gods ruling over humankind is certainly not unique to this myth (see also *The Death of Osiris*), and was quite clearly crucial to the ancient Egyptians' understanding of their own

Isis and the Sun God's Secret Name

The sun god Re had many different names, but the one that held the key to his supreme power was a secret one that only he knew. Anyone lucky enough to discover the secret would be able to claim a position next to Re at the head of the pantheon of gods and goddesses.

Isis, who was very clever, was determined to discover this secret name so she hatched a plan. As an old man, Re drooled, and Isis collected some of his saliva and mixed it with earth to conjure a demon in the form of a snake, symbolizing Re's own strength.

Isis knew that Re was partial to a daily stroll outside his palace, so she familiarized herself with his usual route, and left the snake at the crossroads he was likely to pass. Of course he did walk this way, and the snake bit him, as Isis had intended.

The snake's venom entered Re and he became overwhelmed by a terrible fever. Because he had not created the snake, Re had no idea how to cure himself of the effects of its bite. He cried out in agony and the other gods came running but were unable to help him in his distress. His future was looking bleak, when Isis arrived. She offered to cure him on condition that he told her his secret name.

The sun god is cured

As well as being considered 'great in magic', Isis was known to have impressive medical skills, so Re was tempted, but he knew that having someone else in possession of his secret identity could put him in a vulnerable position. He tried to pull the wool over Isis's eyes by reeling off a long list of his other names, such as 'Moulder of the Mountains' and 'Maker of the Bull for the Cow in order to bring Sexual Pleasure into Being'.

But Isis could not be duped, and Re's symptoms grew even worse – he was sweating, shivering and losing his sight. In desperation, he agreed to Isis's bargain. He told her his secret name, but knowing that she would not be able to resist passing it on to her son, he insisted that she promise to make Horus swear an oath that he would keep the secret.

In receipt of this arcane knowledge, Isis became known as the 'Mistress of the Gods who knows Re by his own name', and recited a spell to cure the sun god's ailment.

▲ *Atum and Re appear as cats on this stela from Deir el-Medina. Below them, a married couple recite a hymn to the 'great cat' and the sun god. 19th Dynasty.*

▶ *The circular motif in front of this winged snake is a* shen, *the ancient Egyptian symbol of eternity. Valley of the Queens.*

Isis and the Sun God's Secret Name in Context

This myth survives on a papyrus dating from the Nineteenth Dynasty (c.1200 BC) which is now in the Turin Museum in Italy; a version of it can also be found in a more fragmentary state on another papyrus, Papyrus Chester Beatty XI, in the British Museum, London.

The main point of the myth was to emphasize the significance of a name, and the fact that knowledge of a name was equated with power. The ancient Egyptians believed the name to be very much part of the personality of an individual or the nature of an object. Generally, the myths served to provide the deities with their names and identities. It was not until a force had a name that offerings and prayers could be made to it by worshippers. But to know a name was to be able to exercise a certain degree of control over the deity (or person or thing) to which it belonged. Knowing the relevant names was particularly crucial in spells and their accompanying rituals (see *Isis and the Seven Scorpions*).

Mystery of the divine

It is significant that, in this myth, although Isis eventually managed to learn the sun god's secret name, the reader (or listener) never does. It was important to the ancient Egyptians that they could, to a certain extent, make sense of, and even identify with, their gods and goddesses, but by its very nature the divine world could not be completely familiar: it always retained a degree of mystery. The gods had to be believed to have their own secrets in order to inspire awe.

Magic and medicine

In this myth, Horus became party to the secret of the source of the sun god's power, so if the king was identified with Horus, he would presumably have been considered to be the only mortal with possession of this hidden knowledge, the key to certain powers.

The myth was obviously used in a ritual 'to ward off poison'. It includes the words of the spell with which Isis cured Re. Because she was successful in her combination of magic and medicine, it was thought that anyone suffering from a poisonous sting could be similarly cured.

As far as the ancient Egyptians were concerned, magic and medicine were not two distinct fields. The ten or so magico-medical texts that have survived show that spells and the use of amulets and other ritual objects were regularly combined with clinical observation and carefully worked-out prescriptions. This particular text stipulates that recitation of the spell is to be accompanied by a remedy of 'scorpion herb' mixed with beer or wine. ◆

Names

Egyptian names were chosen with care as they were considered to be an important aspect of a person's character. They might be derived from words indicating desirable qualities, such as beauty or wisdom, or from the names or attributes of gods to show devotion. Others associate the individual with the king.

From the Old Kingdom (c.2686–c.2181 BC) the king took five names, the first four of which he acquired when he came to the throne. The first was the Horus-name, or chief name. The second was the 'Two Ladies' name, giving him the protection of the goddesses Nekhbet and Wadjet. The third name, the Golden Horus name, referred to his divinity and the fourth, his throne name, introduced by the epithet 'He of the Sedge and the Bee' to his role as ruler. His last name, called the nomen, was the name given to him at birth and was preceded by the title 'Son of Re'.

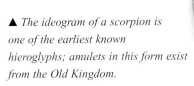

▲ *The ideogram of a scorpion is one of the earliest known hieroglyphs; amulets in this form exist from the Old Kingdom.*

The Journey of the Sun Through the Netherworld

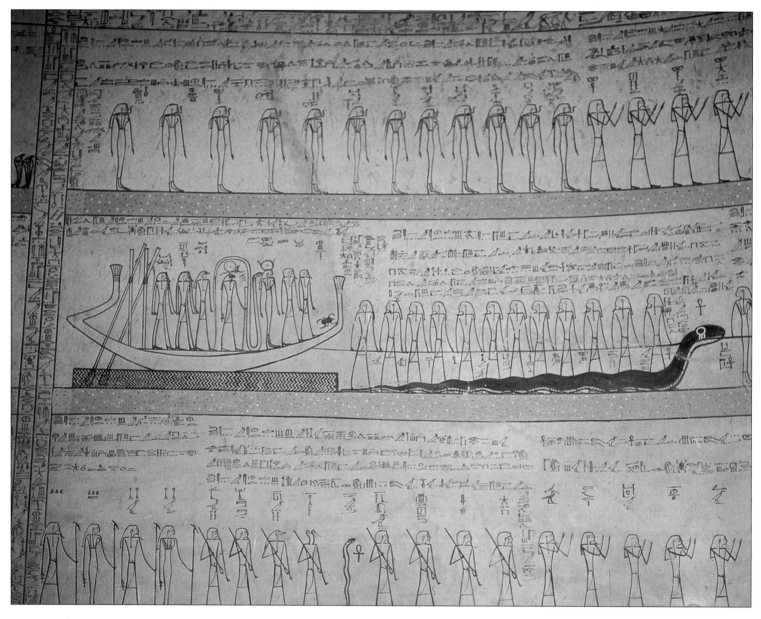

The sun god Re arose each day and, having bathed and fed, began his journey across the sky in his solar day boat. On the way, he spent one of the 12 hours of the day inspecting each of his 12 provinces, as he made a serene progression from east to west. During the night, however, he had to make a perilous voyage through the Netherworld while the land was left in darkness awaiting his return the following morning. The myth that describes his ordeal begins just as night falls.

The sun god had reached the western horizon, ready to begin his nightly journey through the Netherworld. He was all set to travel along the River of Wernes, a journey that would take him 12 hours.

In the first hour of the night he embarked on his journey in his night-boat with a crew of deities, including 'Path-opener' and 'Guide of the Boat'. He was also accompanied by two sets of nine baboons, who sang to Re as he entered the Netherworld and were there to open doors for him, as well as 12

▲ *The tomb of Tuthmosis III is painted with scenes from the Am Duat, 'The Book of that which is in the Netherworld'. Valley of the Kings.*

snake goddesses whose job it was to light up the darkness. In the second hour Re sailed on to the region of Wernes, where he granted land rights to the grain gods. In the third hour, he performed an important ritual act: he revived the god of the Netherworld, Osiris, by bestowing on him two divine forces described as 'Will' and 'Mind'. In the fourth hour, he reached a passage which was the way to

▶ *The fourth and fifth hours of night (the realm of Sokar) are shown on this sarcophagus. 30th Dynasty.*

the underworld from the Gate of the Passageways, the entrance taken by the dead, and the route to the body of the hawk-headed Memphite funerary deity Sokar and the tomb of Osiris. The passage was guarded by a number of fantastic snakes with human heads and several short legs, or with wings and multiple snakes' heads.

The hazards of the journey

In the fifth hour, Re's solar boat was towed across a mound referred to as the Mound of Sokar, but in fact representing the tomb of Osiris and therefore flanked by his two sisters Isis and Nephthys in the form of kites. The tow-rope of the boat was held by a scarab beetle, symbolizing the coming emergence of Re from the night in the form of the scarab beetle deity Khepri. The entrance to the mound was guarded by four heads spurting flames, and even more extraordinary was a primeval embodiment of Re which appeared at this stage of his journey: Sokar balancing on a

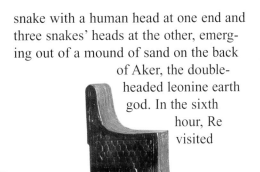

snake with a human head at one end and three snakes' heads at the other, emerging out of a mound of sand on the back of Aker, the double-headed leonine earth god. In the sixth hour, Re visited

Thoth, the god of the moon, wisdom and writing, who appeared in the form of a baboon, but holding his other manifestation, an ibis. Thoth's role in this myth was to found a city for the gods and rulers of Egypt. Re also encountered an image of himself – the dung-beetle, in death

◀ *A model or depiction of a boat was included in tombs to ensure that the deceased would be able to journey with the sun god in the Afterlife. 18th Dynasty.*

the body of Khepri enveloped in the body of a five-headed snake.

In the seventh hour, Re sailed past enemies of Osiris (who his protectors were busily decapitating and lassoing with a rope) before coming face to face with his most terrible of enemies, the serpent demon Apophis, whose main aim was to swallow the sun. Re's magical protection allowed him to come into close contact with Apophis only if the demon was disabled in some way. Apophis had knives sticking into him, and in case this was not adequate disablement, the scorpion-goddess Selket held his head, and the 'Director of Knives' held his tail.

In the eighth hour, Re had to face further enemies, but luckily he had an entourage of human-headed staffs, each

▼ *This bejewelled winged scarab beetle rolling the sun with its forelegs, and resting its hindlegs on a basket, is the hieroglyphic representation of Tutankhamun's throne name Neb-Kheperu-Re, 'Lord of the manifestations of Re'. 18th Dynasty.*

of which had a knife with which to destroy Re's demons. A variety of deities, including gods with the heads of rats and mongooses, called out to Re as he passed their caverns. In the ninth hour, Re met the 12 alarming guardians of Osiris, fire-breathing cobras who lived on the blood of their captives. Decidedly less intimidating were the deities Re sailed past, who were responsible for carving trees and plants, and who held nothing more threatening than palm branches.

▲ *In this wall-painting in the Theban tomb of Inherkha, a knife-wielding cat slays the serpent-demon Apophis near the* ished-*tree. 19th Dynasty.*

The end in sight

In the tenth hour, Re was beginning to prepare for dawn; he ordered his armed escort of 12 gods to seek out the last of his enemies, as he revealed himself as a scarab beetle, the manifestation of the sun god at dawn. In the eleventh hour, the hawk-god Horus presided over the final slaughter of the enemies of the sun god, which took place in pits of fire and was distinctly gory.

Re had survived the perils of the Netherworld, and the final hour before dawn had arrived. In the twelfth hour, the solar boat was towed into the body of an enormous snake, and the sun god emerged from its mouth as the scarab-beetle deity Khepri. Shu, the god of air, sealed the exit to the Netherworld behind him, and the sun god proceeded on his way in his daytime vessel.

The Journey of the Sun Through the Netherworld in Context

This particular myth of the nightly journey of the sun god is found in the 'Book of Am-Duat', or 'Book of What is in the Netherworld'. It is recorded in its most complete form in the Eighteenth-Dynasty tombs of the kings Tuthmosis III (c.1479–c.1425 BC) and Amenhotep II (c.1427–c.1400 BC), both of which are in the Valley of the Kings, the burial ground of the rulers of the New Kingdom (c.1550–c.1069 BC) on the west bank of the Nile at Thebes. In each instance the text is accompanied by a series of weird and wonderful painted images.

Similar, detailed descriptions of the journey of the sun god through the Netherworld are to be found in compositions entitled the 'Book of Gates' and the 'Book of Caverns'. The former can be found in its fullest version on the walls of the tomb of the Twentieth-Dynasty king, Ramesses VI (c.1143–c.1136 BC) in the Valley of the Kings, and inscribed on the sarcophagus of the Nineteenth-Dynasty ruler Seti I (c.1294–c.1279 BC), which was originally in his tomb in the Valley of the Kings but is now in the Sir John Soane Museum in London. The 'Book of Caverns' is the rarest and latest of the three funerary compositions, and it also occurs in its complete form in the tomb of Ramesses VI.

Darkness and death
The story identifies the journey of the sun during the hours of darkness with the passage of the dead (especially the king) into the Afterlife. Sunset is equated with death, and sunrise with rebirth. By recording the successful journey of the sun god in the tomb of the king, it was believed that the king would in turn be reborn without mishap. His enemies were regarded as the same as those of the sun god, and so it was important that they – especially Apophis – should be symbolically destroyed.

The myth also serves to explain the hours of darkness, so it is an alternative to the idea of the sun being swallowed by the sky goddess Nut in the evening, passing through her body during the night, and being given birth to by her in the morning. Other myths include the idea that the earth god Geb grew angry with his consort Nut for swallowing her 'children'. In the temple at Abydos, Nut is compared to a sow which eats its piglets.

The ancient Egyptians believed the Sun god to assume different manifestations at different times in the day. The most

▲ *The Valley of the Kings actually consists of two separate valleys: the eastern valley is the main royal cemetery of the New Kingdom, while the western one contains only four tombs.*

commonly occurring solar deity was Re, who tended to be associated with the midday sun. Atum was associated with the setting sun, and the scarab-beetle deity Khepri was the form taken by the rising sun. The fact that the sun god is imagined travelling in a boat should not surprise us because the chief means of transport both for people and goods would certainly have been by river. ◆

The Days Upon the Year

The myth is set at the time of creation, when the cosmological deities were coming into being. The sky goddess Nut was pregnant (following an illicit sexual encounter with the earth god Geb), but the supreme solar deity Re felt threatened by the prospect of the arrival of more gods and goddesses on the scene. He had convinced himself that his supremacy would be at risk if he did not take precautions, so he cursed Nut, preventing her from giving birth on any day of the year (which at this time still totalled 360 days).

As a result, Osiris, Isis, Seth and Nephthys would never have been born if Re had had his way. Luckily for them and humankind, the lunar deity Thoth decided to intervene. By beating the Moon in a board game, he managed to win enough light to create an additional five days each year (referred to by the ancient Egyptians as 'days upon the year' and as 'epagomenal days' by the Greeks). On each of these days, Nut was able to produce one of her offspring. To explain the existence of the fifth day, in this particular myth Nut is also said to be the mother of 'Horus the Elder' (Harwer; Haroeris in Greek).

The civil year

Even after the addition of the days upon the year, the Egyptian calendar did not coincide precisely with the solar year, which is 365¼ days long. The civil year gradually fell behind the solar year, moving backwards by one month every 120 years and only coming into alignment again after 1,460 years. As the civil calendar fell out of step with the seasons, festivals associated with the natural cycle (such as harvest) continued to be held in their correct season.

▲ *A scene from the Satirical Papyrus, showing a lion and an antelope playing* senet, *the best-known board game from ancient Egypt. Late New Kingdom.*

▼ *This cosmological vignette of Shu separating Nut from Geb comes from the Book of the Dead belonging to Nesitanebeteshru, a 21st Dynasty priestess.*

The Days Upon the Year in Context

This myth has survived in the work of the Greek writer Plutarch (c. AD 46–c.126), in a volume called *Peri Isidos kai Osiridos*. It was obviously originally devised as a means of explaining the five days which were added to the calendar in order to match it more closely to the solar year. The ancient Egyptians were in fact the earliest people to adjust their calendar to a length of 365 days.

Watching the stars

The New Year (*Wep Renpet*, literally 'the Opening of the Year') was celebrated when the dog star Sirius, the brightest star in the sky, was sighted on its heliacal rising. The Egyptians noticed that there was a 70-day period when the dog star could not be seen. During this time the earth, the sun and the dog star are so nearly in line that the light of the star is swallowed up in the sun's brightness and becomes invisible. At the end of this period is a night when, just before dawn, the dog star is momentarily visible just above the eastern horizon, an astronomical event known as its heliacal rising. It so happened that this usually took place at the time when the period of low water was coming to end, and it appeared to herald the inundation.

The Egyptians divinely personified Sirius as a goddess, Sopdet, depicted as a woman with a star on her head. They also created a god of the main southern constellation Orion, named Sah. Stars in general were often depicted as gods sailing on crescent-shaped barques through the body of the goddess Nut.

The calender

Initially, the Egyptian calendar was based on the agricultural cycle, which in turn revolved around the flooding of the Nile. The year was divided into three seasons, each of four months (each month averaged thirty days and was

named after an important religious festival that took place during that period). The first season was that of the flood (*Akhe*t), the second of planting and growth (*Peret*), and the last of the harvest and low water (*Shomu*). All three seasons were divinely personified as male deities.

The days of the demons

In the Calendars of Lucky and Unlucky Days, days were categorized according to the mythical events said to have taken place on them, and they would have been consulted in order to decide whether an activity should or should not be carried out on a particular day. The calendars made it clear that nothing of

▲ *The three seasons were divinely personified. Mereruka, the vizier of the 6th-Dynasty king Teti, is shown at the entrance to his mastaba seated before the seasons. Each is accompanied by four crescent moons symbolizing the four lunar months of each season. Old Kingdom.*

any consequence should be done on any of the 'days upon the year'. These extra days were added to the end of the calendar and did not form part of any month: all the months continued to be thirty days long. Of the five days upon the year, the one on which Seth was supposed to have been born was considered to be particularly dangerous, but all were collectively known as 'the days of the demons'.   ◆

Trees in Egyptian Mythology

The shade of trees afforded the ancient Egyptian people welcome respite from the searing heat of the sun, so it is hardly surprising that sites associated with cults were often situated in groves. Soon the groves themselves came to be regarded as sacred and, according to various local traditions, gods were believed to shelter under, or even live in, particular trees. Trees were also important in the cemetery regions on the edge of the desert. But trees were relatively rare in ancient Egypt and this fact presumably heightened the respect in which they were held. There were no trees native to Egypt that could yield timber suitable for building work, so cedar had to be imported from the Lebanon for such uses as constructing ships and making roof beams.

There are two ways of finding out which trees were considered sacred in each of the nomes (or districts) of ancient Egypt. First, the emblems adopted by the nomes often include trees, and second, there are lists inscribed on the walls of Ptolemaic temples that describe the trees in each of the sacred groves around the country. The most common appear to have been the sycamore, persea (a sacred fruit-bearing tree), date palm and acacia.

Tallying the days

The hieroglyphic sign for 'year' (*renpet*) was a branch from a date palm with all the leaves stripped off (the notches left by the leaves were thought to indicate the passing of time). The presentation of a symbolic palm branch to the king was an important part of his jubilee festival, (see *Royal Jubilee Festivals*). Heh, the god of eternity, was depicted wearing a notched palm branch on his head or holding one in each hand.

Tree deities

Presumably because of the shade and the fruit provided by them, goddesses associated with protection, mothering and nurturing were closely associated with them. Hathor, Nut and Isis appear frequently in the religious imagery and literature. Any of these goddesses might be represented as a woman with a tree on her head, as a tree with the upper half of a woman growing out of it, or as a semi-personified tree with arms. In the tomb of the Eighteenth-Dynasty king Tuthmosis III (c.1479–c.1425 BC), a goddess (probably Isis) is depicted as a sycamore tree with a breast.

Hathor was sometimes referred to as 'Mistress of the Date Palm' (this refers to the male palm, *imaw*), and in the Book of the Dead the goddess was occasionally depicted in front of this kind of tree. She could also be called 'The Lady of the Sycamore' (the *nehet*, which also means 'refuge'), or more specifically, 'The Lady of the Southern Sycamore' – an actual tree that grew at the temple of Ptah in Memphis during the Old Kingdom (c.2686–c.2181 BC).

▲ *Nespawershefi, the 21st-Dynasty Chief of all the Scribes at Karnak Temple, is depicted making offerings before Nut, the sycamore tree goddess, on the side of his coffin. His ba is shown drinking the liquid poured by the goddess.*

According to the Book of the Dead, two 'sycamores of turquoise' grew on the eastern horizon at the place where the sun rises each morning, so the sycamore also had a male aspect as a manifestation of the solar deity Re-Horakhty. According to the Pyramid Texts, gods were thought to live in the branches of the sycamores on the eastern horizon.

In a funerary context, the goddesses Hathor and Nut occurred as sycamore tree goddesses, offering shade, food and water to the souls of the dead who, in the form of human-headed birds (*bas*), enjoyed the sustenance. The *bas* of the dead might be visualized sitting on the branches of a tree, rather as the gods were imagined on the eastern horizon. Sycamores were often planted near tombs, and models of leaves of this tree were used as funerary amulets.

The sacred ished

A tree that grew in the sacred groves of 17 of the nomes was the *ished*, a fruit-bearing, deciduous tree that was probably the same as the persea. Like the sycamore, it was associated with the rising sun and the horizon. And like the sun god, it was protected from the serpent demon Apophis by the 'great cat of Heliopolis'. According to the Book of the Dead, the cat that was said to sit in the shade of the *ished* tree was in fact Re himself. An inscription on the Heliopolitan obelisk known as Cleopatra's Needle in London records that a sacred *ished* grew at Heliopolis from the Old Kingdom through to the Graeco-Roman Period. (There were also *ished* trees at Herakleopolis, Memphis and Edfu.)

From the Eighteenth Dynasty (c.1550 BC), reliefs show Amun-Re, Thoth, the god of scribes, and Seshat, the goddess of writing, inscribing the leaves of the *ished* with the names and titles of the king and the number of years in his reign, so this kind of tree was associated with royal annals. The Egyptian word for 'records' or 'annals' was *genut*, from *genu*, meaning 'branch'.

Trees and rituals

The willow (*tcheret*), often identified as tamarisk, was sacred to Osiris. It was believed to have sheltered his dead body, while his *ba*, in the form of a bird, was said to sit in it. Those towns (including Memphis, Heliopolis and Herakleopolis) where part of Osiris was said to have been buried by Isis (see *The Death of Osiris*) had willow groves, and an annual festival called 'Raising the Willow' was celebrated to ensure the fertility of the land. Representations of the tomb of Osiris sometimes showed a tomb-chamber covered by a mound with trees growing on top of it or beside it.

Inscriptions at Philae record that milk was poured at the foot of trees at what was believed to be the sacred tomb of Osiris. These libations were thought to revive the god so that he might be reborn into the Afterlife. The reliefs show Osiris standing in a tree growing out of a small pool. An inscription at Philae describes Osiris's *ba* as living in the branches of a cedar tree while, according to Plutarch, a tamarisk shaded Osiris's tomb.

Deities were also associated with several other types of trees. The jackal-god Wepwawet was said in the Pyramid Texts to have 'emerged from a tamarisk bush', while Horus was believed to have come forth from an acacia (*shened*). In another myth, Horus was said to have taken refuge under an acacia tree as a child. A sacred acacia appears to have grown at Heliopolis. The crocodile god Sobek was associated with the *kesbet* tree and the moringa tree. Cypresses were deemed sacred to Min, and he was often worshipped under them.

Sacred trees are still important in Egypt. They are usually connected with the tombs of famous sheikhs, whose spirits are thought to dwell in them. They are believed to be able to cure problems such as infertility, and gratitude may be expressed by hanging votive gifts on their trunks. ◆

▲ *This semi-personified tree with a breast, suckling Tuthmosis III, is probably intended to be identified as the mother goddess Isis. Valley of the Kings.*

▼ *Another semi-personified tree offers food and drink to Sekeh, the deceased mayor of Memphis, and his* ba, *or soul.*

Plants and Flowers in Mythology

The papyrus plant (*Cyperus papyrus*) played a key role in the rise of the ancient Egyptian civilization because of the high-quality writing material that could be produced from it. The papyrus reed is a member of the sedge family and needs to grow in soft, easily penetrable soil, with its roots completely submerged in water. For this reason, the Faiyum and Delta districts were ideal habitats, and papyrus thickets were abundant in ancient times. As well as the fine sheets manufactured using strips of its juicy, starchy pith, the outer fibres of the papyrus plant were turned into boats, sandals, basketry, matting, boxes, ropes, jar stoppers and even building materials.

It is not surprising that the papyrus plant was highly prized. It was so closely associated with the northern region, that it came to be regarded as a heraldic emblem of Lower Egypt. In the iconography of the 'Unification of the Two Lands', a Nile deity or the god Horus might be depicted holding (or even wearing) this plant (see *The Concept of Duality*). Because it symbolized Lower Egypt and was believed to have grown on the primordial mound of creation, and in the belief that papyrus 'pillars' held up the sky, temple complexes usually included limestone or sandstone columns carved to represent single or composite papyrus stems, with capitals in the form of open umbels or closed buds.

For the ancient Egyptians, the papyrus plant also symbolized freshness, flourishing, youth and joy. To ensure the presence of these attributes in their lives, they would wear or carry a tiny amulet in the shape of a single stem and umbel of papyrus. It was stipulated that this should be made of green or blue-green faience, and it was referred to as *wadj* (literally 'green'). Goddesses such as Hathor, Bastet and Neith were often depicted holding a papyriform sceptre.

Lotus or lily?

The symbol of the South (Upper Egypt) is generally referred to as the lotus, but was actually the water lily (sometimes called the 'southern plant'). There were two species of lotus or water lily that grew in ancient Egypt, the white *Nymphaea lotus*, and the blue *Nymphaea caerulea*. It was the latter species that was most commonly depicted and was usually described as the sacred lotus. It

▲ *These two red granite pillars form part of the barque sanctuary of Tuthmosis III at Karnak. The pillar in the foreground depicts the lotus/lily and the other the papyrus plant.*

too occurs in the imagery of the 'Unification of the Two Lands', held (or worn) by a Nile deity or by Seth. Because of its significance, the sacred lotus was also an important element in the design of temple columns.

Flowers of life and death

During the New Kingdom the flowers of the *ished* tree were considered life-giving and were called 'flowers of life'. Together with the lotus blossom they were used at funerals for decorating the coffins and statues of the deceased.

The ancient Egyptians observed that the lily flower closed for the night and sank under the water, rising and reopening as the sun rose, and for this reason it was associated with the night-time journey of the sun god Re and his 'rebirth' at dawn. In time it came to be associated with creation and rebirth in general. One version of the creation myth of Hermopolis Magna tells us that the sun rose for the first time out of a primordial lotus bobbing on the waters of chaos (see *Creation Myths*).

Throughout Egyptian history images were created of figures rising out of lotus blossoms, such as the wonderful painted wooden head of Tutankhamun found in his tomb and now in the Cairo Museum. The lotus became so important

▶ *This wooden sculpture of Tutankhamun's head emerging from a lotus blossom has been plastered and then painted. The image likens the boy king to the sun god rising out of a lotus, in accordance with the mythology of creation.*

in ancient Egyptian religion that it was divinely personified in the form of the god Nefertem, 'Lord of Perfumes', who was portrayed anthropomorphically with a lotus growing out of his head (sometimes with two tall plumes extending upwards out of the flower). In the Pyramid Texts of the Old Kingdom Nefertem is described as 'the lotus at the nose of Re', and gods and goddesses are often depicted sniffing lotus blossoms.

Gods and flowers

Deities as well as people were thought to love the pleasurable stimulation of their senses, and flowers were considered to be important offerings to the gods.

We know that the sense of smell was highly regarded by the ancient Egyptians – the nose was the hieroglyphic sign used as a determinative in the writing of the verbs 'to enjoy' and 'to take pleasure in'. Flowers are ubiquitous in the scenes of festivity on the walls of Theban private tombs of the New Kingdom (c.1550–c.1069 BC). They are shown as festoons and garlands worn by the merry-makers, but are also depicted being held to the nose for the pleasure of their scent. It is likely that when added to alcohol they would have released psychoactive properties.

Certain plants were particularly associated with certain deities. The lettuce (*Lactuca sativa longifolia*) was, for example, an emblem of the cult of the fertility god Min at Koptos. This association may have arisen from the resemblance of the milky juice of the lettuce to semen (see *The Contendings of Horus and Seth*). ◆

◀ *The heavy black wigs and fine white linen dresses of these women, together with an abundance of flowers, are typical of the banqueting scenes on the walls of non-royal Theban tombs of the New Kingdom.*

The Concept of Duality

The crux of the ancient Egyptian system of beliefs was the relationship between order (*maat*) and chaos (*isfet*). Although a state of order was considered to be the ideal, it was acknowledged that an opposing yet interdependent state of chaos must exist in order for equilibrium to be achieved. For the ancient Egyptians, a state of order (or harmony or balance) was of such vital significance in their lives that they divinely personified the abstract concept of order in the form of the goddess Maat. She was represented as a woman wearing an ostrich feather, which represented truth, on her head.

A sense of unity was created by the existence of a duality, which was expressed clearly in religious iconography. The god Horus was associated with all that was right and ordered, whereas the god Seth was linked with chaos, as well as with infertility and aridity (see *The Contendings of Horus and Seth*). The presence of both of these deities indicated an idea of

▶ *Maat, the goddess of order, wearing an ostrich feather on her head, is characteristically shown seated on a plinth. The symbol of the plinth is included in the hieroglyphic writing of her name and represents the primeval mound of creation.*

completeness. In the Cairo Museum there is an impressive triad statue which was found at Medinet Habu, the mortuary temple of the Twentieth-Dynasty king Ramesses III (c.1184–c.1153 BC). The king is shown flanked by Horus on one side and Seth on the other – the two gods together constituting a wholeness.

The ancient Egyptians believed that the fertile part of Egypt (the Nile Valley and the Delta) in which they lived was a place of order with a reliable pattern to it – particularly the agricultural cycle hingeing on the annual flooding of the Nile. Maat was present in this, the 'Black Land' (*Kemet*). On the other hand, the desert or 'Red Land' (*Deshret*) was considered to be a place of chaos. A precarious, yet highly important, relationship existed between the two.

Unification

The conventions of Egyptian art were perfect for illustrating the concept of duality, because symmetry was frequently used to create a balanced design. This is best exemplified by the artistic representation of the fundamentally important idea of the 'Unification of the Two Lands' (*sema tawy*). The ancient Egyptians viewed their country as consisting of two distinct parts: Upper Egypt (*Shemau*) and

Lower Egypt (*Ta-Mehu*). These correspond to the South (the Nile Valley from the first cataract north to just south of Memphis) and the North (the Delta), respectively. The people believed that the origins of the state of Egypt could be traced to an act of unification of these two regions by a ruler named Menes (for whom there is no actual archaeological evidence) at the beginning of the early Dynastic Period (c.3100 BC).

The hieroglyphic sign used to express the notion of this unification was a stylized rendering of a pair of lungs, with a windpipe extending straight upwards out of the middle of them. In art this emblem might be flanked by two deities, sometimes Horus and Seth, on other occasions two Nile gods, one with papyrus on his head and the other with the lotus (or water lily) plant (see *Plants and Flowers in Mythology*). The figures on each side are often depicted tying the papyrus and lotus stems in a knot around the hieroglyph. This is further symbolic of the unity of Egypt because the papyrus plant was a heraldic emblem of the Delta, and the lotus was a heraldic emblem of the Nile Valley.

▶ *Snofru sits beneath his cartouche wearing the Double Crown of Upper and Lower Egypt. One of his chief titles, 'He of the Sedge and the Bee', is easily identifiable, and beneath this is his 'Two Ladies' epithet.*

Lord of the two lands

This particular aspect of the notion of duality manifested itself very clearly in the royal titles. The king's chief titles were 'Lord of the Two Lands' (*Neb Tawy*) and 'King of Upper and Lower Egypt' (*Nesw Bity*), which translates literally as 'He of the Sedge and the Bee'. The sedge plant was an emblem of the Nile Valley, and the bee was an emblem of the Delta. Another of his titles was 'He of the Two Ladies' (*Nebty*), which referred to the two goddesses who were thought to protect him: the vulture goddess, Nekhbet, who had her main cult centre at el-Kab in the South, and the cobra goddess, Wadjet, whose principal cult centre was at Buto in the North.

The regalia of kingship also reflected the idea of duality. The king might be depicted wearing the White Crown (*Hedjet*) associated with Upper Egypt, the Red Crown (*Deshret*) of Lower Egypt, or sometimes the Double Crown (*Pschent* or *Sekhemty*), which incorporated the crowns of both regions.

So north and south were distinct but both were necessary to create a whole. Similarly east and west were opposing and yet interdependent. The places of the rising and setting sun resulted in the east being associated with the living, and the west being associated with the dead. But as the sun rose again each morning, so the dead were believed to be reborn into the Afterlife. ◆

▶ *This diadem was found under the bandaging on Tutankhamun's mummy. For safekeeping, the cobra had been detached and placed on Tutankhamun's left thigh, and the vulture on his right thigh.*

Kingship and the Gods

Did the ancient Egyptian people believe that their king was a god? The extent to which they did seems to have varied according to the period of Egyptian history, and also to have depended on context. The king could be regarded as a god, or as somewhere between the divine and mortal world, or as a mere human being. It is safe to say, however, that the concept of kingship – the office, rather than the man himself – was considered divine. It was felt that the king could relate to the gods in a way that none of his subjects would have been able to, which must have enhanced the nature of kingship and inspired respect, if not awe, in the people.

Many sources reveal that the king was identified with a god, both in life and after death. Myths, inscriptions and royal titles all stress the reigning king's identification with the falcon-god Horus. After death, the king was identified with Osiris. The divinity of a dead king was less ambiguous than that of a living one, and is well attested throughout Egyptian history. By the New Kingdom (c.1550– c.1069 BC), the royal mortuary temples were on a par (in terms of size, wealth and administration) with the cult temples of the deities.

◀ *On the wall of a corridor in the temple of Seti I at Abydos, this king and his son, Ramesses II, stand before a list of cartouches representing their royal predecessors.*

Kings of Egypt

All dates are BC unless stated otherwise

Early Dynastic Period
c.3100–c.2686

FIRST DYNASTY	c.3100–c.2890
Narmer	c.3100
Aha	c.3100
Djer	c.3000
Djet	c.2980
Den	c.2950
[Queen Merneith	c.2950]
Anedjib	c.2925
Semerkhet	c.2900
Qa'a	c.2890
SECOND DYNASTY	c.2890–c.2686
Hetepsekhemwy	c.2890
Raneb	c.2865
Nynetjer	
Weneg	
Sened	
Peribsen	c.2700
Khasekhemwy	c.2686

Old Kingdom
c.2686–c.2181

THIRD DYNASTY	c.2686–c.2613
Sanakht (= Nebka?)	c.2686–c.2667
Djoser (Netjerikhet)	c.2667–c.2648
Sekhemkhet	c.2648–c.2640
Khaba	c.2640–c.2637
Huni	c.2637–c.2613
FOURTH DYNASTY	c.2613–c.2494
Sneferu	c.2613–c.2589
Khufu (Cheops)	c.2589–c.2566
Djedefre (Radjedef)	c.2566–c.2558
Khafre (Chephren)	c.2558–c.2532
Menkaure (Mycerinus)	c.2532–c.2503
Shepseskaf	c.2503–c.2494
FIFTH DYNASTY	c.2494–c.2345
Userkaf	c.2494–c.2487
Sahure	c.2487–c.2475
Neferirkare	c.2475–c.2455
Shepseskare	c.2455–c.2448
Raneferef	c.2448–c.2445
Niuserre	c.2445–c.2421
Menkauhor	c.2421–c.2414
Djedkare	c.2414–c.2375
Unas (Wenis)	c.2375–c.2345
SIXTH DYNASTY	c.2345–c.2181
Teti	c.2345–c.2323
Userkare	c.2323–c.2321
Pepi I (Meryre)	c.2321–c.2287
Merenre	c.2287–c.2278
Pepi II (Neferkare)	c.2278–c.2184
Nitiqret	c.2184–c.2181

First Intermediate Period
c.2181–c.2055

SEVENTH AND EIGHTH DYNASTIES	c.2181–c.2125
Numerous short reigns	
NINTH AND TENTH DYNASTIES (HERAKLEOPOLITAN)	c.2160–c.2025
Khety (Meryibre)	
Khety (Wahkare)	
Merykare	
Ity	
ELEVENTH DYNASTY (THEBES)	c.2125–c.2055
[Mentuhotep I ('Tepy-aa')]	
Intef I (Sehertawy)	c.2125–c.2112
Intef II (Wahankh)	c.2112–c.2063
Intef III (Nakhtnebtepnefer)	c.2063–c.2055

Middle Kingdom
c.2055–c.1650

ELEVENTH DYNASTY (ALL EGYPT)	c.2055–c.1985
Mentuhotep II (Nebhepetre)	c.2055–c.2004
Mentuhotep III (Sankhkare)	c.2004–c.1992
Mentuhotep IV (Nebtawyre)	c.1992–c.1985
TWELFTH DYNASTY	c.1985–c.1795
Amenemhat I (Sehetepibre)	c.1985–c.1955
Senusret I (Kheperkare)	c.1965–c.1920
Amenemhat II (Nubkaure)	c.1922–c.1878
Senusret II (Khakheperre)	c.1880–c.1874
Senusret III (Khakaure)	c.1874–c.1855
Amenemhat III (Nimaatre)	c.1855–c.1808
Amenemhat IV (Maakherure)	c.1808–c.1799
Queen Sobekneferu (Sobekkare)	c.1799–c.1795
THIRTEENTH DYNASTY	1795–after 1650

About 70 rulers, of whom the most frequently mentioned are listed below

Hor (Awibre)	
Khendjer (Userkare)	
Sobekhotep III (Sekhemrasewadjtawy)	
Neferhotep I (Khasekhemre)	
Sobekhotep IV (Khaneferre)	c.1725
FOURTEENTH DYNASTY	c.1750–c.1650

Series of minor rulers, probably contemporary with the kings of the Thirteenth Dynasty

Second Intermediate Period
c.1650–c.1550

FIFTEENTH DYNASTY (HYKSOS)	c.1650–c.1550
Salitis	
Khyan (Seuserenre)	c.1600
Apepi (Aauserre)	c.1555
Khamudi	
SIXTEENTH DYNASTY	c.1650–c.1550
Minor Hyksos rulers, contemporary with the kings of the Fifteenth Dynasty	
SEVENTEENTH DYNASTY	c.1650–c.1550

Several rulers based in Thebes, of whom the most prominent are listed below

Intef (Nubkheperre)	
Taa I (Senakhtenre)	
Taa II (Seqenenre)	c.1560
Kamose (Wadjkheperre)	c.1555–c.1550

New Kingdom
c.1550–c.1069

EIGHTEENTH DYNASTY	c.1550–c.1295
Ahmose (Nebpehtyre)	c.1550–c.1525
Amenhotep I (Djeserkare)	c.1525–c.1504
Tuthmosis I (Aakheperkare)	c.1504–c.1492
Tuthmosis II (Aakheperenre)	c.1492–c.1479
Tuthmosis III (Menkhpererre)	c.1479–c.1425
Hatshepsut (Maatkare)	c.1473–c.1458
Amenhotep II (Aakheperure)	c.1427–c.1400

Tuthmosis IV (Menkheperure)	c.1400–c.1390
Amenhotep III (Nebmaatre)	c.1390–c.1352
Amenhotep IV/Akhenaten	
(Neferkheperurawaenre)	c.1352–c.1336
Nefernefruaten (Smenkhkare)	c.1338–c.1336
Tutankhamun (Nebkheperure)	c.1336–c.1327
Ay (Kheperkheperure)	c.1327–c.1323
Horemheb (Djeserkheperure)	c.1323–c.1295
NINETEENTH DYNASTY	c.1295–c.1186
Ramesses I (Menpehtyre)	c.1295–c.1294
Seti I (Menmaatre)	c.1294–c.1279
Ramesses II (Usermaatra Setepenre)	c.1279–c.1213
Merenptah (Baenre)	c.1213–c.1203
Amenmessu (Menmire)	c.1203–c.1200
Seti II (Userkheperur Setepenre)	c.1200–c.1194
Saptah (Akhenra Setepenre)	c.1194–c.1188
Tausret (Sitrameritamun)	c.1188–c.1186
TWENTIETH DYNASTY	c.1186–c.1069
Sethnakhte (Userkhaure Meryamun)	c.1186–c.1184
Ramesses III (Usermaatre Meryamun)	c.1184–c.1153
Ramesses IV (Hekamaatre Setepenamun)	c.1153–c.1147
Ramesses V (Usermaatre Sekheperenre)	c.1147–c.1143
Ramesses VI (Nebmaatre Meryamun)	c.1143–c.1136
Ramesses VII (Usermaatre	
Setepenre Meryamun)	c.1136–c.1129
Ramesses VIII (Usermaatre Akhenamun)	c.1129–c.1126
Ramesses IX (Neferkare Setepenre)	c.1126–c.1108
Ramesses X (Khepermaatre Setepenre)	c.1108–c.1099
Ramesses XI (Menmaatre Setepenptah)	c.1099–c.1069

Third Intermediate Period c.1069–c.747

TWENTY-FIRST DYNASTY	
(TANITE)	c.1069–c.945
Smendes (Hedjkheperre Setepenre)	c.1069–c.1043
Amenemnisu (Neferkare)	c.1043–c.1039
Psusennes I [Pasebakhaenniut]	
(Aakheperre Setepenamun)	c.1039–c.991
Amenemope (Usermaatre Setepenamun)	c.993–c.984
Osorkon the Elder (Aakheperre Setepenre)	c.984–c.978
Siamun (Netjrkheperre Setepenamun)	c.978–c.959
Psusennes II [Pasebakhaennuit]	
(Titkheperure Setepenre)	c.959–c.945
TWENTY-SECOND DYNASTY	
(BUBASTITE/LIBYAN)	c.945–c.715
Sheshonq I (Hedjkheperre Setepenre)	c.945–c.924
Osorkon I (Sekhemkheperre)	c.924–c.889
Sheshonq II (Hekakheperre Setepenre)	c.890
Takelot I	c.889–c.874
Osorkon II (Usermaatre Setepnamun)	c.874–c.850
Takelot II (Hedjkheperre Setepenre amun)	c.850–c.825
Sheshonq III (Usermaatre)	c.825–c.773
Pimay (Usermaatre)	c.773–c.767
Sheshonq V (Aakheperre)	c.767–c.730
Osorkon IV (Aakheperre Setepenamun)	c.730–c.715
TWENTY-THIRD DYNASTY	
(TANITE/LIBYAN)	c.818–c.715
Several contemporary lines of rulers at Herakleopolis Magna, Hermopolis Magna, Leontopolis and Tanis, three of whom are listed below	
Pedubastis I (Usermaatre)	c.818–c.793
Sheshonq IV	c.780
Osorkon III (Usermaatre Setepenamun)	c.777–c.749
TWENTY-FOURTH DYNASTY	c.727–c.715
Bakenrenef (Bocchoris)	c.727–c.715

Late Period c.747–332

TWENTY-FIFTH DYNASTY	
(KUSHITE)	c.747–c.656
Piy (Piankhy)	c.747–c.716
Shabaqo (Neferkare)	c.716–c.702
Shabitqo (Djedkaure)	c.702–690
Taharqo (Khunefertemre)	690–664
Tanutamani (Bakare)	664–656
TWENTY-SIXTH DYNASTY	
(SAITE)	664–525
[Nekau I	672–664]
Psamtek I (Wahinre)	664–610
Nekau II (Wehemibre)	610–595
Psamtek II (Neferibre)	595–589
Apries (Haaibre)	589–570
Ahmose II (Khnemibre)	570–526
Psamtek III (Ankhkaenre)	526–525
TWENTY-SEVENTH DYNASTY	
(FIRST PERSIAN PERIOD)	525–404
Cambyses	525–522
Darius I	522–486
Xerxes I	486–465
Artaxerxes I	465–424
Darius II	424–405
Artaxerxes II	405–359
TWENTY-EIGHTH DYNASTY	404–399
Amyrtaios	404–399
TWENTY-NINTH DYNASTY	399–380
Nepherites I	399–393
Hakor (Khnemmaatre)	393–380
Nepherites II	c.380
THIRTIETH DYNASTY	380–343
Nectanebo I (Kheperkare)	380–362
Teos (Irmaatenre)	362–360
Nectanebo II (Senedjemibre Setepenanhur)	360–343
SECOND PERSIAN PERIOD	343–332
Artaxerxes III Ochus	343–338
Arses	338–336
Darius III Codoman	336–332

Ptolemaic Period 332–30

MACEDONIAN DYNASTY	332–305
Alexander the Great	332–323
Philip Arrhidaeus	323–317
Alexander IV	317–310
PTOLEMAIC DYNASTY	
Ptolemy I Soter I	305–285
Ptolemy II Philadelphus	285–246
Ptolemy III Euergetes I	246–221
Ptolemy IV Philopator	221–205
Ptolemy V Epiphanes	205–180
Ptolemy VI Philometor	180–145
Ptolemy VII Neos Philopator	145
Ptolemy VIII Euergetes II	170–116
Ptolemy IX Soter II	116–107
Ptolemy X Alexander I	107–88
Ptolemy IX Soter II (restored)	88–80
Ptolemy XI Alexander II	80
Ptolemy XII Neos Dionysus (Auletes)	80–51
Cleopatra VII Philopater	51–30
Ptolemy XIII	51–47
Ptolemy XIV	47–44
Ptolemy XV Caesarion	44–30

After the chronology in the British Museum Dictionary of Ancient Egypt *by Ian Shaw and Paul Nicholson*

Was the King Really Divine?

The belief in the divine nature of the position of pharaoh was central to the ideology of kingship in ancient Egypt. The term 'pharaoh' (*per-aa*) actually means 'great house' and it was not used to describe the ruler himself until the New Kingdom period (c.1550–c.1069 BC); before that time it was used to refer to the king's palace or the royal court.

The divinity of kingship was an important part of the Egyptian system of beliefs and social structure from the very beginning of the pharaonic period (c.3100 BC). Some very early inscriptions have been found that describe the king as *netjer* ('god') or, more usually, *nefer netjer* ('good god'), which may in fact indicate a lesser or minor god. Several inscriptions are also known in which the king is referred to as *aa netjer* ('great god').

▼ *Wings were a symbol of protection: Horus protected the king and the earth with his wings, as did the vulture mother and funerary goddesses.*

More is known about the ruler's identification with the god Horus: for example, that the falcon was a symbol of kingship from the Protodynastic Period. On the Narmer Palette, a falcon holds a rope in its talons which is attached to a ring through the nose of a semi-personified papyrus marsh. The falcon presumably symbolizes Narmer, whose victories are commemorated on this schist ceremonial palette, which was found in the 'Main Deposit' at Hierakonpolis and is now in the Cairo Museum.

Royal titles

From the Old Kingdom (c.2686–c.2181 BC), each king had five names, which were each introduced by an important title. Only one name was given to him at birth; the other four were bestowed when he was crowned king. They encapsulated the ideology of kingship. Two of the names were introduced by titles that stressed the rule of the king over two lands that had been united: 'He of the Sedge and the Bee' (*Nesw Bity*) and 'He of the Two Ladies' (*Nebty*) (see *The Concept of Duality*). The other two names – 'Horus' (*Hor*) and 'Golden Horus' (*Hor Nebw*) – could not have more clearly emphasized his identification with the god.

The office of kingship was decidedly male, and during the 3,000 or so years of pharaonic history female pharaohs were few and far between. The best known is probably Hatshepsut (c.1473–c.1458 BC), who necessarily had to make use of the masculine royal titles and regalia. She was even referred to as 'he' in the inscriptions on the walls of her mortuary temple at Deir el-Bahri on

▲ *In the Hypostyle Hall at Abydos the royal Horus image surmounts one of the king's titles, 'Mighty Bull', common during the New Kingdom.*

the west bank at Thebes. This is not to underestimate the political and religious importance of female members of the royal family – in particular the king's mother and wives (especially the 'Chief Royal Wife').

In the ruler's succession and coronation he re-created the myth (parts of which were recorded as early as the Pyramid Texts) of Horus rightfully ascending to the throne of his deceased father Osiris (see *The Death of Osiris* and *The Contendings of Horus and Seth*). On his accession the king was crowned with the Double Crown, which Horus is often depicted wearing in temple and tomb reliefs. The king would also have performed rituals identifying himself with the falcon god. Of particular significance would have been the symbolic triumph over the god Seth.

Festival of victory

Inscriptions and reliefs on the walls of the temple dedicated to Horus at Edfu describe the events of the annual Festival of Victory. Although these scenes date to the reign of Ptolemy IX (116–107 BC), rituals of this kind were probably being enacted as early as the New Kingdom (c.1550–c.1069 BC). The aim of the ritual drama was the annihilation of Seth. The king, identified as Horus, had to pierce Seth with ten harpoons. Seth took the form of a hippopotamus, and it is likely that a model hippopotamus would have been made for the festival; the final ritual certainly involved the eating of a cake in the shape of a hippopotamus. The act of harpooning this wild animal, whether symbolic or actual, was an ancient royal ritual that symbolized the triumph of order over the forces of chaos.

Royal regalia

At the front of his crown, the king wore the *uraeus*, the image of a rearing cobra poised ready to strike down any potential opponent of the ruler, and therefore any threat to the order of the state.

The royal insignia included various sceptres. Two of the most important were the 'crook' symbolising government and the flail, perhaps deriving from a fly whisk. The king might also be represented holding various weapons, such as the mace and the scimitar, to signify his role in the defence of order.

A false beard was another mark of royalty, tied under the chin by a cloth strap.

The king is also seen to play the part of Horus in the Ramesseum Dramatic Papyrus, which is now in the British Museum, London. This document dates to the reign of the Twelfth-Dynasty king Amenemhat III (c.1855–c.1808 BC), although the drama had originally been written down for the Jubilee Festival of king Senusret III (c.1874–c.1855 BC). The king, as Horus, had a conversation with the other gods; he received the 'Sacred Eye' (a powerful protective amulet); he ordered oxen to refrain from trampling on barley because it symbolized his father Osiris, the god of vegetation; and he engaged in mock battle with Seth.

It is clear that in such rituals the king was identified with Horus, but he was also believed to come under his protection. The magnificent diorite seated statue of the Fourth-Dynasty king Khafre (c.2558– c.2532 BC) has a beautifully sculpted Horus falcon on the back of the king's head, with the wings in a protective posture around it. In the Ramesside Period (c.1295–c.1069 BC), the figure of Horus became part of the royal headdress, with his outstretched wings wrapped around the crown.

Son of Re

In accordance with the mythology of kingship, the king's father (and thus by definition the deceased king) was identified with the god of the dead,

▲ *Seti I is depicted at Abydos wearing the Blue Crown* (Khepresh) *and burning incense before a seated deity.*

rebirth and vegetation, Osiris. But the divine parentage of the ruler differed according to the context. In the fivefold titles mentioned earlier, the king's birth name was introduced by the title 'Son of Re' (*Sa Re*) – that is, son of the sun god, whom the king was thought to join on his death. This title was first used by the Fourth-Dynasty king Djedefre (c.2566–c.2558 BC). The birth name (called the nomen) and the throne name (the prenomen), introduced by the titulary 'He of the Sedge and the Bee', were the two names that appeared in the royal cartouche (ancient Egyptian *shenu*). This oval outline represented an encircling rope with knotted ends, and was believed to have protective properties.

▲ *Hatshepsut, represented here as a sphinx, wore the false beard of the pharaoh despite the fact that she was a woman.*

In the New Kingdom Period (c.1550–c.1069 BC), rulers claimed to be the offspring of Amun, the 'king of the gods'. The 'divine births' of the Eighteenth-Dynasty rulers Hatshepsut (c.1473–c.1458 BC) and Amenhotep III (c.1390–c.1352 BC) were documented on the walls of Hatshepsut's mortuary temple at Deir el-Bahri and the temple of Luxor respectively (see *The Divine Birth of the Egyptian King*). These kings continued to use the title 'Son of Re', but this would not have appeared contradictory to the ancient Egyptians because Re, the supreme solar deity, had by this time been merged with Amun to become the principal deity Amun-Re.

A variety of religious texts show that the king might be identified with a range of deities, depending on the context. He was often referred to as being 'like' (*mi*) a particular god. A marvellous example of the comparisons made between a particular ruler and the divine world is the cycle of hymns composed in honour of the Twelfth-Dynasty king Senusret III (c.1874–c.1855 BC) (see *Temple Literature*). The status accorded to kingship is exemplified by the occasional reference to the ruler as a creator god. For example, in the Twelfth-Dynasty tomb inscription of Khnumhotep at Beni Hasan, the king is referred to as Atum. In fact, throughout the Old Kingdom (c.2686–c.2181 BC), the king was said to have the divine powers of Sia (divine knowledge), Hu (divine utterance) and Heka (divine magic), which were usually attributed to the creator gods.

Inescapable mortality

In the eyes of the Egyptian people there must have been strict limitations on the living king's divinity, and clear distinctions were made in references to the king and the gods. During the Middle Kingdom (c.2055–c.1650 BC), the mortality of the man who held the divine office of king was acknowledged for the first time in some of the texts, such as *The Instruction of King Amenemhat I for his Son Senusret I*, the theme of which is regicide. Although written as if it were the advice of the Twelfth-Dynasty king Amenemhat I (c.1985–c.1955 BC) to his son and successor Senusret I (c.1965–c.1920 BC), it must have been composed during the latter's reign because it refers to the assassination of the older king. The tone of the piece is rational, personal and bitter, dealing as it does with the dangers of political office. The new king is warned about the treachery of his subjects in a manner that appears realistic and in conflict with the dogma of divine kingship.

The decision to emphasize the humanity as well as the divinity of the king can be seen in the art as well as the literature of this period. The statues of Senusret III (c.1874–c.1855 BC) and Amenemhat III (c.1855–c.1808 BC) of the Twelfth Dynasty, portray a sense of weariness in the faces, which are lined with age. These are a far cry from the typically stylized features of earlier Egyptian kings who, in representation, always had to appear youthful and vigorous. The fact that being pharaoh was a tough job was publicly acknowledged for the first time. In cases where the king was assassinated in a palace conspiracy, or if several kings died in quick succession, the mortality of the ruler would have been evident to all. Jubilee festivals were celebrated with the emphasis on the revivification of the king (see *Royal Jubilee Festivals*).

▼ *The large ears on this black granite statue of Senusret III might indicate the all-hearing capacity of the king. The more realistic royal portraiture of this era is also apparent.*

Glorification of the king

By the early New Kingdom (from c.1550 BC), the Old Kingdom (c.2686–c.2181 BC) was regarded as the glorious past, and the rulers emulated the heightened status of kingship of the Old Kingdom (whose pharaohs had certainly left their mark in the form of enormous pyramids). The king could be worshipped and supplicated for aid as a god. The Eighteenth-Dynasty king Akhenaten (c.1352–c.1336 BC) elevated himself and his family to the status of a divine royal family, whose members were then worshipped at shrines in households throughout his capital city of Akhetaten (see *Akhenaten's New Religion*). The Nineteenth-Dynasty king Ramesses II (c.1279–c.1213 BC) built throughout Egypt on an incredible scale and covered the country with large images of himself, including four statues 21m (69ft) high fronting his temple at Abu Simbel in Lower Nubia, seemingly attesting to his divinity. He even had a cult worshipping him.

▼ *The wild bull hunt of Ramesses III, illustrated on the temple pylon at Medinet Habu, symbolized the king's control over chaos and potential danger to the Egyptian state. 20th Dynasty.*

▲ *Tutankhamun probably never went into battle but, as this decorated chest reveals, by his reign it had become standard practice to represent the king conquering his enemies, because the triumphant imagery had symbolic value.*

The king as high priest

Throughout Egyptian history the pharaoh was nominally the high priest of every god in every temple throughout the country. (In practice high priests had to be appointed in each of the temples to function on behalf of the king.) In this way, the pharaoh stood as the intermediary between every god and the human world. Reliefs on the walls of the temples showed the king making offerings to the gods, and performing the required rituals before them (see *Temple Rites and Offerings*). It was considered of prime importance that he should be portrayed as the one who presented *maat* (translated as 'truth', 'order' or 'justice') to the gods, because this was what the Egyptian gods lived on. It was the role of the king to ensure the beneficence of the gods and thereby ensure peace, harmony, and prosperity in Egypt.

The king was essential to universal order, and it was his duty to maintain *maat* at all times. This function also involved quelling chaos, which was believed to manifest itself in wild animals and foreigners. Even if the king never actually involved himself in wild bull hunts and military campaigns abroad, the convention was for him to be depicted on temple walls engaged in such activities. In this way the king was symbolically subduing chaos and ensuring order. A common motif was the king smiting the enemy or a bound captive. It was essential for the dogma of divine kingship that the Egyptian ruler should always be portrayed as triumphant. The king's victories in battle were not, however, put down to the fact that he was a god, but that he had been granted them by the divine world, after the appropriate offerings and prayers.

It was traditional for a new pharaoh to have texts composed claiming that the land had been in a state of disorder prior to his ascent to the throne, and that, thanks to his greatness, he had restored it to its former balance and glory. Sometimes these texts did follow a period of upheaval, but they tend to be formulaic and together form a genre of literature that glorified the new king and legitimated his right to rule. ◆

The Divine Birth of the Egyptian King

The reliefs are fading fast in the colonnades of the west Theban mortuary temple at Deir el-Bahri, built in honour of the deceased Eighteenth-Dynasty ruler Hatshepsut (c.1473–c.1458 BC). But it is just possible to make out a series of scenes that tell an interesting story concerning ancient Egyptian ideas about kingship and their gods – the so-called 'divine birth' of their pharaoh.

Amun, the 'king of the gods' in the New Kingdom Period (c.1550–c.1069 BC), is shown being led by the hand to a queen's bedchamber by the ibis-headed Thoth, the 'messenger of the gods'. Amun is depicted in human form wearing the curled beard that was associated with divinity. He wears a tall, double-plumed headdress and holds a was-sceptre (associated with divinity, power, well being and prosperity) in his free hand. The queen in question is Ahmose Nefertari, the wife of the Eighteenth-Dynasty king Tuthmosis I (c.1504–c.1492 BC).

The next scene is a wonderfully modest portrayal of the sexual union between the queen and Amun. They are shown fully dressed, seated upright together on a bed which is supported on the heads of two goddesses. Amun and the queen have their knees entwined and he holds an ankh (the sign of life) up to her nose: thus she takes in his vitality and procreative force.

Following this night of passion, in the next scene Amun passes on his instructions to Khnum, the ram-headed creator god. They both hold was-sceptres and ankhs. As a result of this meeting, Khnum fashions Ahmose Nefertari's

▲ The 'messenger of the gods' Thoth accompanies the 'king of the gods' Amun.

▼ Amun, wearing the characteristic double-plumed headdress, is seated together with Queen Ahmose Nefertan in a euphemistic portrayal of sexual union.

▼ The goddess of childbirth, Heket attends the creation of Hatshepsut on Khnum's potter's wheel.

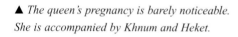

daughter and the ruler-to-be, Hatshepsut, on his potter's wheel (see *Creation Myths*). Alongside the tiny figure of Hatshepsut on the wheel is an identical figure, representing her *ka* or 'spirit'. Heket, the frog-headed protective goddess of childbirth, is also present at this creation of the ruler.

Idealism in art

Ancient Egyptian art is highly stylized and idealized. Women are depicted as slender young beauties regardless of their actual age and looks, and it is almost unheard-of to find a representation of a pregnant woman. The scene of the pregnant queen being led to the birthing chamber by Khnum and Heket is one such rare example, although you have to look very closely to detect any sign of pregnancy – the queen's abdomen is only very slightly rounded. Like the sexual intercourse, the scene of the birth is entirely

▼ *Hatshepsut is presented before Amun, who holds an ankh in his right hand.*

euphemistic. A goddess, presumably acting as midwife, kneels before the seated queen and hands her the newborn child. Kneeling behind the queen is Meskhent, the goddess of the birthing bricks. Finally, Hatshepsut is presented before the gods, the most important of whom is of course her 'father', Amun.

Divine parentage

The idea of Amun being the father of the monarch was not particular to Hatshepsut, but as a woman, she might have felt it necessary to emphasize her legitimacy in this way. On the other hand she may well have felt no need for 'propaganda' of this kind, and in commissioning these reliefs she was merely doing what was expected of her as an Eighteenth-Dynasty ruler, emphasizing an aspect of the divinity of kingship.

Amenhotep III (c.1390– c.1352 BC) had a similar series of reliefs carved in the temple of Luxor on the east bank at Thebes. In this case the queen was Mutemwia, and although Amun was represented in his usual way (as at Deir el-Bahri), the

▲ *The queen's pregnancy is barely noticeable. She is accompanied by Khnum and Heket.*

hieroglyphs indicate that he took the guise of her husband Tuthmosis IV (c.1400–c.1390 BC) for the purpose of this ceremonial sexual union (perhaps to put the queen at ease). ◆

Goddesses of childbirth

Women in ancient Egypt appear to have given birth in a crouching position supported on 'birthing bricks'. Because infant mortality was high and the Egyptians were well aware of the dangers of childbirth, they sought as much divine assistance and protection as possible, and the bricks were divinely personified as the deity Meskhent, one of the goddesses of fate who governed the future of newly born children.

The frog goddess Heket, at one time regarded as the consort of the creator god Khnum, acted as the divine midwife and was said to attend royal births. The protection of the hippopotamus goddess, Taweret, extended to all pregnant women.

Royal Jubilee Festivals

It was important for the king to remain strong and agile in the eyes of his people. This must have been very difficult if the king had been ruling for any length of time and had become noticeably stooped and wrinkly. The Sixth-Dynasty king Pepi II (c.2278–c.2184 BC), for example, supposedly reigned for around 94 years, so towards the end of his reign he can hardly have looked spry at public appearances.

It was traditional to celebrate a royal jubilee festival (*heb sed*) 30 years into the reign, but sometimes a king might choose to hold such a celebration at another time. Amenhotep III (c.1390–c.1352 BC), for example, is said to have ruled for 38 years and yet he celebrated three *heb seds*.

The festival consisted of a number of rituals which were intended to

▼ *This limestone fragment shows two figures of Akhenaten wearing the traditional short cloak of the sed-festival. On the right he is accompanied by his Chief Prophet, who carries the king's sandals. 18th Dynasty.*

rejuvenate the king, to display his fitness to continue ruling, to consolidate his claim to the land over which he ruled, and to ensure the fertility of the land. Reliefs depicting the events of such a festival emphasize the honouring of the enthroned king, who is often shown wearing a very particular short cloak and sitting in a pavilion special to the occasion. He is also depicted ceremonially running (often holding ritual implements) between markers which may well have symbolized the borders of Egypt, thereby staking his claim to the whole territory.

Royal athleticism

A very early depiction of a *sed*-festival can be seen on an ebony label in the British Museum, London. It was found at Abydos in the tomb of the First-Dynasty king Den (c.2950 BC). An illustration carved on the label shows Den wearing a Double Crown, sitting on his throne in a special festival pavilion. He is also shown running between two sets of three boundary markers – an

The Step Pyramid complex

It is still possible to visit the *heb sed* court to the south-east of Djoser's Step Pyramid. This open court is home to a number of 'dummy' shrines representing the ancient chapels of local gods of the nomes of Egypt. At its southern end is the base of what would originally have been a double festival pavilion containing two thrones, one to symbolize the king's rule over Upper Egypt, and the other to symbolize his rule over Lower Egypt.

image that crops up throughout pharaonic history.

The Third-Dynasty ruler Djoser (c.2667–c.2648 BC), for example, is portrayed running on a relief found in the underground chambers of his Step Pyramid complex at Saqqara. In fact various structures in this king's mortuary complex were dedicated to his

▶ *Dummy chapels such as this one were stone replicas of those built for the celebration of the* sed-*festival. Their presence in Djoser's Step Pyramid complex was intended to ensure that the king would be able to celebrate jubilee festivals throughout eternity. Old Kingdom.*

enactment of the *sed*-festival. The Step Pyramid does not stand alone, but is surrounded by a series of courts, temples, and other important buildings. In the large court to the south of the pyramid there are the traces of boundary markers, so perhaps this was where the king performed his ceremonial display of athleticism.

Commemorative buildings

Important religious buildings were still being built and decorated in connection with the royal jubilee festivals very much later in Egyptian history. Examples include the mortuary temple of the Eighteenth-Dynasty king Amenhotep III (c.1390–c.1352 BC) on the west bank at Thebes (of which only the two statues known as the Colossi of Memnon survive), as well as the temple to the Aten at east Karnak built by his successor Akhenaten (c.1352–c.1336 BC) and the *sed*-festival court at Bubastis built by the Twenty-second-Dynasty king Osorkon II (c.874–c.850 BC).

The large lake to the east of Amenhotep III's palace at Malkata on the west bank at Thebes appears to have been the setting for one of this king's splendid jubilee festivals, during which he was rowed in a boat in a ceremony reminiscent of the sun god's night-time journey through the Netherworld. The rejuvenation of the king reflected the rising of the sun (see *The Journey of the Sun through the Netherworld*). ◆

▶ *This false door stela in the South Tomb of Djoser's Step Pyramid Complex, shows the king performing the ceremonial* heb sed *run.*

Temples and Priests

The temples of ancient Egypt have inspired awe throughout the ages. The modern visitor still marvels at their magnificence – their huge size and the beauty and detail of the reliefs on their walls.

To ensure their survival, these grand structures, mostly of stone, were built in the desert fringes, just beyond the reaches of the Nile flood. It is, of course, the most recent structure at any one site that still stands today, and most surviving temples are not pharaonic at all, but date to the Ptolemaic and Roman Periods (332 BC–AD 395). They do, however, comply with the ancient conventions of temple-building. It was possible for a cult centre to have been dedicated to a particular deity for centuries, while the temple itself was rebuilt, perhaps more than once.

The architectural splendour of the great religious buildings is impossible to overlook, but finding out what actually went on inside them involves closer scrutiny. As well as inscriptions on temple walls, hymns, prayers and records of administration and offerings were kept on papyri. Many votive offerings have also survived. From such sources it is possible to build up a picture of the roles of the various priests, and to begin to fathom the rituals of the High Priest, who enjoyed a more intimate interaction with the resident deity of the temple.

◄ *Colossal statues of rulers and elaborately decorated columns were key features of the great temples of Egypt.*

Temple Architecture

The temples that survive in Egypt today tend to date from the New Kingdom onwards (c.1550 BC). They may have varied in size depending on the importance of a particular deity, but whether they were dedicated to gods or kings (living or dead), all Egyptian temples had essential architectural features in common.

The grand approach

Each temple was approached by a processional way or avenue, often flanked by rows of statues. The approach to Karnak Temple is typical, lined on each side by stone sphinxes with ram's heads (the ram was one of the guises of Amun, who was worshipped at this temple). It once connected the great complex at Karnak with Luxor Temple, about 2km (1 mile) to the south.

The processional way led to the main gateway, known as the first pylon (the ancient Greek word for 'gate') of the temple. This consisted of two enormous tapering towers of masonry with an opening between them. Flags on long poles projected outwards from the front of the temple on each side of the entrance. These flags, flying majestically, would have been visible from a long way off and would have been an image closely associated with the temple. It is therefore interesting that the hieroglyphic sign used to write the ancient Egyptian word *netjer*, which means 'god', was possibly intended to represent a flag on a pole. The onlooker would also have been struck by the size of the statues of the king which flanked the gateway, such as those of Ramesses II (c.1279–c.1213 BC) at Luxor Temple. It would certainly have heightened the people's belief in the divinity of kingship to witness these statues of the ruler in such a hallowed setting, and being so colossal they must have seemed like gods. Sometimes an obelisk, or a pair of obelisks, also marked the entrance to the temple.

▲ *There were originally two obelisks in front of the First Pylon at Luxor Temple, but the other is now in the Place de la Concorde in Paris.*

▼ *The roof of the great hypostyle hall at Karnak Temple was originally supported by 134 massive stone columns.*

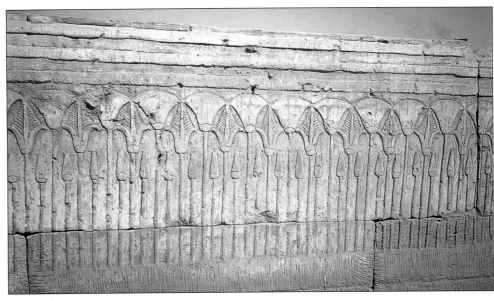

▶ *Plant-life is a common theme of temple decoration, and is seen here at Kom Ombo.*

Inside the great entrance was the peristyle court, a large, open square surrounded by a colonnade. It is likely that some of the population (at least in the later periods of Egyptian history) would have been allowed at certain times into this 'public' area of the temple, although all who entered the temple's confines would have had to comply with the criteria of ritual purity (see *The Temple Complex*).

The temple lay on a straight axis. On the other side of the great court, opposite the back of the first pylon, was a smaller gateway known as the second pylon. Access through this inner entrance was restricted to those with priestly titles, and the rooms within were used for storing cult equipment and for performing the secret rituals of the temple (see *Temple Rites and Offerings*).

The inner sanctum
On the other side of the second pylon was the hypostyle hall, with a roof supported by rows of columns. This was usually broader than it was deep. To walk through it was like wandering through a forest. Gaps at the top of the outer walls provided clerestory lighting – shafts of light piercing the mysterious darkness. It would have been only just possible to make out the painted reliefs and inscriptions on the walls and columns. The gloom and the dense columns formed a perfect screen between the outside world and the secluded dwelling-place of the god.

The number of peristyle courts and hypostyle halls depended on the size of the temple, as did the number of storerooms, antechambers, vestibules, offering halls and shrines which led off the inner hypostyle hall. But deep within every temple lay the 'holy of holies' – the sanctuary where the god lived. The

god or goddess resided in a cult statue, which stood in a raised shrine or *naos* (the ancient Greek word for the innermost part of a temple or shrine), usually of stone or wood with wooden doors. From the New Kingdom onwards (c.1550 BC) the shrine often took the form of a boat, as at the temple of Horus at Edfu, and was known as a barque shrine. Only the High Priest could enter the presence of the god.

The god's home
The temple was very much the house of the god. The ancient Egyptian for 'temple' was *hwt netjer*, 'the god's mansion', or *per netjer*, 'the god's house'. The temple was also regarded as a model of the place where creation was believed to have taken place. The floor level rose gradually from the temple entrance to the shrine in the innermost sanctuary, and the *naos* was thought to reflect the mound projecting from the primordial waters, with the deity standing on it as the creator god had first done.

The primordial waters (Nun) were symbolized by a 'sacred lake', such as at Karnak, where the priests made their ablutions. The Victory Stela of Piy (c.747–c.716 BC) in the Cairo Museum records that when this Twenty-fifth-Dynasty king visited Heliopolis and ritually cleansed himself in the sacred lake there, he claimed that he had washed his face in 'the river of Nun', as the sun god was believed to do each day before dawn. It is also possible that the

undulating mudbrick wall surrounding some of the temple enclosures was meant to represent the waters of chaos.

The cosmological theme was extended elsewhere inside the temple. A marsh was evoked by the halls with their rows of papyrus- and lotus-form columns. The flat ceilings were often painted dark blue and covered with yellow stars. The hieroglyphic sign for 'horizon' was a tract of land with the sun rising between two mountains, and it is possible that the great pylon forming the entrance to the temple was meant to represent this. ◆

▲ *The monolithic* naos *of highly polished syenite in the sanctuary at Edfu Temple is the oldest part of the building, dating to the 30th-Dynasty reign of Nectanebo II.*

Different Types of Temples

There were two main types of temple: cult temples dedicated to deities, and mortuary temples built in honour of dead kings. Both were very similar in design and function: offerings were made to the gods in the former, to ensure the beneficence of the divine world; and to the spirits (*kas*) of the deceased kings in the latter, ensuring their continued existence in the Afterlife. Both procedures were seen as crucial to the maintenance of order and peace (see *Temple Rites and Offerings*).

Cult temples were usually dedicated to a triad of deities, whereas mortuary temples were concerned with the deceased king and his identification with a number of gods. A king's mortuary temple was clearly also intended to be used for ceremonies during his lifetime, and provided the focal point for a complex of buildings built in celebration of divine kingship, including a royal palace which could go

▲ *The columns in this colonnade at Karnak are papyriform: their capitals resemble stylized papyrus buds.*

▲ *Statues of Ramesses II in the form of Osiris stand before pillars in this king's mortuary temple, the Ramesseum.*

on to serve as a dummy palace for the dead king's spirit.

In all temples, priests officiated (see *The Role of Priests*), offerings were made and rituals performed. The focal point of any cult temple was the statue of a god, whereas in a royal mortuary temple it was the statue of a king.

Cult temples

Very little has survived of cult temples built before the New Kingdom (c.1550 BC). During the Old Kingdom (c.2686–c.2181 BC) it is likely that temples to the deities were built of mudbrick, which is obviously a less durable building material than stone. (Today, Egyptian farmers make use of the ancient mudbrick as a fertilizer, called *sebakh* in Arabic.) During the Middle Kingdom (c.2055–c.1650 BC) cult temples were apparently built of stone, but little has survived. Usually the stone from these structures was re-used in the buildings of the New Kingdom (c.1550–c.1069 BC) and later temples located on the same sites as the earlier ones. The ancient Egyptians were great recyclers, as modern Egyptians are today. Why go

to the bother of quarrying in the searing heat of the desert, transporting heavy loads across vast distances and working stone with stone and bronze tools, when ready-dressed blocks were available on the site from an earlier structure that had perhaps fallen into disrepair? A good example of such re-use is a stunning relief of the Twelfth-Dynasty king Senusret I (c.1965–c.1920 BC) and the god Min which presumably once graced the walls of an important Middle Kingdom temple. Now in the Petrie Museum of Egyptian Archaeology, it was discovered by the 'Father of Egyptian archaeology', William Matthew Flinders Petrie (1853–1942), turned face down and re-used as a paving slab in a much later Ptolemaic temple at the site of Koptos.

Mortuary temples

Royal mortuary temples (referred to in the ancient texts as 'mansions of millions of years') have survived from

the Early Dynastic Period onwards (c.3100 BC). They became larger and grander as time went on. The earliest examples are simple offering chambers adjoining the earliest royal tombs, called mastabas (Arabic for 'bench') at the royal burial sites of Abydos and Saqqara. By the Third Dynasty they were more complex. The mortuary temple in the burial complex of King Djoser (c.2667–c.2648 BC) was attached to the north face of his pyramid. It was made of stone and consisted of two courts, one of which was presumably dedicated to Djoser as king of Upper Egypt, and one to him as king of Lower Egypt. By the Fourth Dynasty, the mortuary temple had been shifted to the east face of the pyramid, so that it could be joined via a straight causeway to a 'valley temple' at the edge of the cultivation, usually at a quay on a canal. The best preserved mortuary temples from the Old Kingdom (c.2686–c.2181

▼ The unusual altar in the sun temple of Niuserre at Abu Gurab is sculpted out of calcite and is some 6m (20ft) in diameter. 5th Dynasty.

BC) are those of king Khafre (c.2558–c.2532 BC) at Giza.

By the New Kingdom (c.1550–c.1069 BC), the mortuary temples were separate from the tombs of the kings. The tombs were in the Valley of the Kings on the west bank at Thebes, whereas their accompanying temples were some distance away on the desert fringes, more conveniently sited close to the cultivation and the river. They were imposing structures, elaborately decorated and on a par with the contemporary state cult temples.

A variation on the theme of the mortuary temple were the 'cenotaph temples' at Abydos, the legendary burial

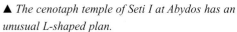

▲ The cenotaph temple of Seti I at Abydos has an unusual L-shaped plan.

place of Osiris, god of the dead, rebirth and vegetation. These temples were closely associated with the cult of Osiris, and their function was to associate the dead king with various gods. The earliest royal cenotaph at Abydos was built by the Twelfth-Dynasty king Senusret III (c.1874–c.1855 BC), but by far the best preserved and thus best known is that of the Nineteenth-Dynasty ruler Seti I (c.1294–c.1279 BC).

Sun temples

The remains of stone sun temples date from the Fifth Dynasty (c.2494–c.2345 BC). They were dedicated to the sun god Re, but were also closely associated with royal burials. They were built by the first six rulers of this dynasty and were connected with their pyramids (which, like the obelisk, were presumably solar symbols) and with the cult of the sun god at Heliopolis. Six sun temples are known from inscriptions, but only two have actually been discovered; they are those of Userkaf (c.2494–c.2487 BC) and Niuserre (c.2445–c.2421 BC), and are both situated at Abu Gurab, north of Abusir (part of the necropolis of ancient Memphis). The sun temple of Niuserre houses the remains of an enormous squat stone obelisk, and a gigantic altar in the form of four hieroglyphic signs for 'offering' (*hetep*). ◆

The Temple Complex

The purpose of the ancient Egyptian temple was to reflect and maintain the divine order of creation. It was not a place of organized public worship, comparable with a mosque, synagogue or church. No form of service was held, and rather than everyone being welcomed into the temple, the public were generally excluded from it. A large number of priests was employed by each temple but very few of them actually performed religious rituals.

The temple was rather like a medieval European monastery, in that it was a great landowning institution and functioned very much as the hub of the local economy, and as a place of learning. It was run by a large and complex bureaucracy, and temple workers included farmers, builders and scribes as well as priests.

▲ The ears on this painted stela were included to ensure that the god would hear the prayer.

Ritual purity

All who entered the confines of the temple had to comply with the strict rules regarding ritual purity. According to inscriptions on the walls of the temple at Esna, all those entering temples from the Late Period (c.747 BC) were expected at least to have cut their fingernails and toenails, shaved their heads and removed other body hair, washed their hands with natron (a naturally occurring salt), be dressed in linen (they were forbidden from wearing wool), and to have not had sexual intercourse for several days. Priests were not required to remain celibate outside the temple.

Much ritual purification would subsequently have gone on inside the temple, making use of ablution tanks and the Sacred Lake.

Public access to the deity

During much of Egyptian history most people would have been allowed only as far as the gateway of the temple complex. They did, however, come to the outer precincts of the temple to say prayers and enlist the help of the gods. At the mortuary temple of Ramesses III (c.1184–c.1153 BC) at Medinet Habu, for example, the corridor inside the entrance gateway had an image of 'Ptah who hears prayers' on its wall. In this way, people who would only ever be granted access to this part of the temple could petition, or give thanks to, the god. No member of the public would ever have laid eyes on the cult statue of the god housed in the inner shrine. However, by the later period of Egyptian history, the peristyle court (see *Temple Architecture*) appears to have become available to a certain degree of public access, and was a place where offerings and supplications could be made before statues of gods and kings (see *Temple Rites and Offerings*). The emphasis was on the gods hearing the prayers of the people, so stelae, statues and even walls might be inscribed with numerous ears in order to ensure this would happen. Sometimes stelae and statues set up in the outer parts of the temple were covered in hieroglyphs. These were often spells to help to cure, or protect against, scorpion stings, snake bites, and other such hazards and illnesses.

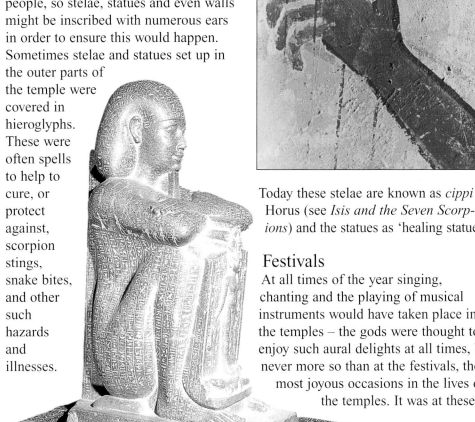

Today these stelae are known as *cippi* of Horus (see *Isis and the Seven Scorpions*) and the statues as 'healing statues'.

Festivals

At all times of the year singing, chanting and the playing of musical instruments would have taken place in the temples – the gods were thought to enjoy such aural delights at all times, but never more so than at the festivals, the most joyous occasions in the lives of the temples. It was at these

▲ *Musical instruments of all kinds were played in the temples. Paintings and reliefs reveal that male harpists were often blind. 18th Dynasty. Tomb of Nakht, west Thebes.*

celebrations that the statue of the deity emerged from his or her secluded shrine, carried on the shoulders of priests, but always still concealed from the eyes of the masses, sometimes in a carrying shrine in the form of a boat (known as a barque shrine). The oracle of the god could then be consulted. His or her answer might be sought to questions such as whether it was sensible to make a difficult journey north, or who, out of a list of suspects, was responsible for stealing an article of clothing.

◀ *This basalt 'healing statue' of the priest Djedhor is covered in hieroglyphs of incantatory texts. The priest sits behind a* cippus *of Horus, and the basin in the plinth is for the collection of water which was ritually poured over the statue to be imbued with the potency of the magic spells. 30th Dynasty.*

▲ *The foreleg of the ox was the choice cut of meat for offering to the gods and to the dead. 6th Dynasty. Tomb of Idut, Saqqara.*

The god's needs

The daily rituals of the temple took place in the darker, more secluded parts of the building on the far side of the hypostyle hall (see *Temple Architecture* and *Temple Rites and Offerings*). Every need of the deity was tended to, directly by a minority of the priesthood and indirectly by a large number of temple workers. According to the longest known papyrus from ancient Egypt, Papyrus Harris (40.5m or 133ft long), which dates to the day the Twentieth-Dynasty king Ramesses III died

▶ *The migdol gateway of Ramesses III's mortuary temple at Medinet Habu was a quasi-defensive feature borrowed from the design of Syrian fortresses.*

▲ *Windows in the inner parts of temples were usually clerestory, allowing shafts of light to filter down from the tops of the walls, as here in the hypostyle hall at Edfu.*

(c.1153 BC), the estate of Karnak Temple employed a total labour force of 81,322 people (see *The Role of Priests*). The papyrus also records that this great temple of Amun exercised control over 2393sq km (924sq miles) of arable land, 433 orchards, 421,362 head of livestock, 65 villages, 83 ships and 46 workshops.

Temple economy

The ancient Egyptian temple was the economic hub of the locality. The temple complex would have had its own landing quay, giving it easy access to the river for transporting produce. In the larger temple complexes, food production would have taken place on a grand scale in the temple butcheries, breweries and bakeries.

By a process known as the 'reversion of offerings', a large proportion of the population could in practice be fed via the temple. Much of the produce of

Egypt passed, by various requirements, to the temples throughout the country, especially in the big cities such as Thebes and Memphis where there were huge temple complexes, each with a number of different deities to be offered to on a daily basis. The greater the quantity of offerings, it was hoped, the greater the beneficence of the gods. Food offerings of all kinds were made to the gods, but most of what was offered eventually reverted to the priests. From them it was passed to their families and to the many workers and dependents of the temple and temple estates, not to mention the poor at the temple gate (see *Temple Rites and Offerings*).

A place of scholarship

The temple was also a place of learning, providing education for those boys who would go on to hold administrative or priestly positions. During the New Kingdom (c.1550–c.1069 BC), it is known from texts that there were at least two schools in Thebes, one in the temple of the goddess Mut at Karnak, and one behind the Ramesseum, the mortuary complex of the Nineteenth-Dynasty king Ramesses II (c.1279–c.1213 BC), although no excavated structure has been found which can be identified as having been used as a school.

The local temple was the storehouse for local records, which were written on papyrus rolls kept in locked chests. In general, the temple, with its high surrounding walls and massive gateway, would have functioned as the local safe place. The temple at Medinet Habu, for instance, was one of the most defensible places in western Thebes. The east gate was fortified with guardhouses flanking the entrance, and in the late Twentieth Dynasty, when the people of the west Theban workmen's village of Deir el-Medina felt threatened by marauding foreigners, they hid themselves in the precincts of the temple. ◆

The Role of Priests

If, as is stated in Papyrus Harris (c.1153 BC), the temple of Amun at Karnak employed 81,322 people towards the end of the New Kingdom, it is clear that the temples must have been the chief places of employment in the country. There is no implication that those 81,322 individuals could possibly all have been priests. In fact it is a matter of dispute whether any of these temple employees would actually have been priests in the modern sense of the term.

The conventional translations of ancient Egyptian terms can be misleading when they employ words that have very specific meanings and associations for us today. The ancient Egyptian term *hem netjer* is normally translated as 'priest', but it literally means 'servant of the god' and not all those described in this way were necessarily trained in theology. They certainly would not have conducted the kind of worship or services performed by priests in any of the religious traditions that are familiar today. It is possible that most of those described as 'servants of the god' would not have performed any kind of ritual in the temple.

Priestly garments

Apart from the obligation to be clean shaven, priests of lower ranks who are depicted in reliefs and paintings are indistinguishable from ordinary people. However, some priests did wear distinctive clothing as a sign of their office. The *sem*-priests who performed the final purification and revivification rites at funerals, wore cloaks made of leopardskin. When the king was portrayed officiating in his priestly role he was sometimes shown wearing this form of dress.

A priestly rota

The number of temple employees depended on the size of the temple, which in turn depended on the status of the deity to whom it was dedicated and the size of the town or city. Throughout Egyptian history, the main body of priests was made up of people who spent much of the year engaged in their

▲ *Tuthmosis III wears a leopardskin to identify his role as High Priest.*

own, different, occupations. A rota system was devised whereby the priests of each temple were divided into four groups (usually referred to today by the Greek word *phyle*). The members of each group performed their temple

▲ *A libation of water (indicated by a zig-zag line, the hieroglyphic sign for water) is poured from a heset-jar on to a heaped offering table in this relief at the temple of Kom Ombo.*

▼ *An enormous variety of foods, including beef, fish, duck, bread, fruit and vegetables, were offered to the gods and to the spirits of the dead. Tomb of Horemheb, Saqqara.*

duties for one month, then returned to their own jobs for three months, so that they worked for the temple for a total of three months in every year. At the end of each month-long shift, a stock taking was carried out, and records were made on papyri or wooden boards.

For most members of the community, it would have been well worth their while to perform this temple service because the priests received a proportion of the temple revenue (this would have been given in kind, because there was no coinage in ancient Egypt). The ancient Egyptians believed that the deity consumed the essence of the food given to him or her as an offering, and it could then be passed on to the priests. This system was known as the 'reversion of offerings' (see *The Temple Complex*). The practice could at times prove lucrative – as it did during the New Kingdom (c.1550–c.1069 BC) when tithes and war booty created huge temple incomes – to the extent that it was sometimes even considered worth purchasing a priestly office.

Priests were also exempted from some taxes, and could often avoid undertaking state labour that was otherwise a compulsory service, such as the digging of irrigation systems.

The purified ones

Most of the priests had very little contact with the cult statue of the deity, the focal point of any temple, although tending the statue was the most important temple rite and would have been carried out by the most senior priests. The reliefs on temple walls can be misleading because it was believed that it was only the king who was worthy of being depicted standing opposite a deity, so priests are never shown making offerings to the gods.

All those working in the temple had to be considered ritually pure in order to do so. In fact the majority of the priests

▲ *The calendars of festivals carved on the walls of temples such as this one at Kom Ombo, were based on the lunar months, stellar sightings and the annual inundation of the Nile.*

◀ *The 18th-Dynasty king Ay (c.1327– c.1323 BC) is depicted on the north wall of Tutankhamun's burial chamber wearing the leopardskin of a priest and performing the ritual of the Opening of the Mouth on the mummy of the dead king; thus Ay legitimized his accession to the throne as Tutankhamun's heir.*

were called *wab* ('purifier' or 'purified') priests. The Greek historian Herodotus, writing in the fifth century BC, stated that Egyptian priests washed twice daily and twice nightly, that they were clean-shaven, had no body hair, were circumcised, abstained from sexual intercourse for several days before entering the temple, wore no wool or leather clothing, and had sandals made of papyrus. In addition, priests seem to have had to rinse out their mouths with a solution of natron (a natural compound of sodium carbonate and bicarbonate, found as crystals at the edges of certain lakes) and rub their bodies with oil. A judicial document now in the Turin Museum tells us that a *wab* priest of Khnum was brought to justice because he had sworn not to enter the temple at Elephantine until he had spent ten days drinking natron, but in fact he had entered after only seven days and was considered ritually impure.

A variety of jobs

Most priests would not have come into direct contact with the divine cult image, so although their job might have been to see

to the needs of the god, it would have been only by indirect means. The man who was able to interact most closely with the god was the High Priest (see *The High Priests*). His deputy was the Second Prophet, who was in charge of the economic organization of the temple. He oversaw its provisioning from estates and endowments, and he made sure that the right amount of offerings were delivered each day. He would have had a host of administrators working with him.

The majority of the priests were occupied with ensuring the maintenance and security of the temple. They ran the workshops, storerooms, libraries and other affiliated buildings, as well as acting as doorkeepers and porters. The daily tasks of washing, dressing and feeding the cult statue of the deity appear to have been carried out by Stolist Priests (see *Temple Rites and Offerings*). They would have worked closely with the Lector Priests, whose job it was to recite the words of the god. They chanted magic spells while important rituals were

carried out; for example, they would recite spells from the Book of the Dead while a dead body was being embalmed and mummified.

The *sem*-priest, who can be distinguished in images by the leopardskin he wears, was also very important at death. This priest's function developed in the New Kingdom out of the duties performed by the first-born son at his father's funeral. These included the final rites of purification and the Opening of the Mouth ceremony, which was performed on the mummified body to revive its senses, so that the deceased could be reborn.

All those people who worked in the temple confines had to swear not to spread the secrets or mysteries of the temple, and were considered to occupy a privileged position.   ◆

◀ *This priest has a figure of the god Amun tattooed on his upper arm. He kneels behind an image of the god. As is often the case, an inscription accompanies the statue.*

The High Priests

The king was nominally High Priest of every cult in Egypt, but basic logistics clearly prevented him from performing the daily rituals in many places at once, and so in practice he had to delegate the day-to-day duties of High Priest to men stationed at temples throughout the country. Thus the position of High Priest (or Chief Priest or First Prophet) was by royal appointment and was a highly esteemed title, both religiously and politically.

Acting on behalf of the king, the High Priest had closer contact with the cult statue of the god than anyone else in the temple complex. It is likely that only the High Priest would have been allowed to stand before the image of the god in the shrine. Temple reliefs illustrate what was expected of the High Priest, but because the presence of the king was still considered necessary in the temples, even if only symbolically, it was the ruler who was shown performing the rituals in the various reliefs and statuary (see *Temple Rites and Offerings*). Superb reliefs on the walls of the sanctuaries in the temple at Abydos, for example, depict the Nineteenth-Dynasty king Seti I (c.1294–c.1279 BC) carrying out his priestly duties.

Nepotism

In the Old Kingdom (c.2686–c.2181 BC) all senior positions, whether in the temples, the administrative system or the army, were held by the same small group of people, more specifically members of the royal family – especially brothers, sons and uncles of the reigning monarch – who held multiple honorary titles, each accompanied by privileges granted by the king. As priests these men would certainly have played a role in the temple structure, but would probably not have worked full-time within the temple confines. During the Middle Kingdom (c.2055–c.1650 BC) these three sources of employment for the élite became more distinct, but the highest ranking priests continued also to sit on councils of state in the royal palace, and clearly had political influence.

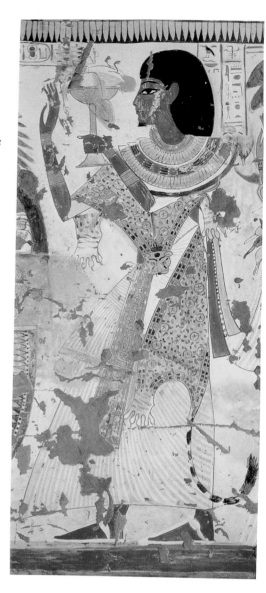

▲ *The leopardskin was a priestly robe usually associated with the sem-priest.*

During the Eighteenth Dynasty (c.1550–c.1295 BC) the wealth of the largest temples grew dramatically, mainly augmented by booty and tribute resulting from successful military campaigning in Syria-Palestine. The Temple of Amun at Karnak received the bulk of this new source of income, and its High Priest became more and more powerful, thanks to the wealth and manpower under his control. According to Papyrus Harris, by the end of Ramesses III's reign (c.1153 BC) the king had relinquished control over the finances of the estate of Amun. The Wilbour Papyrus, dating to the reign of Ramesses V (c.1147–c.1143 BC), records that this land was not subject to royal taxation, and that its dependents

▲ *The ruler Hatshepsut wears a false beard, the* nemes *headdress – a striped linen headcloth – and a* uraeus *on her brow. She holds two* nw *pots, characteristically used for offering wine and milk to the gods. 18th Dynasty.*

▲ *In the cenotaph temple of Seti I at Abydos, the king burns incense before a seated figure of Horus. The god holds an* ankh *in his left hand and a crook, flail and* was-*sceptre in his right.*

were exempt from compulsory military service and state labour.

Priestly power

If the reigning king was strong and successful, the excessive power of the High Priest of Amun at Karnak did not necessarily cause any real problems. But if a weak and ineffective king succeeded to the throne there was likely to be trouble, and this is exactly what happened towards the end of the Twentieth Dynasty (c.1186– c.1069 BC). Because of the exceptionally long reign of Ramesses II (c.1279–c.1213 BC), many of the last kings of the New Kingdom succeeded to the throne when they were already elderly and feeble. They chose to pass their days in their palace at Per-Ramesses in the Delta, thus distancing themselves from their people and, more significantly, from the Theban region. Generally their reigns

appear to have been fairly ineffectual. But the people of the south of Egypt needed a strong leader, and rather than look to the king they decided it would be most sensible to show allegiance to the High Priest of Amun at Thebes.

At the end of the Twentieth Dynasty, a High Priest of Amun named Herihor was able to get away with claiming royal titles even though Ramesses XI (c.1099– c.1069 BC) was still on the throne. There are inscriptions in the Temple of Khonsu at Karnak which show Herihor's name written in royal cartouches, and his adoption of the full regal titles, including the royal epithet 'Victorious Bull', the rare title 'Great Ruler of Egypt' and even 'Son of Amun', thereby claiming divine descent (see *The Divine Birth of the Egyptian King*). This High Priest was militarily and economically incredibly powerful, and during Ramesses XI's reign he effectively controlled Egypt from its southern border at Aswan north to Herakleopolis near the Faiyum. Despite this, at no time did Herihor claim complete royal power. ◆

▲ *It was unheard of for a high priest to have himself represented with royal titles and his name in cartouches, face-to-face with the god Amun, until Herihor brazenly usurped these royal prerogatives here at Karnak.*

The Role of Women in the Temples

◄ *The design of the hooped* sistrum, *or ceremonial rattle, often incorporated the face of Hathor with her cow ears. Tomb of Sennefer.*

and Pakhet, and during the Old Kingdom a certain queen Meresankh held the office of High Priestess of the god Thoth.

Music and dance

An important part of the cult of Hathor was music and dance – the priestesses accompanied ceremonial dances and rituals by shaking their *sistra* (rattles), instruments whose handles were often decorated with the carved head of Hathor, and rattling their broad, beaded necklaces with long counterpoises, called *menat* necklaces.

From the Old Kingdom onwards, women often functioned as the cult singers, dancers and musicians, playing instruments such as harps, tambourines and clappers in the temples of both

▶ *Amenirdis, the daughter of the Kushite ruler Kashta, was adopted as 'God's Wife of Amun' at Thebes.*

There were far fewer women than men working in the temples of ancient Egypt, but the title 'priestess' (*hemet netjer*, literally 'wife of the god') certainly existed. These women, who functioned in the temple cults, tended to be from the upper echelons of society and were usually married to priests, and as a result their position relied heavily upon the status of their husbands. During the Old and Middle Kingdoms (c.2686–c.1650 BC), the title *hemet netjer* was most usually associated with the cult of Hathor, the goddess of fertility. It was a priestess who was in charge of the management of the estates of this goddess, and even some of the High Priests were women. We also know of female High Priests serving the cults of the goddesses Neith

▲ *This painted limestone stela depicts Nefretiabet seated before an offering table laden with bread and surrounded by other commodities such as oil, incense and meat. A list of types of linen appears on the right. 4th Dynasty.*

The Chief Concubine

The Ramesside sources tell us that the wife of the High Priest of Amun-Re at Karnak held the title 'Chief Concubine of Amun-Re'. She had ritual responsibilities, such as leading the female musicians of the temple, and seems to have wielded a certain amount of power. One record mentions that the Chief Concubine acted to ensure the prompt delivery of overdue rations to the protesting necropolis workers of Deir el-Medina. On another occasion a Chief Concubine arranged for the murder of a troublesome policeman.

gods and goddesses. By the beginning of the New Kingdom (c.1550 BC) the title 'Chantress of Amun' was in fairly common use – once again it was usually the wives of priests who gained positions of this kind.

Funerals

Women played an important role at funerals and, during the Old Kingdom (c.2686–c.2181 BC), in the rituals of the mortuary cults of the deceased. Two of the female mourners took the titles 'Great Kite' and 'Little Kite' and impersonated the goddesses Isis and Nephthys. According to the myth of Osiris, these goddesses had taken the guise of kites as they pieced together the body of the god in order to mummify him (see *The Death of Osiris*). At least during the Old Kingdom, priestesses could hold the title '*Ka*-servant' (*hemet-ka*). It was their responsibility to perform rituals in the tomb-chapels of the deceased.

The most prestigious religious title held by a woman was 'God's Wife of Amun', which was also, from the Eighteenth Dynasty, a position of great political significance. This office was based at Thebes, and was held by a daughter of the king in order to ensure royal control of the Theban area. From the reign of the Twenty-third Dynasty king Osorkon III (c.777–c.749 BC), the 'God's Wife of Amun' was expected to remain celibate, so she had to adopt a daughter and successor. She was also given the second title 'Hand of the God', possibly giving her a symbolic role in the act of creation. According to one version of the creation myth of Heliopolis, the god Atum had brought the gods Shu and Tefnut into existence by masturbating.

By the Late Period the God's Wife was more important than the High Priest. She controlled the vast estates of Amun, employed huge numbers of people, and had access to great wealth. ◆

Temple Rites and Offerings

Temple rites revolved around the cult statue of the deity, which resided in each temple shrine. We can guess that these cult statues would often have been made of precious materials such as gold and silver, because very few have survived to this day, at least not in situ. Each statue was believed to house the very essence of the deity in question. A ritual ceremony known as the Opening of the Mouth had been performed on every statue in order to animate it symbolically. As a result, the god, together with his or her family, was believed to live in the temple which was regarded as his or her house (*hwt netjer*, 'the god's mansion' or *per netjer*, 'the god's house').

King lists

In a royal mortuary temple, offerings of food were made to the deceased ruler. The accompanying rituals included prayers that it was believed would allow the king's *ka* or spirit to be nourished by the food. Endowments of land to the temple enabled these rituals to continue for generations after the death of the king to whom it was dedicated.

Some cenotaph temples, including those of the Nineteenth-Dynasty kings Ramesses II and Seti I at Abydos, contained kinglists recording almost all the rulers of Egypt, as well as shrines to various deities. After an offering of food had been made to a deity or the king and he was judged to have finished with it, it would be placed on an altar set before the kinglist so that it could also nourish all the previous kings. Once they were deemed to have been satisfied by the offering, it would be removed and given to the priests serving in the temple.

Tending the god

The most important temple rites were concerned with the washing and feeding of the god in the form of his statue. Every morning at dawn, the clay seal on the shrine was broken, and the door opened. Two purification rituals were performed before the god: incense was burnt and a libation of water was poured. He was believed to need a good breakfast, so food was brought to him as

▲ *Reliefs on the walls of Hatshepsut's mortuary temple at Deir el-Bahri show incense and other exotic goods being imported by boat from Punt. 18th Dynasty.*

an offering. The ancient Egyptians would certainly have agreed with the saying that cleanliness is next to godliness. The next stage of the proceedings was to remove the god so that his shrine could be cleaned. The

▶ *The two cartouches above Ramesses III's incense burner frame his throne name ('He of the Sedge and the Bee') and birth name ('son of Re'). Amunherkhopeshef's Tomb.*

statue was then undressed, cleansed with incense and water, re-dressed in clean linen, and adorned with jewellery, before being returned to his shrine. The rituals were accompanied by chanting and singing. Similar but less elaborate rituals were carried out at midday and in the evening. The rites were depicted on temple walls in the hope that even if the priesthood failed to perform them, the service would be guaranteed for eternity.

The god's shrine

The Greek word *naos* is generally used to refer to the shrine of the god. It was a rectangular box carved from a single block of wood or stone (often basalt or granite), with wooden doors. If the god needed to leave his *naos* to travel to a particular ceremony or festival, he would be carried on the shoulders of priests in a divine boat (a model of a real Nile vessel). If he needed to

travel, his barque was placed on an actual boat. Amun, for example, crossed the river at Thebes to the west bank for the Valley Festival, and Hathor travelled from her temple at Dendera to that of Horus at Edfu for the Feast of the Beautiful Meeting. Very often these barques had an *aegis* (a broad necklace surmounted with

the head of the deity in question) attached to the prow and stern. The barque of Amun, for example, was adorned with the head of a ram at each end. At the temple of Edfu the sacred barque stood on a plinth in front of the *naos*, while at the temples of Luxor and Karnak the gods had their own barque shrines.

▶ *Pediu-Imenet is depicted in his Book of the Dead making an offering of incense to Osiris. The fine quality of the dead man's linen clothing is indicated by its transparency. 21st–22nd Dynasty.*

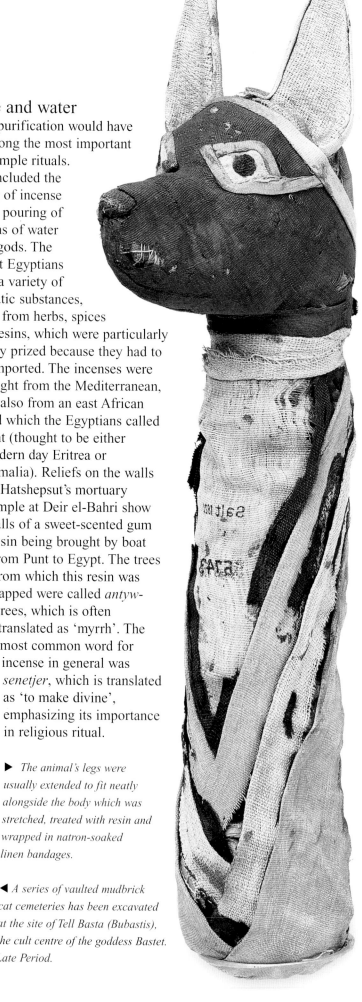

Incense and water

Rites of purification would have been among the most important of the temple rituals. These included the burning of incense and the pouring of libations of water to the gods. The ancient Egyptians burnt a variety of aromatic substances, made from herbs, spices and resins, which were particularly highly prized because they had to be imported. The incenses were brought from the Mediterranean, and also from an east African land which the Egyptians called Punt (thought to be either modern day Eritrea or Somalia). Reliefs on the walls of Hatshepsut's mortuary temple at Deir el-Bahri show balls of a sweet-scented gum resin being brought by boat from Punt to Egypt. The trees from which this resin was tapped were called *antyw*-trees, which is often translated as 'myrrh'. The most common word for incense in general was *senetjer*, which is translated as 'to make divine', emphasizing its importance in religious ritual.

▶ *The animal's legs were usually extended to fit neatly alongside the body which was stretched, treated with resin and wrapped in natron-soaked linen bandages.*

◀ *A series of vaulted mudbrick cat cemeteries has been excavated at the site of Tell Basta (Bubastis), the cult centre of the goddess Bastet. Late Period.*

Pure water was also considered sacred by the ancient Egyptians, explaining the importance of the sacred lake within the temple complex (see *Temple Architecture*). The most common type of lake was called *she netjeri* ('divine pool'). It was a rectangular, stone-lined reservoir filled by groundwater, and examples have been found at temples such as Karnak, Dendera, and Medinet Habu. The remains of ablution tanks have also been discovered in temple confines, such as in the first court (now ruined) at Abydos; and near to chapels, such as the T-shaped pools close to the chapels in the workmen's village at Tell el-Amarna. Water drawn from the lake was used in the temple both for purification and as offering.

Everlasting offerings

The ancient Egyptian word for 'offering', *hetep* was also their word for 'satisfaction'. The idea was that the gods and spirits of the dead were satisfied by the offerings of food and drink (and other things such as linen) that would be made to them.

The hieroglyphic sign for an offering, and an altar, was a mat (the forerunner to the more sophisticated offering table of stone) with a loaf of bread placed on it. In addition to the actual offerings that would have been placed on these tables, representations of them were carved on the stone surface – these were seen as magical substitutes for the real thing, thereby ensuring an eternal supply of symbolic sustenance for the gods.

▶ *Not only might a dead animal be intricately mummified, but it might also be placed in a plastered and painted wooden coffin imitating the shape of the animal.*

The offerings that were depicted on the altar tables include jars of water, beer, wine and milk, trussed ducks and loaves of bread. Grooves that had been cut into the surface of the offering tables were intended to receive the libations that were poured from ceremonial vases. The most highly prized offerings made in the temples and tomb chapels consisted of the meat of oxen, the choice cut being the foreleg. It is clear that the animal itself was not sacrificed in the temple before the god, but was butchered in the temple butchery, and then the choice piece of meat was offered to the god (or the deceased person). The ritual significance of the ox's foreleg is emphasized by the fact that the oxen was also used as a symbol of royal and divine strength or power. ◆

Mummified animals

From the Late Period (c.747 BC) pilgrims to certain temples could purchase a mummified animal to offer to the gods. The animals were bred specially for this purpose, and were considered sacred. Having been dedicated to the particular deity, they were ritually buried at the cult centres, where they have been discovered literally in their millions. Subterranean chambers at Saqqara, for example, have yielded an estimated four million embalmed ibises. Today these animal mummies are scientifically studied, but as recently as the nineteenth century hundreds of tons of mummified cats were shipped from Egypt to the English port of Liverpool to be turned into fertilizer.

Temple Literature

We know that hymns, prayers, and incantations were sung, chanted or recited in the temples. These have been found inscribed on temple walls and on stone stelae erected in temple and burial complexes, as well as written on papyrus. It is most likely that they were composed and copied by the priesthood in a temple room such as the House of Life, where the most able scholars studied texts in all fields of knowledge, from funerary rituals to astronomy.

Ancient Egyptian prayers commonly took the form of a bargain made between the priest, deputizing for the king, and the god. The deal was that offerings were made to the deity in return for the granting of tangible favours or rewards, such as victory in battle or a long life.

Some ancient musical instruments have survived, together with representations of musicians. The title 'Temple Musician' is also found in texts, so hymns were presumably sung with an accompaniment, but no musical notation has survived from ancient Egypt – although we know the words we can have no idea of the kind of tunes to which they were set.

Hymns provide us with a great deal of information concerning the ancient Egyptian perception of the divine world – including the names, titles and epithets of gods and goddesses. In fact, some of the mythological details referred to in them add to our understanding of the myths themselves.

A huge number of funerary stelae have been found inscribed with a hymn to Osiris, the god of the dead and the Afterlife; many of the Nineteenth- and Twentieth-Dynasty royal tombs in the Valley of the Kings have inscribed on their walls a hymn to the sun god, known as the *Litany of Re*, which refers to the king as the son of the god.

▲ *The royal scribe Nebmertef writes on a papyrus roll under the auspices of the god Thoth, the patron deity of scribes, in the form of a baboon. New Kingdom.*

▼ *Granite statues of Senusret III from Deir el-Bahri display youthful, athletic bodies typical of royal statues, but the realistic portraiture of the aging faces is unusual.*

▶ *Offering bearers process with an array of offerings that include the foreleg of a ceremonially slaughtered ox, fish, and the spoils of desert hunting. 18th Dynasty.*

The Abusir Papyri

Of the more secular temple documents that have survived, perhaps the most informative are those known as the Abusir Papyri. These were the administrative documents of the mortuary cult of the Fifth-Dynasty king Neferirkare (c.2475–c.2455 BC), so they would have formed part of an archive housed in the funerary temple complex associated with this ruler's pyramid at Abusir,

Hymns to the king

A particularly splendid example of a collection of hymns is the cycle of six hymns sung in honour of the Twelfth-Dynasty king Senusret III (c.1874–c.1855 BC). All six hymns were written on one side of a large sheet of papyrus measuring 114cm (45in) across, discovered at the town of Kahun, which was home to those who worked on the pyramid construction and for the mortuary cult of Senusret III at el-Lahun. They were probably composed to be sung on the occasion of a royal visit, or perhaps they formed part of the service of the cult at the pyramid complex. The ruler was eulogized in poetic and – as one might expect – exaggerated, terms. He was identified with the supreme solar deity, Re:

He is Re, little are a thousand other men!

and with the ferocious lioness goddess Sekhmet:

He is Sekhmet to foes who tread on his frontier!

which was part of the necropolis of Memphis. The documents provide many details of the daily routine and organization of a mortuary temple, which would have continued for generations after the death of the king.

The numerous fragments that have been discovered feature lists of temple staff and their duties, including guard duties, corresponding to the regular daily and monthly rituals as well as the special arrangements for festivals. They outline the general organization of the temple workforce, and stipulate the offerings to be made. They also include inventories of the temple furnishings and cult objects, such as knives, vessels, boxes and jewellery, as well as records of the daily income and expenditure of the temple – accounts of all produce and materials arriving at the temple, their use or storage, and any financial transactions made. They record the quantity and variety of goods that poured into the temple from the royal estates and other institutions. There are also records of temple inspections, including checking for any damage to the stonework. ◆

Scribes and Writing

Most scribes (*sesh*) were educated in schools housed in the temple complexes. They played an important role in the daily life of the temples, and their work involved the composition and copying of literary texts, as well as record-keeping on a grand scale, particularly at the larger complexes. There is a statue of an official and high priest named Bekenkhons in the Staatliche Sammlung Agyptischer Kunst in Munich that has his life story and route to success inscribed on it. He lived during the reign of the Nineteenth-Dynasty king Ramesses II (c.1279–c.1213 BC), and we learn that he spent four years at a school in the temple of Mut at Karnak before

▶ *The 'block statue' provided a useful surface area for inscriptions. Details of Bekenkhons' life are revealed by the hieroglyphs on his statue.*

spending 11 years as an apprentice scribe in the royal stables. He went on to become a priest of Amun at Karnak for four years, finally achieving the exalted position of High Priest.

Patron deities

The patron deity of scribes was the baboon or ibis deity Thoth, who was also considered the god of wisdom. There was also a goddess associated with writing. She was called Seshat, and was depicted as a woman wearing a pantherskin dress and with a seven-pointed star and a bow on her head. She was also associated with measurement. Temple reliefs of the Old and Middle Kingdoms (c.2686–c.1650 BC) show her recording numbers of foreign captives and quantities of booty taken after battles and raids. New Kingdom (c.1550–c.1069 BC) reliefs depict her in a more peaceful environment, that of the *sed*-festival (see *Royal Jubilee Festivals*), where she is shown holding the notched palm rib that symbolized the passing of time or sometimes writing the names

of the king on the leaves of the *ished* tree (see *Trees in Egyptian Mythology*).

Tools of the trade

A scribe was typically portrayed in statue form seated cross-legged on the ground, holding a papyrus roll in his left hand, stretched across his lap on his starched kilt, and writing with his right hand from right to left. Scribes wrote with a fine brush made from the stem of a rush (*Juncus maritimus*): the end was cut at a slant and the fibres split. The reed pen was not used in Egypt until it was introduced by the Greeks at the end of the third century BC. The stem of the reed (*Phragmites aegyptiaca*) was cut to a point and split in two like a quill. The scribal palette contained two cakes of ink, one of red

▶ *Seshat was venerated under the epithets 'She who is Foremost in the House of Books' and 'Lady of Builders'. Late Period.*

▲ *Hesire was Chief of Dentists and Physicians, but on this panel from his tomb at Saqqara he is portrayed not with the tools of his trade, but with staffs of office and a writing kit over his shoulder. 3rd Dynasty.*

Papyrus

Papyrus grew in abundance in the marshes of the Faiyum and Delta regions. The inner pith of the stems was used to make fine quality, light-coloured sheets for writing.

Although the word 'papyrus' is the root of our word 'paper', papyrus sheets were made using a different method. One layer of stems was arranged side by side horizontally and a second layer was laid vertically on top. The two layers were then beaten together until the juice that was released bonded the fibres of the stems. A typical sheet measured about 25 x 40cm (10 x 16in), but many sheets could be joined together to create long rolls.

(finely ground red ochre, usually from the Aswan region) and one of black (carbon, often the fine soot from cooking pots). These pigments were mixed with a solution of gum and were applied with water.

Writing had a sacred quality for the ancient Egyptians, and this is clearly indicated by their phrase for hieroglyphs: *medw netjer*, 'the god's words'. We use the word 'hieroglyphs', from the Greek words *hieros* ('sacred') and *glypho* ('carved'), because, in the Graeco-Roman Period at least, this form of writing was almost exclusively used for religious inscriptions on temple walls or public monuments. Throughout Egyptian history, hieroglyphs were used for religious and royal or monumental purposes, so they were often carved in stone, whether on temple or tomb walls, or on stelae or the sides of sarcophagi, for example. But they could also be found on other surfaces, such as wooden coffins, gold jewellery, calcite vessels and papyrus. Whatever the material or context, they were usually highly detailed and elaborate.

From as early as the First Dynasty (c.3100 BC), a method of writing cursive or simplified hieroglyphs was used by the scribes for writing more easily and speedily in ink on papyrus or *ostraca* (flakes of limestone and sherds of pottery). This cursive script is known as hieratic (from the Greek, *hieratika*, 'sacred') because it was the script used by the Egyptian priests during the Graeco-Roman Period. During the Dynastic Period, it was the script used for all administrative and literary documents up until the Twenty-sixth Dynasty (664–525 BC), when an even more cursive script was devised, known as demotic (from the Greek *demotika*, 'popular') or as *sekh shat*, ('writing for documents') to the ancient Egyptians. ◆

Akhenaten's Religious Revolution

Akhenaten (c.1352–c.1336 BC) was the tenth ruler of the Eighteenth Dynasty. His wife was the beautiful Queen Nefertiti. Akhenaten's reign saw enormous innovation and change. He chose to alter the state religion and mode of worship, and changed the style and content of art and temple architecture to such an extreme that his actions and beliefs have been heralded as revolutionary (he was considered heretical by later rulers).

He began his reign as Amenhotep IV – with the same name as his father, which meant 'Amun is Satisfied', but five years later he had changed his name to Akhenaten ('Beneficence of the Aten'), had extended the name of his wife to Neferneferuaten ('Fair is the beauty of the Aten'), and had founded a new capital called Akhetaten ('Horizon of the Aten'). At the centre of all this innovation and upheaval was the Aten (a manifestation of the solar deity, represented as the sun's disc) which Akhenaten elevated to the status of sole god in an attempt to eliminate the traditional pantheon. The plethora of gods and goddesses, with all the myths, festivals and rituals associated with them, were set aside for the duration of one king's reign. Or were they?

◄ Nefertiti kisses her daughter. The art of the Amarna Period is characterized by a more intimate portrayal of the royal family than is found at any other time in ancient Egypt. 18th Dynasty.

Akhenaten's New City

When Akhenaten began his reign, the administrative capital was Memphis and the greatest religious centre was Thebes, which was the home town of the ruling family of the Eighteenth Dynasty. Thebes was also home to the largest and wealthiest temple complex and the most powerful priesthood in the country – that of Amun at Karnak. It had benefited enormously from royal favours, vast quantities of tithes and the booty of war, especially resulting from the military campaigns of Tuthmosis III (c.1479–c.1425 BC) in Syria-Palestine. Because its might had consequently become overwhelming, it was in the interest of the status of kingship for Akhenaten to remove power from the temple of Amun and its High Priest. He achieved this by elevating a deity named the Aten to a position of supremacy and excluding from the state religion all other deities, including (and perhaps especially) Amun (see *Akhenaten's New Religion*). He also founded a new religious centre of Egypt, which became his administrative capital and the site of his royal palace.

In the fifth year of his reign, Akhenaten founded his new capital at the border between Middle and Upper Egypt, on the east bank of the Nile, about 280km (175 miles) south of Cairo. His decision to move the capital was probably politically motivated, but the site he chose was a virgin one, which meant that it had no existing religious associations. It was a wide plain approximately 10km (6 miles) long and a maximum of 5km (3 miles) wide, with perfect natural boundaries: the river lay to the west and desert cliffs formed a semicircular bay to the north, east and south (almost descending into the river at each end). Akhenaten had boundary

▶ *The ancient city of Akhetaten once stood on this desert plain on the east bank of the Nile, sheltered by a bay of cliffs.*

◄ *This vignette at the top of one of the boundary stelae at Tell el-Amarna illustrates that the Aten was worshipped in the open air in broad daylight, rather than within darkened temple sanctuaries as was the custom with other cults.*

► *The remains of this house in the central city exemplify the perennial problem of windswept sand in Egypt.*

stelae erected to designate the site of his city-to-be. The inscriptions on them dedicated all the buildings and their inhabitants to the Aten.

A large city, including housing of all sizes, palaces, temples, workshops, factories, bakeries and administrative buildings, was swiftly erected on the site. Many of the structures were enormous, elaborate and highly decorated, but because of the speed with which they had to be built, they were largely of mudbrick, and consequently very little has survived. The buildings were decorated using sunk relief, rather than the favoured, but incredibly time-consuming, raised relief.

The horizon of the Aten

Akhenaten called this city, with its columned halls, lush gardens, painted pavements and open courts, Akhetaten, 'The Horizon of the Aten'. Today the site is known as Tell el-Amarna, a name fabricated by nineteenth-century European visitors to the area. It is a misnomer because the site is not on a *tell* (Arabic for 'mound') created by successive building, as is usually the case with ancient settlement sites. Not only was Akhetaten built on virgin soil, but when the city was abandoned not long after Akhenaten's death it was never again built on or inhabited. The name Tell el-Amarna was probably derived from the names of the modern village of et-Till (and possibly the village of el-Amariya), and an Arab tribe called the Beni Amran, which had

settled and given its name to the district and a town on the west bank that belonged to it. The name Amarna has come to be used to refer to this particular period of Egyptian history.

Estimates of the ancient city's population range between 20,000 and 50,000, but it is usually said to have been about 30,000. (It has been worked out that the agricultural land at the city's disposal could have supported a population of 45,000.) As well as the city itself, archaeology at the site has revealed a walled village in the desert, about 1.2km (³/₄ mile) east of the main city, today known as the Workmen's Village. Further east still there is a collection of drystone housing, as yet unexcavated, called the Stone Village.

Akhenaten was not to know that his new capital would be abandoned after his death, and so provisions were made for the burial of the royal family and high officials in the desert cliffs surrounding the city. Two sets of rock-cut tombs, one to the north and one to the south, have been discovered, as has the royal tomb complex a short distance to the east of the desert cliffs. Most of the tombs were never finished. ◆

Excavating the site

Archaeologists have been working at the site of Tell el-Amarna pretty much systematically and continuously for the last century. The first significant excavations of the city were carried out by Sir William Matthew Flinders Petrie during the 1891/92 season. In 1911 a German team went on to gain the concession at the site for four seasons, under the direction of Ludwig Borchardt. The concession was regained by the British Egypt Exploration Society in 1921, and its excavations continued until 1936 (under the direction of Eric Peet, Leonard Woolley, Henri Frankfort and, lastly, John Pendlebury). In the 1960s the Egyptian Antiquities Organization carried out some work. But the most accurate and scientific archaeological excavation of the site and analysis of the material has been carried out on behalf of the Egypt Exploration Society by Barry Kemp and his colleagues since 1977.

Akhenaten's New Religion

▲ *In exchange for the offerings made by the royal family, the hands at the ends of the Aten's rays hold* ankhs *to the noses of the king and queen on this sculpted block from the Great Palace at Tell el-Amarna.*

▲ *High officials were usually represented as proud and upright in Egyptian art, but during the Amarna Period they were shown bowing before the king. 18th Dynasty. Tomb of Ramose, Thebes.*

The imagery and inscriptions of Akhenaten's reign reveal that he elevated one god to the unique position of sole deity, and instituted measures to eliminate all other deities. The emphasis on the importance of the sun god was not new, but his sole worship was unprecedented. Later in his reign, Akhenaten sent agents throughout Egypt to destroy the cult statues of other deities and excise their names (even that of Amun in his father's cartouche). By dispensing with the representations of a multitude of deities as weird and wonderful combinations of humans and animals, and with the myths associated with them, Akhenaten seems to have been attempting the creation of a purer and simpler religious doctrine, void of mysticism.

There was nothing innovative about the expression of devotion to the sun god, but Akhenaten took the age-old solar worship to an extreme never before experienced in Egypt. The sun, in the divine personification of Re, had been associated with kingship from at least as early as the Fourth Dynasty (c.2500 BC), when the king first took the epithet 'Son of Re' (see *Was the King Really Divine?*).

The Aten

Akhenaten chose to worship the simplest manifestation of the sun – the disc of the sun itself – the Aten. The Aten was not new; in fact, one of the best-known pieces of Egyptian literature, the Twelfth-Dynasty *Tale of Sinuhe* (c.1900 BC), tells us that when Amenemhat I died he ascended to join the Aten in the heavens. The popularity of the Aten had been growing since the beginning of the New Kingdom: Tuthmosis I (c.1504–c.1492 BC), for example, had taken the title, 'Horus-Re who comes from the Aten', and Amenhotep III (c.1390–c.1352 BC) had named his royal boat 'Glorious is the Aten'. There was certainly a temple to the Aten at Karnak by the reign of Amenhotep III.

▲ *This stela from Tell el-Amarna clearly shows the informality of royal portraiture. Akhenaten gives an earring to his daughter Meritaten, while two princesses sit on Nefertiti's lap. 18th Dynasty.*

▶ *This colossal sandstone statue of Akhenaten from the site of the Gempaaten temple at Karnak shows the unorthodox representation of the king (a style that was more exaggerated at the beginning of his reign). 18th Dynasty.*

The Aten had come to be represented as the solar deity Re-Horakhty – a hawk-headed man with a sun disc on his head – but early in his reign, Akhenaten put an end to this, and the Aten was to be represented purely as a sun disc. However, the disc did have some of the attributes of the deities that had been rejected. Its rays ended in hands, some of which held *ankhs* (the sign of life). Like the king, the disc wore a *uraeus* (a rearing cobra ready to spit venom at the king or god's enemies), had its names written in

cartouches, and a pharaonic titulary. In fact it could be said that the focus of Akhenaten's new religion was really the royal family, whose divine status he stressed. In art, the Aten was depicted holding out *ankhs* only to the mouths and nostrils of immediate members of the royal family. It appears that only the royal family was believed to benefit from the life-giving powers of the sun, and only they might worship the sun directly. Families throughout the city of Akhetaten had household shrines, not

with a stela or figurine depicting one of the traditional deities, or one of their ancestors, as we might expect, but a stela or figure of the king and/or his wife and children. They, in turn, were shown interacting with the Aten. The focus of these shrine images was quite clearly the royal family, and there is no expression of an individual's direct relationship with the god.

Bizarre bodies

Akhenaten claimed to 'live on *maat*' ('truth', 'order', 'justice') as previously only the gods had been said to. He also chose to have himself (and members of his family) depicted in a decidedly unconventional and distinctive character – with full lips, snake eyes, a long neck, pendulous breasts, a paunch, spindly limbs and swollen hips, buttocks and thighs – a far cry from the strong athletic bodies of the traditional depictions of kings. We do not know why Akhenaten chose to have himself represented in this way, but it may have been an attempt to conjure up a divine persona for himself.

His reign also saw the construction of temples of a new design. We must forget the characteristic style of Egyptian temples – the dark inner sanctuary and cult statue – and must imagine instead large open courts with innumerable altars, so that the Aten was very much worshipped in the open air. The shadowy mystery of the traditional temple had gone. Temples dedicated to the traditional deities were closed down throughout Egypt, and as the temple would have been the centre of the local economy it can be assumed that this heavy-handed policy would have resulted in a certain amount of social unrest and hardship.

▲ *The two princesses sitting at the feet of their mother Nefertiti in this wall painting display the extended skull characteristic of Amarna-period portraiture.*

King of the Afterlife

Because Akhenaten had done away with the traditional funerary deities, and the myths associated with them, the concept of the Afterlife had to be cast aside (at least at an official level). With Osiris abandoned, Akhenaten claimed to be the ruler not only of the living, but also of the dead. The funerary rites previously deemed necessary for entrance into the Afterlife no longer applied, and the rock-cut desert tombs at Amarna for the administrative elite were very differently decorated to those at Thebes. The private individual was no longer the protagonist in his own tomb. There were no more scenes of funerary rituals, or the Afterlife, or of daily life in the Nile Valley, or of the tomb owner in the presence of the deities. Now Akhenaten and his family were the centre of attention in every tomb, in scenes illustrating their daily activities, and the tomb owner himself was depicted tiny and humble before the king.

Realistically there is no way that Akhenaten could have obliterated the religious beliefs and superstitions of his people. Despite the dogma issued by the government, and the public displays of devotion to the royal family and acknowledgement of the supremacy of the Aten, in private the people of Egypt must have continued to worship the traditional deities, particularly the household gods and goddesses to whom they felt able to relate directly. In fact many amulets, stelae, rings, pendants and other objects representing the traditional deities of Egypt have been found at Tell el-Amarna dating from this period. How could a pregnant woman forget Taweret, for example, when this goddess might be able to help her through a difficult birth?　　◆

Thutmose the sculptor

The prize possession of the Egyptian museum collection in Berlin is a painted limestone bust of Queen Nefertiti wearing a tall blue crown (48cm [19in] high), which was found at Akhetaten. It is the work of a sculptor called Thutmose and was found in his studio, close to his house in a part of the south suburb of the city where other sculptors lived and had their workshops.

The Restoration of Traditional Religion

There is archaeological evidence for the increasing importance of the Aten, and interesting changes in artistic style, during the reign of Akhenaten's predecessor Amenhotep III (c.1390– c.1352 BC) – whether or not the two shared a co-regency is still disputed. But it is Akhenaten (c.1352–1336 BC) who was – and still is – regarded as the innovator, if not revolutionary. Soon after his death he was branded a heretic and his ideas and style were quashed.

On Akhenaten's death, he was succeeded by an ephemeral ruler named Smenkhkare (c.1338–c.1336 BC) who, it has been argued, might actually have been Nefertiti, and who was probably sole ruler for only a few months. Smenkhkare's successor probably grew up at Akhetaten, and began his life as Tutankhaten ('Living Image of the Aten'). He was, of course, Tutankhamun (c.1336–c.1327 BC), whose name means

◀ *Tutankhamun and his wife are depicted seated beneath the rays of the Aten on the back of this gold-plated and inlaid wooden throne. 18th Dynasty.*

'Living Image of Amun'. He must have changed his name to distance himself from the Atenist cult and the heretical practices of Akhenaten, who was quite possibly his father (his mother being a minor wife, Kiya). Tutankhamun had married one of Akhenaten's daughters by Nefertiti, Ankhsenpaaten, who in turn changed her name to Ankhsenamun.

Tutankhamun's reign witnessed the reinstallation of the traditional religion of Egypt. Akhetaten was abandoned and Memphis once again became the administrative capital of Egypt, with Thebes as the main religious centre. Tutankhamun issued a decree regarding the return to polytheism; his reforms have been found inscribed on a stela at Karnak temple. This is known as the Restoration Stela and is now in the Cairo Museum.

It was not until the reign of Horemheb (c.1323–c.1295 BC), who had been the Great

▲ *Gold necklaces were bestowed as rewards by the king on his loyal entourage. Here Horemheb receives such a gift in his post as Tutankhamun's Commander of the Army and King's Deputy.*

Commander of the army under Akhenaten but became the last ruler of the Eighteenth Dynasty, that Egypt experienced a violent backlash to the Amarna Period. The eradication of Akhetaten began, and the cartouches and images of Akhenaten and Nefertiti were defaced. The aim was to remove all traces of the cult of the Aten, to the extent that Akhenaten's name was missed out of later New Kingdom lists of kings (together with those of Smenkhkare, and even Tutankhamun and Ay, his successor). When Akhenaten's name did come up, he was referred to as 'the heretic' or 'the rebel').

Ironically, the demolished stone blocks, or *talata* (from the Arabic 'three handbreadths', describing their dimensions) from Akhenaten's temples did survive. They were used as rubble infill in the walls and pylons of later temples dedicated to traditional deities, such as Horemheb's ninth and tenth pylons at the temple of Amun at Karnak. ◆

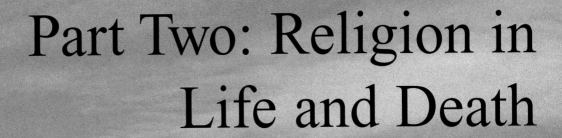

Part Two: Religion in Life and Death

While the state religion of ancient Egypt concerned itself with the well-being of the gods and their interaction with the king, popular religion permeated every aspect of the people's daily lives. Religious beliefs and practices accompanied the ancient Egyptians through life and into death. They were terrified by the prospect of dying away from their beloved Egypt in case this meant they would not be buried close to the Nile, and would not receive the all-important funeral.

The intriguing process of mummification developed because of the belief that the survival of the body was necessary in order to be reborn into the Afterlife. Many other beliefs concerning spiritual life after death influenced Egyptian funeral rites. Mummified bodies have been found in a wide variety of tombs, with elaborate funerary equipment.

The importance of religion in day-to-day existence sheds light on many details of Egyptian life, and evidence remains of all manner of popular beliefs and rituals, as well as moral values and social etiquette.

Modern myths have also developed about ancient Egypt. Is there really a Curse of Tutankhamun? And can one gain immortality by sleeping in the burial chamber of the Great Pyramid? Such legends underline our ongoing fascination with ancient Egypt.

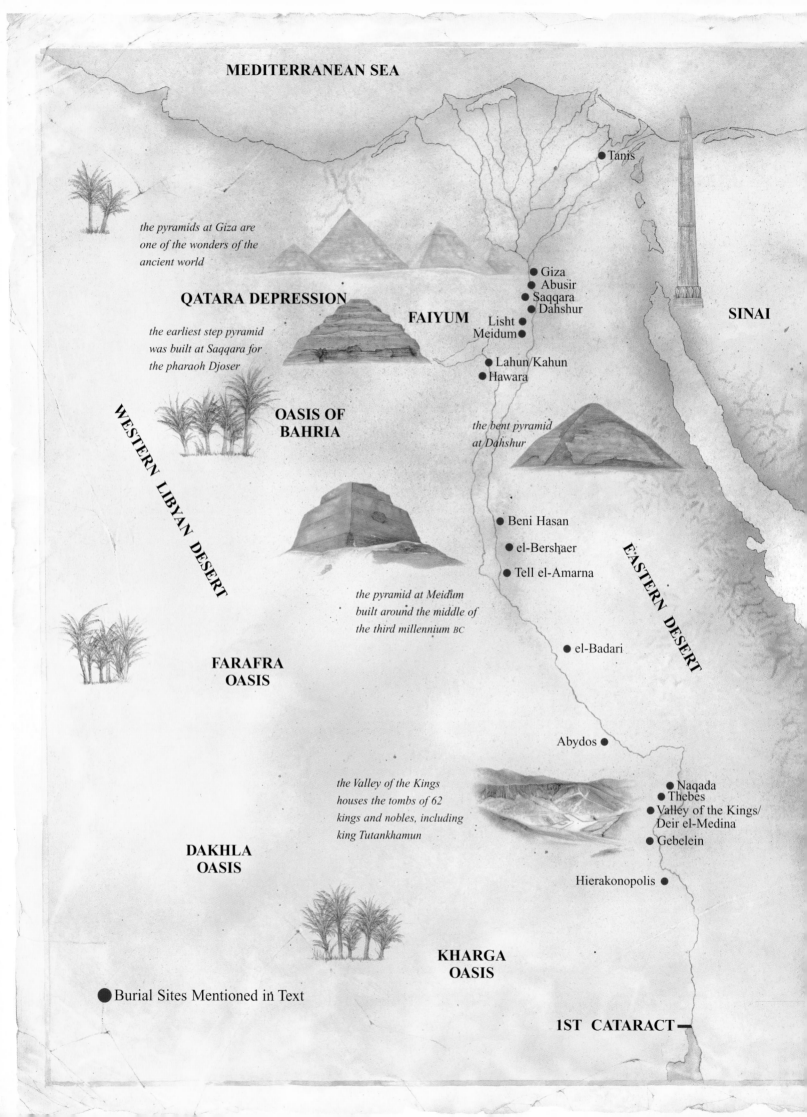

MEDITERRANEAN SEA

• Tanis

*the pyramids at Giza are
one of the wonders of the
ancient world*

• Giza
• Abusir
• Saqqara
• Dahshur

QATARA DEPRESSION

FAIYUM

Lisht •
Meidum •

*the earliest step pyramid
was built at Saqqara for
the pharaoh Djoser*

• Lahun/Kahun
• Hawara

SINAI

*the bent pyramid
at Dahshur*

**OASIS OF
BAHRIA**

WESTERN LIBYAN DESERT

• Beni Hasan

• el-Bershaer

• Tell el-Amarna

EASTERN DESERT

*the pyramid at Meidum
built around the middle of
the third millennium BC*

• el-Badari

**FARAFRA
OASIS**

Abydos •

*the Valley of the Kings
houses the tombs of 62
kings and nobles, including
king Tutankhamun*

• Naqada
• Thebes
• Valley of the Kings/
  Deir el-Medina

• Gebelein

**DAKHLA
OASIS**

Hierakonopolis •

**KHARGA
OASIS**

● Burial Sites Mentioned in Text

1ST CATARACT ━

Burial Sites

The pyramids of Egypt are one of the seven wonders of the ancient world. Each was built as a mortuary – the eternal resting place of a monarch. Such magnificent monuments stand testament to the unwavering belief of the ancient peoples in a life after death. Later kings were buried below ground in tombs no less grand, which were cut into the surface of rock faces. These mortuaries, like the pyramids, housed precious treasures as well as everyday items that would help the monarch assume his rightful role in the Afterlife.

Yet only the very wealthy could afford grand funerals, and mummification did not exist for the masses. For the ordinary people, a burial alongside the Nile river would ensure that they obtained a place in the Afterlife. Here they would assume a more prosperous and bountiful lifestyle than that which they held on earth.

NORTH

RED SEA

PALESTINE

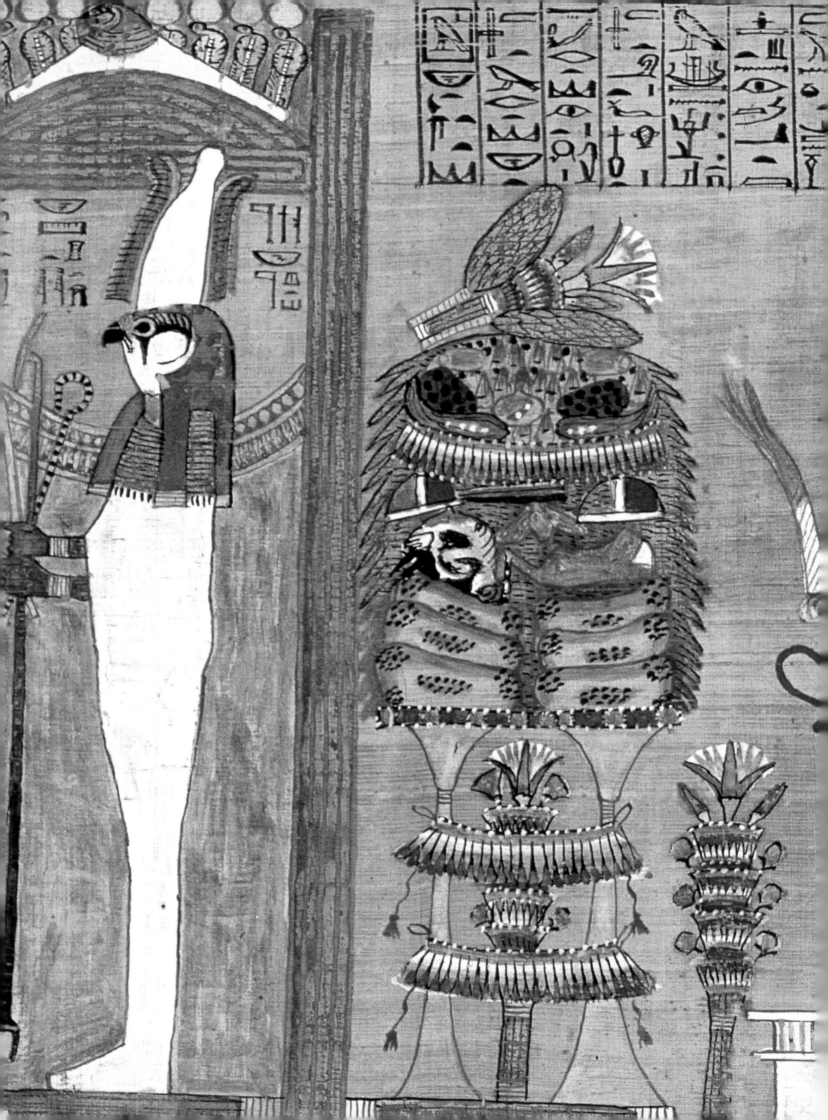

Funerary Religion

The ancient Egyptians clearly believed in an Afterlife long before the advent of writing and a formalized state religion. Burials dating from the Predynastic Period (c.5500–c.3100 BC) contain a range of objects of daily use, such as storage jars, flint knives, ivory combs and slate palettes. Their presence suggests the belief that such 'funerary equipment' was required for the Afterlife.

These excavated burials reveal that the bodies were buried in shallow oval graves at the edge of the desert. The hot dry sand rapidly absorbed moisture, so that bacteria could not breed and cause decay. The body in the British Museum, London, now known as 'Ginger', was buried in the sand at Gebelein in c.3200 BC, and survived intact for more than 5,000 years.

With the emergence of a social élite demanding grander burials, bodies began to be buried in coffins and underground chambers lined with wood, mudbrick or even stone, and they quickly began to rot. Mummification was developed and continued in use until the rise of Christianity in the early fourth century AD. But an elaborate burial was a luxury – although a belief in the Afterlife was no doubt universal, the people of Egypt were equipped for it to varying degrees.

◄ *From the New Kingdom (c.1550–c.1069 BC) it was customary for wealthy Egyptians to include a papyrus roll inscribed with spells and vignettes from the Book of the Dead in their tombs.*

Beliefs About the Afterlife

The preparations that accompanied burials from as early as Predynastic times (c.5500–c.3100 BC) reveal that the ancient Egyptians must have had beliefs about the existence of an Afterlife from very early on. These ideas were certainly formed well before the emergence of Pharaonic Egypt as we know it; that is, before the country was unified into an influential state with a sole ruler and an efficient, centralized government. Pre-dating any evidence for social stratification and the existence of a wealthy minority, there is evidence for burials involving the deposit of funerary goods in the grave alongside the body.

These items were not elaborate or specially crafted ceremonial artefacts, but basic objects of daily life, such as pots, tools and weapons. Presumably the people buried with these things believed that they would need them in a practical way after death. After all, a simple pot is unlikely to have been a token of sentiment or a prized possession; its presence in a tomb must have been considered functional.

▼ *An Egyptian lady would have been buried with a selection of objects intended to ensure that she would be able to eat, adorn herself with jewellery, cosmetics and perfumed unguents, and perform rituals in the Afterlife. New Kingdom.*

▲ *In a land of extreme heat and vast desert expanses, a pool and the cool shade of a date palm were heavenly. By depicting them on the wall of his tomb, Pashedu hoped to enjoy their benefits in the Afterlife. 19th Dynasty. Thebes.*

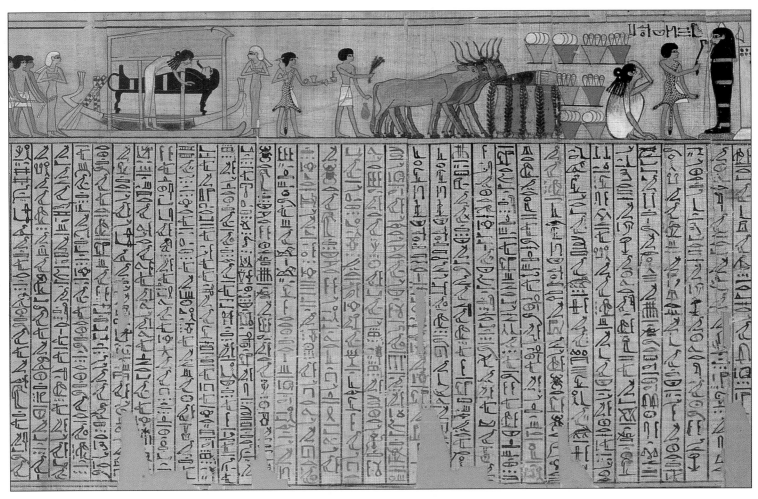

Journeying into the Afterlife

The predynastic custom of burying dead bodies in the foetal position may suggest a belief in the concept of rebirth. Also, the accidental or deliberate unearthing of perfectly preserved bodies may have led the early Egyptians to believe that the dead were living on in some way. The emergence of the practice of mummification early in the Dynastic Period reveals the strongly held belief that the body was required to be intact for the Afterlife.

We can have no idea of what the ancient Egyptians imagined the Afterlife to be until they were able to write down a description of it. The funerary texts that were buried with the dead tell us that they ascended to the Afterlife and that it was located in the heavens – the realm of the sun. Several methods of ascent appear to have been possible. These included riding on the back of a falcon, goose or other bird; being wafted upwards with burning incense; climbing up a ladder formed by the outstretched arms of the gods; or travelling on a reed float or barque that was sailed, rowed or towed. The journey into the Afterlife was no mean feat – all manner of demons and other hazardous obstacles had to be bypassed and overcome. The funerary texts provided guidelines and directions for the routes to be taken, and certain spells and recitations to be uttered at the appropriate time.

Domains of the dead

The ancient Egyptians imagined the Afterlife as a perfect version of life as they knew it in the Nile Valley, with a constant superabundance of produce. The vignettes on papyrus that accompany the text in the Book of the Dead, and the scenes painted on the walls of non-royal tombs, also provide us with a picture of the Afterlife. They tend to show the tomb owner and his wife toiling in the fields, which they did not for one moment expect actually to do (or at least they hoped not to). They certainly would have taken precautions to safeguard against the possibility of any hard work (see *Shabtis*).

▲ *The Book of the Dead includes illustrations of the final procession of the mummified body to the tomb and the last rites before burial, such as the Opening of the Mouth ceremony. The chain of events is depicted here on the papyrus of the high official Nebqed. New Kingdom.*

Egyptian paradise

The Egyptian paradise was called the Field of *Hetep* ('satisfaction' or 'offerings') – the land of Osiris, the god of the dead. The Coffin Texts (spells 464–468) and Chapter 110 of the Book of the Dead describe this land. It was associated with the western horizon (the place of the setting sun) and was imagined as a luscious place. Its fields were irrigated by channels full of water; its crops of emmer wheat, barley and flax grew tall and strong; its fruit trees were heavy with their loads of ripe dates and figs.

▶ *Sennedjem is depicted standing at the gate of the other world. A similar illustration was used to represent the vertical tomb shaft that separated the tomb chapel from the subterranean burial chamber below. 19th Dynasty. Thebes.*

The iconography of the ancient Egyptian religious belief system was strongly influenced by an underlying concept of duality – the importance of opposite but interdependent entities. The two horizons occurred frequently in both the solar and funerary aspects of the religion. Coupled with the Field of *Hetep*, which was associated with the western horizon, was the Field of *Iaru* ('reeds'), a place of purification that was associated with the eastern horizon, the site of the purification and 'rebirth' of the sun each dawn. Two other names that crop up in the funerary texts are '*Duat*' and '*Imhet*'. They were identified as separate locations in the sky: *Duat* referred to the eastern horizon, and *Imhet* to the western one. These terms might best be translated as 'Afterworld'. They are often rendered as 'Underworld' or 'Netherworld', but these translations can be misleading because the deceased appears to have ascended to them. Another name that came to be used as a general term for the Afterworld was *Rosetau* (literally, 'passage of dragging'). It originally referred to the sloping entranceway of a tomb; it was later used as the name for the necropolis of Memphis, and afterwards of Abydos.

Coming closer to the gods

The ancient Egyptians used strong visual images to illustrate, and even animate, their beliefs. The Afterworld was divinely personified as Aker. This was an earth divinity represented as a narrow tract of land with a human or lion head at each end, or sometimes in the form of two lions seated back to back, one facing east and one west (sometimes with the symbol for the horizon between them). These two creatures were thought to guard the entrance and exit to the Afterworld.

There is also evidence that the ancient Egyptians had a concept of an 'undersky' (*Nenet*) and an underworld where demons lived upside-down. As a result, because their mouths were where their anuses should have been, they had to eat their own faeces. Luckily, spells existed to avoid having to face what this place had to offer.

By dying and passing into the Afterlife, an individual was thought to become closer to the gods, and perhaps even influence the divine world. There is evidence to show that the dead were believed to possess supernatural powers that could solve various problems for the living. However, as well as proving helpful, the dead could cause serious disturbances for the living. The unsettled dead were often blamed for causing all kinds of distress, including illness. ◆

Ka, *Ba* and *Akh*

There are three important words which crop up repeatedly in the ancient Egyptian funerary texts, and which are variously translated as 'spirit' and 'soul'. It is probably best to leave them untranslated, because it is very difficult to be sure exactly what these terms meant to the ancient Egyptians, and a word such as 'soul' has connotations that would have been unfamiliar to them.

The hieroglyph used to write *ka* was a pair of arms, but in art the *ka* was represented as an individual's slightly smaller double. For example, in the 'divine birth' scenes on the walls of Hatshepsut's mortuary temple at Deir el-Bahri, two small and identical figures are depicted on a potter's wheel. These are the Eighteenth-Dynasty ruler Hatshepsut (c.1473–c.1458 BC) and her *ka* being created by the ram-headed creator god Khnum.

The *ka* was thought to come into being at the birth of an individual. Dying was sometimes described as 'joining one's *ka*'. The *ka* was intimately linked with the physical body, which was regarded

▲ *Funerary statues were seen as images of the* ka *of the dead, and might incorporate the* ka *symbol on their head, as in the case of this statue of Awibre Hor.*

as the vessel for the *ka* after death. This explains the belief in the need for the survival of the body, and the measures taken to preserve it whenever possible. *Ka* is often translated as 'spirit' or 'vital force', as in the creative life force of an individual that enabled the generations to continue through the ages. It was believed that the *ka* required food and drink, so offerings were made to it for as long as possible after death. In fact the word *ka* sometimes means 'sustenance', depending on the context.

The hieroglyph used to write *ba* was a Jabiru stork, while in funerary art it was represented as a bird with a human head, and sometimes with human arms. The ancient Egyptian idea of the *ba* appears to have been similar to our concept of personality, that is the non-physical attributes that make any human being unique. It is possible that it also implied the moral essence of a person's motivation and movement. It was considered more mobile than the *ka* and it enabled the dead person to move about in the Afterlife. The ancient Egyptian word for 'ram' was also *ba*, and it was probably for this reason that the ram-headed deity Khnum was regarded as the *ba* of Re, the sun god.

The hieroglyph used to write *akh* was a crested ibis, although it was often portrayed as a *shabti*-like mummiform figure (see *Shabtis*). It may well have been considered the result of the successful reunion at death of the *ba* and the *ka*, and it is sometimes translated as 'transfigured spirit'. Those who failed to achieve this transfiguration were condemned to eternal death.

Together with the *ka, ba,* and *akh*, two other important elements of a person's being, in both life and death, were their name and their shadow. It was believed vital to ensure that these two elements were remembered and protected after death in order that the deceased should survive in the Afterlife.

▼ *The* ba-*bird not only represented the concept of the 'soul', but also anonymous gods or powers, and as such was present on the walls of New Kingdom royal tombs.*

▼ *The crested ibis symbolizing the* akh *is distinguished by its characteristic ruff of head feathers. 19th Dynasty. Luxor.*

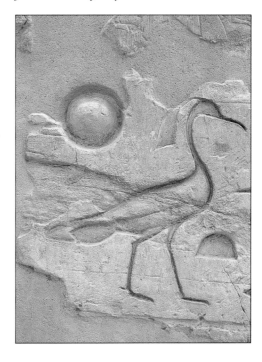

The Weighing of the Heart

The ancient Egyptians believed that, when they died, they would be judged on their behaviour during their lifetime before they could be granted a place in the Afterlife. This judgment ceremony was called the Weighing of the Heart, and was recorded in Chapter 125 of the funerary text known as the Book of the Dead. For this reason it is most commonly recorded and illustrated on papyrus.

The ceremony was believed to take place before Osiris, the chief god of the dead and the Afterlife, and a tribunal of 42 deities. Standing before the tribunal, the deceased was asked to name each of the divine judges and swear that he or she had not committed any of a long list of possible offences, ranging from raising the voice to stealing. This was the 'negative confession'. If found innocent, the deceased was declared 'true of voice' and was allowed to proceed into the Afterlife. The proceedings were recorded by Thoth, the scribe of the gods, and the deity of wisdom and the scribal profession. He was often depicted with an ibis head, writing on a roll of papyrus. His other animal form – the baboon – was sometimes depicted sitting on the pivot of the scales of justice.

Gobbling the heart

The symbolic ritual that accompanied this trial was the weighing of the heart of the deceased on a pair of enormous scales. It was weighed against the principle of truth and justice (*maat*), represented by a feather, the symbol of the goddess of truth, order and justice, Maat. If the heart balanced against the feather then the deceased would be granted a place in the Fields of *Hetep* and *Iaru* (see *Beliefs about the Afterlife*). If it was heavy with the weight of wrongdoings, the balance would sink, and the heart would be grabbed and devoured by a terrifying beast that sat ready and waiting by the scales. This beast was Ammit ('the gobbler'), a composite animal with the head of a crocodile, the front legs and body of a lion or leopard, and the back legs of a hippopotamus.

Ensuring success

The ancient Egyptians considered the heart to be the centre of thought, memory and emotion. It was thus associated with intellect and personality and was considered the most important organ in the body. It was deemed to be essential for rebirth into the Afterlife. Unlike the other internal organs, it was never removed and embalmed separately, because its presence in the body was crucial.

If the deceased was found to have done wrong and the heart weighed down

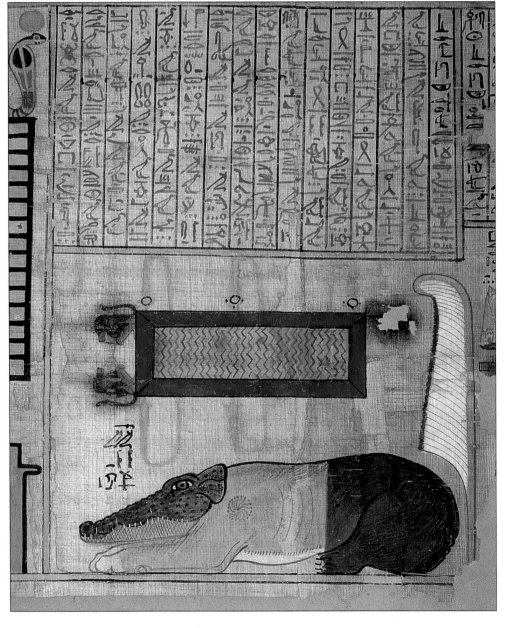

◀ *The Book of the Dead of Nebqed includes one of the earliest depictions of the composite beast Ammit, part crocodile, part lion and part hippopotamus. 18th Dynasty.*

▲ *The Weighing of the Heart took place in the Hall of Double Maat. In this scene from the Book of the Dead of Hunefer a lotus flower grows out of a pool beneath Osiris's throne, and on it stand the Four Sons of Horus.*

the scales, he or she was not thought to enter a place of torment like hell, but to cease to exist at all. This idea would have terrified the ancient Egyptians. However, for those who could afford to include Chapter 125 of the Book of the

▼ *'Heart scarabs' were important protective amulets placed on the mummy to prevent the heart from bearing witness against the deceased. New Kingdom.*

Dead in their tombs, it was almost guaranteed that they would pass successfully into the Afterlife. This is because the ancient Egyptians believed in the magical qualities of the actual writings and illustrations in funerary texts. By depicting the heart balancing in the scales against the feather of Maat (sometimes with the aid of a little adjusting on the part of Anubis, the jackal-headed god of cemeteries and embalming), they ensured that would be the favourable outcome. The entire ceremony was, after all, symbolic.

Following the Weighing of the Heart, the organ was returned to its owner. To make quite sure that this did happen, Chapters 26–29 of the Book of the Dead were spells to ensure that the heart was returned and that it could never be removed again.

Heart scarabs

Those ancient Egyptians who could afford the luxury of extensive funerary equipment took every precaution possible to ensure their survival through the judgment ceremony. A particularly useful addition to the burial would have been a large 'heart scarab' wrapped up in the bandaging (see *Funerary Amulets*). This form of protection was invented at least as early as the Thirteenth Dynasty and, according to the Book of the Dead, should be made of a specific green stone (*nemehef*), which has not been identified with certainty.

The scarab was inscribed on the underside with Chapter 30 of the Book of the Dead, a short text which was thought to prevent the heart from owning up to any crimes the person had committed in life:

O my heart which I had upon earth…do not speak against me concerning what I have done…

Mummification

The ancient Egyptians mummified the dead bodies of those who could afford such an elaborate and costly procedure. It is important to remember that this was a practice followed only by the royal family and the wealthier classes of Egyptian society. The word used to describe an embalmed and wrapped body is of course 'mummy', but this is in fact a misnomer because it comes from the Arabic *mummiya,* meaning pitch or bitumen, neither of which were actually used in Egyptian mummification. However, bodies mummified during the Late

▼ *The standing lion was a symbol of protection and defence, and so embalming tables such as this one painted on the wall of Sennedjem's tomb were carved in this way.*

Period (c.747–332 BC) were often so badly embalmed that they were blackened and brittle, and as they were found to burn well it was assumed that they had been dipped in bitumen.

The Greek writer Herodotus made a slightly erroneous account of the mummification process in c.450 BC, and two damaged papyri have survived from the first century AD outlining the final stages of the process. Unfortunately no embalmer's handbook has survived from the Pharaonic Period. Consequently, our understanding of the procedure, and how it developed, is based mainly on examination of the bodies themselves.

In the Early Dynastic Period (c.3100–c.2686 BC) dead bodies were tightly wrapped in strips of resin-soaked linen.

This did not prove to be wholly successful, because although the bandages hardened in the form of the body, the body itself decayed, so during the Third Dynasty (c.2686–c.2613 BC) methods of preserving the body itself were explored. The ancient Egyptians came to realize that if they wanted the body to survive they had to dehydrate it from the inside and the outside at the same time, and that to do this effectively they had to remove the internal organs. Up until this time, the dead had been buried in a contracted foetal position, but it was found to be easier to reach the internal organs if the body was stretched out, so the dead came to be buried in this position.

The oldest surviving mummy dates to the late Fifth Dynasty (c.2400 BC), but it is known that the ancient Egyptians were removing the internal organs, and embalming and burying them separately, at least as early as the Fourth Dynasty, because the internal organs of Queen Hetepheres, the mother of the Great Pyramid builder, Khufu (c.2589–c.2566 BC), were found in a canopic chest.

Purifying the body

Once a successful procedure was arrived at, it appears to have been as follows.

The body was taken to a 'place of purification' (*ibu*). This would probably have been located on the west bank of the Nile, the bank associated with the setting sun and thus the place of the dead. It would need to be sited close to the river for easy access to a good water supply, and undoubtedly as far away as possible from populated sites owing to the nature of its business.

The initial washing of the naked corpse had both a ritual and a practical importance. The body was washed, as was the cult statue in a temple each morning, and as was the sun god Re in the waters of Nun each morning before

being 'reborn' at dawn. The washing was done using a solution of natron, so it would have aided the first stage of preservation. Natron is a salt (a natural compound of sodium carbonate and bicarbonate) that the ancient Egyptians found as crystals along the edges of lakes in the Wadi Natrun, 65km (40 miles) north-west of Cairo. One of the ancient Egyptian names for natron was *neteryt* ('belonging to the god'), presumably because of its use in ritual purification. It was particularly useful in the embalming process because it is a mild antiseptic as well as being an effective dehydrating agent (it absorbs water, thus drying out the body but leaving it flexible).

Preparing the body

The purified body was then removed to the actual place of embalmment (*wabt* or *per nefer*), which was originally an enclosure containing a tent or booth. By the Late Period (c.747–c.332 BC)far more bodies were being embalmed than ever before, so for the first time permanent embalming houses were built of mudbrick. The chief embalmer was known as 'He who Controls the Mysteries' (*hery seshta*), and it is very likely that he would have worn a jackal mask during the rituals accompanying

▲ *This man was not mummified but thanks to his body's direct contact with the hot, dry sand it has survived since c.3200 BC , intact but for the top of one of the forefingers.*

the embalming process in order to imitate the jackal-headed god of embalming, Anubis. His deputy bore the title 'God's Seal-Bearer' (*hetemu netjer*), which had originally been a title held by priests of Osiris, the god of the dead and the Afterlife. According to ancient Egyptian mythology, Osiris had been the first person to be mummified, after his death at the hands of his brother Seth.

Once in the embalming house, the body was stretched out on four wooden blocks on a wooden board (an example of which was found at Thebes). The first priority was to preserve the face, and so the head was probably coated with molten resin. From the Eighteenth Dynasty (c.1550 BC) the brain was removed and discarded, because it was considered to be merely stuffing for the head. Sawdust, resin or resin-soaked linen was pushed inside the skull to ensure that it kept its shape. The ancient Egyptians really had no idea about the function of the brain; they thought that the heart was the seat of thought and emotion in the human body.

▲ *It is uncertain whether depictions of jackal-headed men in the funerary art represent the god Anubis himself, or priests wearing masks in order to represent the deity.*

▲ *Roman encaustic portraits were combined with the Egyptian tradition of mummification in Egypt for about 200 years from the middle of the 1st century AD. In this portrait of Artemidorus he wears a wreath of leaves and berries applied in gold leaf.*

Consequently they never deliberately removed the heart from the body because they believed its presence was crucial at all times and it played a vital part in the judgment of the deceased before he or she was able to pass into the Afterlife.

The major internal organs were removed, but they were embalmed separately and kept safely because the Egyptians believed they were necessary for the continued functioning of the body in the Afterlife. The stomach and intestines were removed through an incision in the lower abdomen (usually on the left side), then the diaphragm was punctured so that the lungs and liver could also be extracted. According to Herodotus and the Sicilian-born historian Diodorus Siculus (c.40 BC), a knife of Ethiopian stone or obsidian was used to make the incision.

Once removed, the internal organs were dried out in crystalline natron, rubbed with sweet-smelling unguents, coated in molten resin and wrapped in linen bandages in four separate packages. These packages were usually then placed in special jars that accompanied the body to the tomb (see *Canopic Jars*), but from the Twenty-first Dynasty (c.1069 BC) they were often placed back in the original positions of the internal organs inside the body. During the Ptolemaic Period (332–30 BC) they were usually placed between the corpse's legs before wrapping.

Embalming

The body, without its internal organs, was packed with temporary stuffing, and covered over with natron for forty days, after which time it would have turned a much darker colour and have become as much as 75% lighter in weight. The temporary stuffing was removed, and the corpse was rinsed out, washed down, dried to prevent mould forming and re-stuffed with wads of linen, linen soaked with resin, bags of natron crystals, sawdust and other materials to help the body keep its shape. During the Late Period (c.747–c.332) bodies were often filled completely with resin.

For both ritual and functional reasons, the body was anointed again, this time with juniper oil, beeswax, natron, spices, milk and wine. The abdominal incision was stitched up, and often covered with gold foil or wax. It was adorned with a protective 'Eye of Horus' – the *udjat* or

▼ *Networks of beads arranged over the entire body of the mummy are typical of the end of the Third Intermediate Period and Saite Era. Images such as winged pectoral scarabs and the Four Sons of Horus were often woven into them. 25th Dynasty.*

wadjat-eye (see *Funerary Amulets*). The nostrils, ears, and mouth were usually plugged with linen, wax, or sometimes onion skins or whole bulbs. Today people use onion to soak up nasty smells, and in folklore it is believed to help combat infection. In ancient Memphis, during the festival of the hawk-headed funerary deity Sokar, his devotees were accustomed to wearing strings of onions. Depending on the wealth and extravagance of the deceased's family, a piece of gold leaf might be placed over the tongue. The whole body was then coated with resin in order to toughen it and make it waterproof.

As well as the practical measures taken, at all times the emphasis was also very much on creating a pleasing appearance to the body. The soles of the feet and palms of the hands might be stained with henna; the cheeks might be rouged; and the lips and the eyebrows might be painted. Sometimes the body was dressed in clothes, sandals and a wig. The bodies of men were often painted with red ochre and that of women with yellow ochre, because these were the standard pigments used to create the skin colour of men and women in art. The bodies of wealthier people were covered in jewellery before the bandaging began. Mummies have been found, dating to the Graeco-Roman Period, with gold leaf on their faces, chests and nails.

Bandaging the body

At last the body was ready for bandaging. This intricate process was carried out by the bandagers (*wetyw*) and took 15 days, beginning with the fingers and toes. It was accompanied by the recitation of magical spells by a Lector Priest (*hery heb*). The bandages

▲ *Anthropoid coffins of the 21st Dynasty often incorporate a pair of crossed red 'braces', over an enlarged collar, in their design. Thebes.*

were linen and were often made out of old clothes, towels, and so on. The most sought-after bandages would have been recycled from the cast-off garments worn by divine statues in the temples and shrines. A vast quantity of linen – up to 375sq m (450sq yd) – was used to wrap one body.

The embalmed body was enveloped in a yellow shroud before being bandaged. Each stage was painted with melted resin. Every attempt was made to ensure that the body looked as perfect as possible so if, for example, a hand was missing, an artificial hand would be inserted into the bandaging. Men were usually wrapped with their arms extended and their hands crossed over their genitals, whereas women's hands were usually placed on their thighs. From the early New Kingdom (c.1550 BC) onwards, kings were wrapped with their arms crossed over their chest, in the manner of Osiris, the god of the Afterlife.

The bandaged body was then inserted into one or more shrouds (usually dyed

red), which were knotted at the top and bottom and held in place by several more bandages. An interesting feature can be found on top of the bandaging (or just below the surface) of mummies dating to the Twenty-first and Twenty-second Dynasties (c.1069–c.715 BC): two red leather straps crossed over the chest, resembling a pair of braces. A peculiarity of many of the mummies dating to the Twenty-fifth Dynasty (c.747–656 BC) and later is a shroud of blue faience beads, very like the Fifth-Dynasty bead net dress from Qau, now in the Petrie Museum of Egyptian Archaeology, London.

Finally, a mummy mask was fitted over the head and shoulders of the body. The mask was usually made of cartonnage – linen or papyrus stiffened with plaster. In the case of royalty it would have been made of gold, and the upper classes sometimes imitated the costliest of masks by having their cartonnage ones gilded. ◆

Funeral preparations

The entire, complicated process of mummification, from the arrival of the corpse at the *ibu*, lasted 70 days. This was the time permitted for the funeral preparation.

It is likely that a period of 70 days was chosen deliberately in connection with the 70 days when the dog star Sirius (divinely personified as the goddess Sopdet) could not be seen because of its alignment with the earth and the sun prior to its heliacal rising. This annual astronomical occurrence heralded the inundation of the Nile and marked the start of the ancient Egyptian New Year (*wep renpet*).

Pyramid Texts

The oldest surviving funerary texts – collections of spells or 'utterances' that accompanied a burial – are those known today as the Pyramid Texts. These were exclusively the prerogative of the king during the Old Kingdom and First Intermediate Period (c.2686–c.2055 BC). They dealt with his protection while he was still alive (particularly against dangerous animals), but were mainly concerned with his death and what was believed to happen to him afterwards. Later versions of funerary texts – known as the Coffin Texts and the Book of the Dead – were not confined to royal burials, and demonstrate the gradual democratization of funerary religion.

Written in hieroglyphs, the earliest appearance of the Pyramid Texts is as inscriptions on the inner walls of the corridors and chambers of the pyramid of Unas (c.2375– c.2345 BC), the last ruler of the Fifth Dynasty. It was built at Saqqara, one of the great cemeteries of the capital city of Memphis. A further eight pyramids of the Sixth Dynasty and early First Intermediate Period (c.2345–c.2125 BC) have been found to contain very similar inscriptions. Five of these pyramids belonged to kings, and the other three to wives of the Sixth-Dynasty ruler Pepi II (c.2278–c.2184 BC). The Pyramid Texts totalled some eight hundred spells, but no one pyramid was inscribed with all of them, the largest collection being the 675 texts found in the pyramid of Pepi II.

The funeral of the king

It has been suggested that the sequence of the spells relates to the funeral of the king, and the procession of his mummified body from the Valley Temple connected with his pyramid to his burial chamber within the pyramid. The king is identified with Osiris, the god of the dead and the Afterlife, and many of the spells in the burial chamber

By the 5th Dynasty the emphasis was no longer on enormous grandeur but on the hieroglyphic inscriptions within pyramids such as that of Teti, and the reliefs on the walls of the associated mortuary temples. Saqqara.

would probably have been recited by the Lector Priest at the funeral. The earliest known recording of the Opening of the Mouth ceremony and early offering rituals are to be found in these texts. The purpose of many of the spells was to protect the dead king in the Afterlife. Because the language in which they are written is archaic in places, it is likely that these were in fact very ancient spells, recorded for the first time in the Old Kingdom.

The emphasis on the cult of the sun god in the texts implies that perhaps they were composed by the priests at Heliopolis, the cult centre of Re. This temple and its priesthood had had close associations with the king since at least the Fourth Dynasty. Utterance 264 is one of many spells that refer to the king's ascension to the realm of the sun. It ends:

The Nurse Canal is opened, the Winding Waterway is flooded, the Fields of Reeds are filled with water, so that the king is ferried over on it to that eastern side of the sky, to the place where the gods fashion him, where he is born again new and young.

The idea was that when the king died he went to join the sun god on his journey through the sky by day and the Netherworld by night. This journey was thought to be made by boat, and it was believed that when the sun god reached

◀ The behaviour attributed to Nut of swallowing and giving birth to the sun – depicted here in Ramesses IX's burial chamber – was ultimately an enigma, as indicated by her epithet shetayit, which means 'mysterious one'.

the eastern horizon, just before dawn, he was purified in Nun, the waters of creation. The rising of the sun was identified with the dead king's rebirth.

Rebirth of the king

It has been suggested that names such as the 'Nurse Canal', 'Winding Waterway' and 'Field of Reeds' found in the Pyramid Texts refer to parts of the sky goddess Nut's anatomy. One mythological explanation as to where the sun went at night described it as being swallowed by the sky goddess in the evening, and being given birth to by her at dawn. Nut was often depicted on the ceiling of burial chambers and inside the lid of sarcophagi, displaying the idea that the dead person, like the sun, would be reborn. It may be that, in the Pyramid Texts, the idea of the dead king passing through the body of the goddess is being expressed in metaphorical terms.

The imperishable stars

The Pyramid Texts imply that the king was believed to join the circumpolar stars in the northern sky – the 'imperishable stars' that never disappear

▲ The ceiling of the burial chamber in the pyramid of Teti is a vault of stars. The Pyramid Texts are inscribed in columns of hieroglyphs on the chamber walls.

from view. In this way these early royal funerary texts equate the dead king with Osiris, the sun and the stars. They also include hymns to the gods and a long list of offerings of food, drink and clothing. These were to be made at the time of the burial and renewed after the king's death, ideally for eternity, because it was believed that they would sustain the king in the Afterlife. ◆

Fifth-Dynasty pyramids

Instead of the solid limestone blocks used for the great monuments erected during the Fourth Dynasty, the pyramids of the Fifth Dynasty were built from small, roughly-dressed stones, but the inner decoration of their burial chambers and funerary complexes was more lavish than ever before.

Coffin Texts

By the Middle Kingdom (c.2055 BC), it was not only kings and queens who were thought to benefit from having funerary texts included in their burials, but also members of the administrative élite. This fortunate minority was not buried in pyramids but in rock-cut tombs. The spells to aid their transition into the Afterlife were recorded in cursive hieroglyphs on the interior walls of their wooden coffins. This accounts for the

▼ *Vignettes in the* Book of Two Ways *show that features of the waterway and landway were guarded by demons brandishing knives. This coffin belonged to Gua, Chief of Physicians. 12th Dynasty.*

origin of the modern term 'Coffin Texts' – although they have also been found on tomb walls, sarcophagi, statues and stelae in offering chapels.

The Book of Two Ways

More than 1,000 Coffin Texts have been collected. They are derived from the body of royal funerary texts known as the Pyramid Texts, with some careful editing and important additions. The chief component of the Coffin Texts is a detailed guidebook to the Afterlife, known as the *Book of Two Ways*. It has been found drawn inside the bottoms of wooden coffins discovered at el-Bersher, the cemetery of Hermopolis Magna, and the cult centre of Thoth, the lunar deity

of scribes and wisdom. The occupant of the coffin was promised an Afterlife like that of the deceased king, and the chance to travel in the sun god's solar barque. But there was a condition: he had to be able to reel off the right spells and a brief rendition of the theology of the sun god Re. At the end of the *Book of Two Ways* we find the pledge:

> *As for any person who knows this spell, he will be like Re in the east of the sky, like Osiris in the midst of Duat.*

Like the king in the Pyramid Texts, the dead person was assured that he would be reborn into the Afterlife, just as the sun rose at dawn above the eastern horizon, and he would become one not only with the sun god but also with Osiris, god of the dead. It would have been a useful *aide-mémoire* for the deceased to have the words of the spells (which he was expected to know by heart) written on the inside of his coffin.

Map of the Afterlife

There are two versions of the *Book of Two Ways*, and both are thought to have been composed at Hermopolis Magna. Both include references to the non-royal deceased becoming stars in the sky, alongside Thoth. The Coffin Texts were accompanied by the earliest known map of the Afterlife, and on it the Mansion of Thoth is located in the Place of Maat. This map was specifically designed to guide the spirit of the deceased on its journey into the Afterlife. Knowledge of the spells and possession of the map meant that the deceased might become an *akh aper* ('equipped spirit').

The map located the Mansion of Osiris and the Field of *Hetep* (the Egyptian paradise), where the deceased might continue to serve Osiris. However, as in the Pyramid Texts, the Heliopolitan

influence is unmistakable because the largest part of the plan indicated the path followed by the sun god on his voyage. First it moved from east to west along a blue waterway through the inner sky, then it went back again from west to east on a black landway through the outer sky. As in the myth of *The Journey of the Sun through the Netherworld*, found on the walls of royal tombs in the Valley of the Kings dating from the New Kingdom (c.1550–c.1069 BC), the Coffin Texts described the path of the sun god (and thus the deceased) as beset by demons, often wielding knives, throw sticks, spears or nets. If trapped by a demon, it was believed that the dead person might be beheaded, hacked to pieces or burned to death. The most dangerous was the giant serpent Apophis, who threatened to devour the sun every day before dawn, and so had to be symbolically destroyed by the sun's entourage every 24 hours. The only way for the spirit of the deceased to safely pass these obstacles (and others such as mounds, rivers, and gates of fire) was by learning their names and characteristics beforehand.

▲ *Eyes painted on the coffin wall allowed the deceased to see out. Middle Kingdom.*

◄ *The inner coffin of the Commander Sepi is painted with a false door beneath the eyes.* Middle Kingdom.

Seeing eyes

Rectangular coffins of the Middle Kingdom were oriented in the tomb with the head to the north. Eyes were painted on the side of the coffin so that the mummy, whose face was positioned behind them, could see out. The body was therefore laid on its left side, facing east towards the rising sun.

Often the eyes were painted above a niched palace façade (*serekh*) design, or a false door, through which the spirit could pass in and out of the coffin.

The Book of the Dead

The end of the Second Intermediate Period (c.1550 BC) witnessed still further democratization of the Afterlife (see *Coffin Texts*), with the emergence of a collection of nearly 200 spells (or chapters). Today these are known as the Book of the Dead, but they were known to the ancient Egyptians as the '*Formulae for Going Forth by Day*'. These funerary texts came to accompany more people to the grave than ever did the Pyramid Texts (a purely royal prerogative) or Coffin Texts, since they were available to anyone who could afford to have them copied. The text was in fact an edited and supplemented version of the Coffin Texts (as the Coffin Texts had been of the Pyramid Texts), which continued to be included in the burials of wealthy people well into the Graeco-Roman Period (332 BC–AD 395).

Although there were 200 or so spells altogether, each burial contained only as many as the deceased or his family chose (or could afford) to have copied. They have mainly been discovered written on papyrus rolls, although certain spells have also been found recorded on coffins, amulets (such as Chapter 30A inscribed on heart scarabs – see *Funerary Amulets*), tomb walls, figurines (for example Chapter 6 on *shabtis* – see *Shabtis*) and statuary.

The papyrus rolls were often placed in the coffin alongside the body, or they might be wrapped up in the mummy bandaging or inserted into a hollowed-out statuette of Ptah-Sokar-Osiris, the Memphite funerary deity, which was then deposited in the tomb along with a range of other funerary goods. These funerary texts were usually written in hieroglyphs, but Books of the Dead in the more cursive scripts, hieratic and demotic, have also survived. The texts were usually accompanied by brightly coloured illustrations or vignettes, ranging from depictions of the amulets to be included in the mummy wrappings to detailed scenes of the Afterlife.

▶ *This painted wooden* shabti *from the tomb of Ramesses IV is equipped with a hoe in each hand ready to break up heavy soil in the Afterlife on behalf of the deceased king. 20th Dynasty.*

The form of the book

No one copy of the Book of the Dead contained all the spells that were available, although by the Late Period the sequence had become relatively fixed. Egyptologists refer to the spells as numbered 'chapters', following the system imposed in 1842 by Karl Richard Lepsius (1810–84), when he edited the text of the Book of the Dead of Iufankh from the Ptolemaic Period. This example contained 165 chapters. The most significant texts, such as that concerned with the Weighing of the Heart ceremony, were the most lavishly illustrated.

Towards the end of the Ptolemaic Period, the funerary texts grew shorter and the Book of the Dead tended to be replaced by the Book for Breathing or the Book for Outlasting Eternity. These short compositions could be written on single sheets, to be placed at the head and feet of the deceased. They still provided safeguards for his or her passage into the Afterlife, such as the requisite denial of short-comings for the deceased to present at the Weighing of the Heart ceremony.

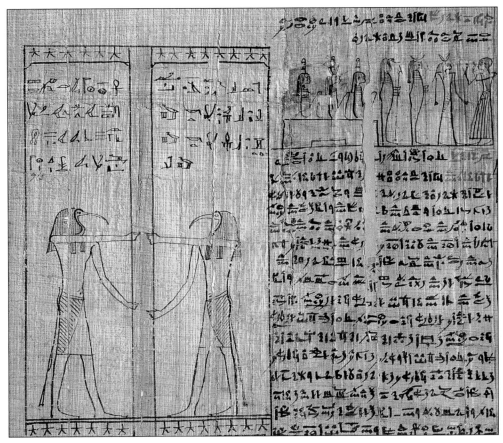

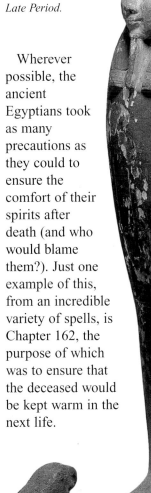

◄ In the funerary and other religious texts, it is rare to find lines or columns of writing without illustrations alongside. Vignettes tend to accompany the spells throughout the Book of the Dead. These spells in Kahapa's Book of the Dead are written in hieratic, a cursive form of hieroglyphs. Late Period.

Becoming Osiris

Like the Pyramid Texts of the Old Kingdom (c.2686–c.2181 BC) and the Coffin Texts of the Middle Kingdom (c.2055–c.1650 BC), the main purpose of the Book of the Dead was to provide the deceased person with a collection of spells that would ensure his or her safe passage into the Afterlife. But, unlike the earlier texts, the spells included in the Book of the Dead were dominated by the cult of Osiris, the god of the dead and the Afterlife, rather than that of the sun god Re. Dead people came to be referred to as Osiris, and identification with this god was clearly considered to be the desired goal. It was also Osiris who sat in supreme judgment over the dead, determining their fitness for acceptance into the Afterlife.

Amulets and demons

The texts and their accompanying illustrations provide information on where and when amulets or papyri were to be placed on the body during embalming. Some objects were to be wrapped up in the bandaging, others were to be only temporarily brought into contact with the body. The texts also convey an idea of how the ancient Egyptians imagined the Afterlife they hoped to enter (see *Beliefs about the Afterlife*). As recorded in the Coffin Texts, there were a whole host of threatening demons and other obstacles that stood between the deceased and his or her arrival in 'paradise'. Probably the most crucial section of the Book of the Dead was Chapter 125, which described the final judgment of the dead person before Osiris. His or her lifetime was assessed to check that he or she had behaved well enough to be reborn into the Afterlife (see *The Weighing of the Heart*). If an ancient Egyptian could afford the inclusion of only one chapter of the Book of the Dead in the burial, he or she would have been well advised to choose this one.

▶ By the Middle Kingdom, Sokar had been syncretized with the gods Ptah and Osiris, and prayers were being addressed to him as a funerary deity. Here, he is accompanied by the Horus falcon. Ptolemaic Period.

Wherever possible, the ancient Egyptians took as many precautions as they could to ensure the comfort of their spirits after death (and who would blame them?). Just one example of this, from an incredible variety of spells, is Chapter 162, the purpose of which was to ensure that the deceased would be kept warm in the next life.

Funerary Equipment

From Predynastic times (c.5500 BC), the ancient Egyptians chose to include in their burials as much funerary equipment as they could afford. From the Dynastic Period (c.3100 BC), this equipment included the dead person's personal possessions, items made especially for the tomb, ritual objects linked specifically with the funeral and burial, funerary texts (often on papyrus rolls), figurines, statues, coffins, sarcophagi, amulets, food and drink. If the individual concerned was wealthy, as much as possible was included in his or her tomb.

A variety of goods

We know from several sources what was included in burials. First, the objects themselves have been discovered during the excavation of tombs; second, information about the goods to be buried with the dead is provided by the funerary texts; and third, scenes of funeral processions painted on the walls of non-royal tombs, especially during the New

▶ *Osiris boxes (or beds) were planted with grain intended to grow in the tomb. Only seven are known, but associated with them are Osiris bricks and corn mummies.*

Kingdom (c.1550–c.1069 BC), include people carrying a range of goods to the burial.

A selection of funerary goods to accompany the deceased into the Afterlife might have included: a bed with a mattress and a headrest; a couple of chairs and stools with cushions; tables and stands (together with the wine jars to stand in them); boxes and chests; linen clothing, wigs, sandals, walking-sticks and staffs of office; draw-neck bags; stone vessels; jewellery; mirrors; fans; and boardgames. In some cases, equipment related to the dead person's profession was included. For example, a scribe might be buried with his scribal equipment; a painter with his brushes, paints and the string he used to mark out a grid with which to proportion figures; and a soldier with his weapons, shield, horse and chariot.

Magical paraphernalia

Much of the equipment placed in the tomb would have been objects of daily use, still familiar to us

◀ *The circular end of the funerary cones found in New Kingdom tombs may have represented the sun as part of the solar iconography of rebirth.*

all. But there would also have been a considerable number of magical and ritual items, some of which would have been inscribed with spells or details about the deceased. From the Late Period (c.747 BC), a flat disc made of bronze or cartonnage (plaster-stiffened linen), known as a *hypocephalus*, was placed under the head of the mummy. It was inscribed with vignettes of various gods and the text of Chapter 162 of the Book of the

▲ *About 30 'reserve heads' have been found, all from private mastaba-tombs in the Memphite necropolis (mainly at Giza), and primarily from the reigns of Khufu and Khafre. 4th Dynasty.*

Kingdom, an Osiris-shaped box might be deposited in the burial chamber. This was filled with Nile silt and planted with grain, which was watered and was intended to sprout in the darkness of the tomb. This 'Osiris box' would have emphasized the role of Osiris as god of the dead, rebirth and vegetation, and the sprouting of the grain would have symbolized the rebirth of the deceased into the Afterlife.

Also during this period of Egyptian history, four 'magic bricks' of unbaked mud were set on the four sides of the tomb. Each brick had an amulet inserted in it: the one beside the western wall had a faience *djed*-pillar (see *Funerary Amulets*); the one by the eastern wall incorporated an unfired clay figure of the god Anubis; the one by the southern wall contained a reed with a wick, resembling a torch; and the one by the northern wall contained a mummiform *shabti*-like figure. The bricks were inscribed with sections of Chapter 151 of the Book of the Dead, which described the role they played in protecting the dead person against the evil enemies of Osiris. Their positions guarded against such an approach from any of the four cardinal directions.

Dead, the purpose of which was to ensure that the deceased would be kept warm in the Afterlife.

Some New Kingdom tombs in the Theban area had as many as 300 'funerary cones' at their entrances. These were made of clay, and measured 10–15cm (4–6in) in length. Their flat circular end was usually stamped with the name, title, and sometimes a short inscription or genealogy of the tomb owner, in hieroglyphs. Although these were not necessarily found

in situ, their tapering ends were probably set in plaster, with only their broad ends visible.

Symbols and amulets

Some types of funerary equipment have been found in tombs from a particular period of Egyptian history. During the Old Kingdom (c.2686–c.2181 BC), for example, a roughly life-sized model stone head, referred to as a 'reserve head', was placed near the entrance to the burial chamber. Its function was probably to serve as a substitute head for the deceased in the event of his or her actual one being destroyed after burial (perhaps by tomb robbers). During the New

Imiut

Certain objects that were placed in the tomb were closely associated with a particular deity. One example is the model of an *imiut*, discovered in the tomb of the Eighteenth-Dynasty ruler Tutankhamun (c.1336–c.1327 BC). The *imiut* was a fetish of the cult of Anubis, the jackal-headed god of embalming and cemeteries. It consisted of the headless skin of an animal (usually a feline), which was inflated or stuffed and tied to a pole in a pot.

Funerary Amulets

mulets were positioned in specific places on the dead body, held in place by the mummy wrappings. Their function was to protect the dead person, and it appears that the greater the number included in the bandaging, the greater the degree of protection they afforded. Often, as many as several hundred amulets have been found on one body. A list of 104 funerary amulets can be found on a doorway in a complex of rooms dedicated to Osiris, in the Temple of Hathor at Dendera.

Sections of both the Coffin Texts and the Book of the Dead are concerned with instructions detailing where and when amulets or papyri should be placed on the body during the embalming process. Some of these objects were to be wrapped up in the bandaging, while others were to be brought into contact with the body temporarily to enable their magical properties to take effect. Pictures of certain amulets might also be drawn on the bandaging.

The ideal, for those who could afford it, was to have a huge variety of different amulets made of precious stones and metals. Amulets that had been worn during life incorporated in items of jewellery were often included in the burial. Of particular importance were the golden vulture collar, the scarab worn over the heart and the Eye of Horus. Chapter 157 of the Book of the Dead was the 'spell for the vulture of gold placed at the throat of the deceased'. The vulture was an incarnation of the protective mother goddess Isis, who kept her son Horus safe within her large encircling wings.

▶ *Four ancient Egyptian words are translated as 'amulet': meket, nehet and sa derive from verbs meaning 'to guard' or 'to protect', and wedja has the same sound as the word meaning 'wellbeing'.*

▶ *The protective Eye of Horus amulet was probably used in greater numbers on mummies than any other amulet. It is first found in the late Old Kingdom, and continued in use until the Roman Period. This glazed-composition example dates from c.600 BC.*

The scarab beetle

The protective amulet for the heart was in the form of the scarab beetle, the manifestation of the creator and solar deity Khepri. It was a symbol of new life and resurrection. The scarab beetle was seen to push a ball of mud along the ground, and from this came the idea of the beetle rolling the sun across the sky. Subsequently, the young beetles were observed to hatch from their eggs inside the ball of mud, hence the idea of creation: life springing forth from primordial mud.

The heart scarab was a large scarab amulet which was wrapped in the mummy bandaging over the deceased's heart. It was made out of a range of green and dark-coloured materials, including glazed stearite, schist, feldspar, haematite and obsidian. It was inscribed with Chapter 30 of the Book of the Dead. The gist of the inscription was an instruction from the dead person to his or her heart that, when it was brought before the tribunal of the gods led by Osiris for judgment, it should not confess to any of the wrongs that the dead person might have committed during his or her lifetime (see *The Weighing of the Heart*). As a further precaution, heart-shaped amulets might

The sign of the embalmer

An amulet in the shape of two fingers was placed on the left side of the mummy's pelvis, and it is possible that it symbolized the two fingers of the chief embalmer.

also be included in the bandaging, to ensure that the heart remained at all times in the body (except during the actual Weighing of the Heart ceremony). Chapter 29B of the Book of the Dead stated that these amulets should be made of cornelian, but they have also been found made of other materials, such as glass.

Amulets and the gods

The Eye of Horus (the *udjat-* or *wadjat*-eye, literally 'the eye which is whole or sound') was an amulet in the shape of an eye. It was placed over the incision usually cut in the left side of the abdomen of a dead body for the removal of the internal organs. In one version of the myth of Osiris, his son Horus offered his healed eye to his dead

father, and it was such a powerful charm that it brought Osiris back to life. The myth of *The Contendings of Horus and Seth* tells us that Horus had his eyesight cured, and so his eye symbolized healing and the process of making whole. The Eye of Horus was used as a protective amulet, symbolizing in particular strength and perfection.

A whole range of other amulets were also included in burials. The detailed instructions accompanying the spells in the Book of the Dead often specified the material out of which the amulet should be made, whether or not it should be strung, and if so the type of stringing to be used. They also specified exactly where on the

◀ *The* djed-*pillar may originally have represented a stylized tree-trunk with the branches lopped off. It is first known to have been used as an amulet in the late Old Kingdom. Ptolemaic Period.*

body the amulet should be placed, and at which stage of the mummification process this should be done.

The *djed*-pillar amulet was associated with Osiris, god of the dead and the Afterlife (it has been interpreted as his backbone), and was thought to symbolize stability. Chapter 155 of the Book of the Dead contains:

...words to be spoken over a djed-*pillar of gold, strung upon a fibre of sycamore...and placed at the throat of the deceased on the day of burial.*

Another amulet associated with Osiris was the staircase amulet, which represented the stepped dais where his throne stood.

The *tyet*-amulet was a protective amulet associated with the goddess Isis. It was knot-shaped and may have represented the knotted girdle of the goddess, or perhaps a tampon inserted into Isis when she was pregnant. This was

done so that she would not miscarry or so that her wicked brother Seth could not harm the son she was carrying. Chapter 156 of the Book of the Dead specified that the *tyet*-amulet should be made of red jasper (the colour of the blood of Isis).

Chapters 159 and 160 were to be said over a *wadj*-amulet made of green feldspar. The ancient Egyptian word for 'green' was in fact *wadj*, and this amulet was in the shape of a single stem and flower of papyrus. In a funerary context its purpose was to ensure that the deceased enjoyed eternal youth.

Models and tiny figures

Other amulets included the headrest amulet, to ensure the head of the deceased would be eternally raised up (like the sun that rose each day); the animal-headed *was*-sceptre amulet, which granted well being and prosperity; the mason's plummet amulet, which guaranteed perpetual

▲ *Amulets such as the* djed-*pillar,* ankh *and heart amulet, as well as figures of deities, were included in the decoration of coffins.*

equilibrium; and the carpenter's square amulet, which guaranteed eternal rectitude.

Amulets of small figures of deities such as the scorpion-goddess Selket and the jackal-god Anubis, were also included for protection. Tiny models of parts of the body seem to have endowed the deceased with their properties – such as action, movement or use of the senses – and could act as substitutes if the real parts went missing. Models of animals were also considered of magical use for granting the deceased the particular characteristics associated with them: for example, the virility of a bull or ram, the speed of a hare or the fertility of a cow, cat or frog. More enigmatically, a serpent's head made out of a red material was believed to ensure cool refreshment for the throat.

Shabtis

From the Middle Kingdom (c.2055 BC), the ancient Egyptians were buried with small human statuettes known as *shabti*-figures, an incredible number of which have come to light over the years. They were usually mummiform, and were made out of faience, stone, wood, pottery, bronze, wax or glass. They were inscribed with Chapter 6 of the Book of the Dead. This was a spell to ensure that the *shabti*, and not the deceased, would end up doing any hard work that he or she might be called upon to do in the Afterlife:

▼ *One type of* shabti-*box had a vaulted lid and raised ends. During the 19th Dynasty a multiple form appeared with a dividing partition.*

O shabti, *if the deceased is called upon to do any of the work required there in the necropolis at any time…you shall say, 'Here I am. I will do it.'*

By the Late Period (c.747 BC), the term *shabti* (and the variant *shawabti*) had been largely replaced by the word *ushabti*, meaning 'answerer'. Now the emphasis in the spell was very much on the role of the figure to answer instead of the dead person when his or her name was called. The hard toil anticipated was that of food production – the funerary text specifies the preparation of the land ready for cultivation, the irrigation of the fields, and the clearing of sand from east to west. To ensure the efficiency of

▶ *During the Ramesside and Third Intermediate Periods the overseer* (reis) *shabtis, who were sometimes referred to as 'chiefs of ten', were represented in living form, as in this faience figure from Memphis, while their workforce were represented as mummiform. 22nd Dynasty.*

these figurines, during the early New Kingdom (c.1550 BC), they were sometimes equipped with a model hoe and basket, and later on they were modelled holding these tools.

By the New Kingdom a person might be buried with as many as 365 *shabtis* – one for every day of the year – accompanied by a further 36 'overseers'. From the Third Intermediate Period (c.1069 BC), these 'overseer figures' were sometimes equipped with whips to make absolutely sure that the workers performed their tasks quickly and satisfactorily. The growing numbers of *shabtis* made it necessary for them to be stored in special *shabti*-boxes.

Canopic Jars

Canopic jars were the containers used to hold the internal organs that were removed from the body before mummification and embalmed separately. During the Old Kingdom (c.2686–c.2181 BC), when mummification was in its infancy, the jars that served this purpose were stone vessels with flat lids. It was not until the First Intermediate Period (c.2181–c.2055 BC) that the four jars each acquired a human-headed

stopper. From this time, too, the packages of viscera placed inside them were sometimes decorated with human-faced masks. Then from the late Eighteenth Dynasty onwards, the stoppers of the jars were each shaped like the head of one of the minor funerary deities known as the 'Four Sons of Horus'. These were the baboon-headed Hapy, the human-headed Imsety, the jackal-headed Duamutef, and the falcon-headed Qebehsenuef.

The Sons of Horus

It was the job of these four deities to protect the internal organs of the deceased. These would have been removed from the body, embalmed, anointed and wrapped in linen ready to be placed in the jars for safe keeping,

◀ *The use of stone and ceramic canopic jars seems to have come to an end around the beginning of the Ptolemaic Period (332 BC). This limestone jar belonged to Prince Hornakht (c.850–c.825 BC) of the 22nd Dynasty.*

▲ *By the New Kingdom (c.1550–c.1069 BC) the Four Sons of Horus had become members of the group known as the 'seven blessed ones' who were said to guard Osiris's coffin in the northern sky. They are shown here on the wall of Queen Nefertari's tomb in west Thebes. 19th Dynasty.*

because the ancient Egyptians firmly believed that the deceased required his or her organs in order to be reborn into the Afterlife. Hapy guarded the lungs, Imsety the liver, Duamutef the stomach and upper intestines, and Qebehsenuef the lower intestines.

The ancient Egyptians went to such great lengths to ensure the preservation of the entire body for the Afterlife that each of the four organs, together with the Son of Horus who was its particular guardian deity, was under the further protection of four of the most important of the Egyptian goddesses, who guarded the jars themselves: Nephthys protected the jar containing the lungs, Isis the jar containing the liver, Neith the jar containing the stomach and upper

▲ *By the late Middle Kingdom (c.1650 BC), a set of canopic equipment might consist of a carved stone outer chest and a wooden inner one holding the four jars. This jar stopper belonged to the canopic equipment of Nefertari. 19th Dynasty.*

was placed in a niche in the burial chamber, close to the coffin.

The ancient Egyptians upheld their longstanding funerary traditions and continued to include canopic jars in their burials, but from the Twenty-first Dynasty (c.1069 BC) the jars were no longer functioning receptacles, in that they were left empty, or were not hollowed out, so their presence in the tomb became purely symbolic. Although the internal organs were still removed for the actual embalming of the body, they were no longer entombed separately but were packaged and returned to the body for burial. The Four Sons of Horus, in the amuletic form of wax figures, were also often inserted into the body together with the packaged organs.

Canopus of Osiris

The term 'canopic jar' is actually a misnomer arrived at by early Egyptologists. They considered that the jars resembled the form in which Osiris, the god of the dead and the Afterlife, was worshipped in the Delta city of Canopus – a port on the Mediterranean coast. The city is said to have been named after the pilot of the ship belonging to the Greek hero Menelaus. According to Homer, Menelaus died on the Egyptian coast after a storm wrecked his ship on his way home after the Trojan wars.

This manifestation of Osiris as a human-headed jar with a foot and a swollen belly was referred to as the 'Canopus of Osiris'. The form has been found on some Roman coins minted at Alexandria, so it must have been a fairly well-known image during at least the Roman period of Egyptian history.

intestines, and Selket the jar containing the lower intestines. These four goddesses were also associated with the four cardinal points: north, south, east and west, respectively.

In the Pyramid Texts of the Old Kingdom, the Four Sons of Horus were described as the 'friends of the king' because they were said to assist him in his ascent into the sky. In funerary art, for example in tomb paintings and

vignettes of the Book of the Dead on papyrus, the Four Sons of Horus occurred as small mummified human figures with their respective heads. They were often depicted close to Osiris, sometimes standing on an open lotus blossom. They might also be included as amulets in the burial – these took the form of small modelled figures of mummified human bodies, again with their respective heads.

Empty jars

By the late Middle Kingdom (c.1650 BC), the set of four canopic jars were commonly stored in a wooden chest which in turn was placed inside a stone outer chest. The whole ensemble

Coffins and Sarcophagi

D uring the Early Dynastic period, (c.3100–c.2686), if the ancient Egyptians did not bury their dead in direct contact with the sand they used baskets, large pots or square crates. This did not interfere with the age-old tradition of burying the dead in the foetal position. But with the advent of effective artificial preservation of dead bodies, the corpses had to be stretched out to facilitate the removal of the internal organs, and so wooden coffins became full-length and rectangular in shape. By the end of the Old Kingdom (c.2181 BC), food offerings were often painted on the inside of the coffin, in order to provide symbolic sustenance for the *ka* of the deceased (see *Tomb Scenes and Models*). Two eyes were painted or carved on one of the longer sides of the coffin at the head end so that the deceased might magically be able to look out through them. This followed from the ancient Egyptian belief that the dead had their faculties returned to them

at the 'Opening of the Mouth' ceremonies (see *Funerals*). The coffin was positioned in the tomb so that the eyes faced east – the place of the living and the rising Sun. These eyes were *udjat*-eyes (or Eyes of Horus), so they symbolized completeness, well being, strength and perfection.

Decoration and design

Royalty and the wealthiest people were buried in sarcophagi of granite, basalt, limestone or calcite, some of which were carved with a design known as a *serekh*. This was a pattern of recessed panelling thought perhaps to imitate the architecture of the earliest royal palaces. The design can also be found painted on wooden coffins.

By the beginning of the Middle Kingdom (c.2055) the key features of the coffins of the higher echelons of society were the Coffin Texts and maps of the Afterlife which were painted on the interior walls and bases (see *Coffin*

◀ The rishi *coffin of Nubkheperre Intef was made from a hollowed-out log overlaid with gilded gesso. 17th Dynasty.*

▼ The stone sarcophagus of King Amenhotep II, *carved in the shape of a cartouche, decorated with divine figures and an eye-panel. 18th Dynasty.*

▲ *Many coffins and sarcophagi of later periods, such as that of the priest Ken-Hor (c.750 BC) were made in the shape of the* Per-nu *or Lower Egyptian shrine.*

Texts). Those who could afford it were buried in an inner rectangular coffin placed inside an outer one, both of which would have been made from well-cut planks of imported timber. Anything imported was regarded as a luxury item and thus an indicator of wealth and a symbol of status. The timber native to Egypt was decidedly more flimsy than, for example, the cedarwood that could be imported from the Lebanon. Poorer people naturally had no choice but to use the local timber, such as sycamore or tamarisk, in their burials, and it was often roughly cut with attempts made to disguise it using a coating of plaster.

The Middle Kingdom also saw the emergence of the anthropoid coffin. This appears to have been regarded as a substitute for the body itself, in case the body was destroyed at some stage after burial. Anthropoid coffins were usually made of cartonnage (layers of linen stiffened with plaster) rather than wood, but were placed inside a rectangular wooden outer coffin.

A rather beautiful type of anthropoid coffin appeared at Thebes late in the Second Intermediate Period (c.1650–c.1550 BC). The surface was covered in a pattern of feathers (hence the name *rishi*, from the Arabic word for 'feathered'). This was possibly to indicate that the body was being protected by the enveloping wings of a vulture – a manifestation of the mother goddesses Mut and Isis. Alternatively, it may have

been intended to represent the *ba* – the personality or moral essence – of the deceased, which was symbolized as a bird with a human head.

The anthropoid coffins of the Eighteenth Dynasty (c.1550–c.1295 BC) displayed another new feature – the arms on the coffins were carved in high relief. They were usually depicted crossed over the chest like those of the god Osiris, and some coffins had modelled beards like Osiris. These coffins tended to be covered in depictions of deities, with bands of hieroglyphic extracts from the funerary texts. By the Ramesside Period (the Nineteenth and Twentieth Dynasties, c.1295–c.1069 BC), the fashion was to bury the dead inside a nest of anthropoid wooden coffins, which for royalty and noblemen might sit inside an outermost stone sarcophagus. Then by the Twenty-second Dynasty (c.945–c.715 BC) it became usual for the innermost of the coffins to be made of cartonnage with a wooden footboard.

The goddess Nut

Nut, the sky goddess, was closely associated with coffins and sarcophagi. From the late New Kingdom onwards this goddess was often depicted stretched out inside the lid. She was believed to swallow the sun in the evening and give birth to it at dawn. In keeping with the solar aspect of funerary religion, the deceased was believed to be reborn from her (and thus the coffin or sarcophagus) into the Afterlife.

Sarcophagi

The term 'sarcophagus' is derived from the Greek word for 'flesh-eater'. This reflects the Hellenic belief that the type of stone used to make coffins actually consumed their contents.

Tomb Scenes and Models

For the ancient Egyptians, two- and three-dimensional representation and the written word were charged with magical potency, especially within the context of the tomb and temple or chapel. They believed that by depicting something they might magically animate it and make it happen, at least in symbolic terms. But the ancient Egyptians were also a rational and realistic people. They knew that family, friends and passers-by (or the priesthoods of funerary cults if they were particularly important members of society), would eventually give up leaving food offerings at the tombs or associated funerary chapels, so they took further precautions to provide magical substitutes for the actual food supplies. Tomb reliefs, paintings and models representing agriculture and food

▲ *The hieroglyphs beneath Nebamun's raised arm in this fragment of wall painting from his tomb describe him as 'taking recreation and seeing what is good in the place of eternity'. 18th Dynasty.*

▼ *'Soul houses' (symbolic homes for the* kas *of the dead) were placed beside the mouths of shaft-burials. Middle Kingdom.*

production served to ensure an adequate and eternal supply of food and drink for the *ka* of the deceased in the Afterlife. The images were expected to work their magic in conjunction with the '*hetep-di-nesw* ('an offering which the king gives') formula'. This was a prayer inscribed on funerary furniture such as coffins, stelae and the false doors in tombs which served as a link between the worlds of the living and the dead. It asked for the king to placate the funerary deity Osiris or Anubis with gifts on behalf of the deceased, and then for offerings such as bread, beer and linen to be made to the *ka* of the dead

person. During the First Intermediate Period and Middle Kingdom (c.2181–c.1650 BC), 'soul houses' were often included in the burials of less wealthy people. These were pottery houses (often quite crudely modelled), with courtyards covered in models of food offerings.

Scenes of daily activity, agriculture and food production occurred on the walls of non-royal tombs throughout Egyptian history. Painted limestone figurines of servants brewing beer, grinding corn and so on, have been found in burials dating to the late Old Kingdom (c.2686–c.2181 BC). Of particular note, because of their superb craftsmanship and the incredible number that have survived, are the wooden tomb models of the Middle Kingdom (c.2055 – c.1650 BC). The most famous of these models were discovered in the tomb of

the Eleventh-Dynasty chancellor
Meketre (c.2000 BC) at Deir el-Bahri.
They are now in the Cairo Museum and
include absolutely exquisite models of a
weavers' and a carpenters' workshop, a
butcher, a bakery, boats, a cattle count,
and two models of Meketre's house and
garden with trees and a pool.

Imagining the Afterlife

The people who were able to afford the
extreme luxury of a decorated tomb
were highly unlikely ever to have
actually toiled on the land. But in a
funerary context they were depicted
ploughing the land, sowing seeds and
reaping the harvest. The emphasis was
clearly on the fundamental principle of
the importance of an individual's
relationship with, and acknowledgement
of, his dependence on the fertile silt of
the Nile Valley. To ensure that the
deceased would not really have to
perform these tasks in the Afterlife, they
included *shabti*-figures in their burials to
do the work for them.

The hope appears to have been that the
Afterlife was like this life, but free from
worry and hard work. Paintings and
reliefs portrayed the tomb owner and his
wife, family and friends enjoying
themselves at parties and various leisure
activities, such as hunting hippopotami
or waterfowl. Such scenes were laden
with symbolism, particularly connected
with fertility and the suppression of

▶ *Models showed the production
of food, such as this
woman grinding barley,
using a saddle quern
and rubbing stone, to
make bread and beer.*

▶ *The false door was a stone or wooden
imitation doorway which first appeared in tombs
of the Old Kingdom. It was usually carved with a
figure of the deceased seated before an offering
table. Here the dead man is Sheshi.*

evil or chaos. Symbols of sexuality and
fertility (the two being considered far
more interconnected by the ancient
Egyptians than by us today) such as
ducks, monkeys, cats, heavy wigs,
almost transparent clothing, and
vegetation crop up in the scenes. The
ancient Egyptian terms for some of the
activities portrayed are also worth
considering in this context, for the verb
'to throw a throwstick' (*qema*) is the
same as that for 'to father a child' or 'to
create', and the verb 'to harpoon' (*seti*)
is the same as that for 'to impregnate'.

Idealized portrayals

The portrayal of the tomb owner
hunting birds, hippopotami and
crocodiles (or wild bulls and lions in the
case of kings) showed him taking part
in activities that he had probably
enjoyed during his lifetime and hoped to
enjoy in the Afterlife. But it was also
the display of the deceased as a good
man who had been assessed as 'true of
voice' at the divine tribunal (see *The
Weighing of the Heart*), overcoming
symbols of evil or chaos,
as Horus had conquered
Seth in *The Contendings
of Horus and Seth*.

At all times, the style
and content of the artistic
representation was
extremely idealized. The
tomb owner was
always shown as
strong and
athletic, even if
he had died in
extreme old
age,

and his wife was always young and
slender despite the fact that giving birth
to many children had no doubt wreaked
havoc with her body. But anyone who
could afford such scenes in their tombs
chose to be depicted in this idealized
way in the hope that this would indeed
be how they might look in the Afterlife.

The Book of the Dead

From the New Kingdom (c.1550 BC)
onwards, scenes from the Book of the
Dead also appeared. By depicting the
funerary rituals taking place it was
hoped that they would happen after
death. When representing the dead
person's heart balancing against the
feather of Maat at the Weighing of the
Heart ceremony, it was believed that,
magically, this would occur. It was as
though portraying the deceased and his
family in the Afterlife would guarantee
entry into paradise.

Funerals

We know how the ancient Egyptians conducted their funerals because they depicted the proceedings on the walls of their tombs during the New Kingdom (c.1550–c.1069 BC). The most detailed portrayals of events are to be found in non-royal tombs.

The mummy passed in procession from the embalming house to the tomb, the attendant grandeur depending on the wealth and status of the individual concerned. The mummy usually lay in an open booth shaped like a shrine and bedecked with funerary bouquets. This was mounted on a boat-shaped bier which in turn sat on a sled drawn by oxen. A priest walked in front of the bier, sprinkling milk and burning incense. The canopic chest was dragged or carried behind the bier. All manner of funerary goods and food offerings were also carried in the procession, destined for burial alongside the body. One of the more enigmatic components of the procession was the *tekenu*, a human-headed sack-like object usually depicted in wall paintings and reliefs being drawn by cattle on a sled. Its significance is very uncertain but it has been suggested that this was a sack containing those parts of the body that were not actually mummified or placed in the canopic jars, but were nevertheless regarded as essential for the rebirth of the deceased into the Afterlife.

Mourning the deceased

Professional female mourners dressed in pale blue were an important presence at every funeral. They let down their hair and tore at it, bared and beat their breasts, wept, wailed and threw dirt from the ground over themselves. The two chief mourners were often identified with the goddesses Isis and Nephthys who, according to mythology, had pieced together the body of their brother Osiris (whose dead body had been hacked apart

by their wicked brother Seth), mummified it, and mourned his death. Just as Osiris had been mummified in order to preserve his body and had then been reborn, it was expected that the deceased and mummified person would be reborn into the Afterlife. Dancers also accompanied the procession. These were the *muu*-dancers, who wore kilts and tall white headdresses, rather like the White

▲ *The strict conventions of Egyptian art allowed women to be depicted displaying hysterical behaviour, such as these mourners in the tomb of Ramose, but men had at all times to be portrayed as upright and in control. 18th Dynasty.*

▼ *This vignette from the Book of the Dead of Ani is one of a series of scenes illustrating the role of the* ba *after death. Here the* ba *is united with the body of the deceased.*

▲ A number of different ritual implements were used in the Opening of the Mouth ceremony (shown here on the papyrus Book of the Dead of Hunefer). Their use was believed to restore the dead person's ability to see, breathe, eat and drink. 19th Dynasty.

Crown of Upper Egypt. There were also priests, distinguished by their shaven heads.

The key rituals performed at the funeral were the final act of purifying the mummified body with water (probably a natron solution) and incense; the anointing of the mummy with sacred oils; and the ceremony known as the Opening of the Mouth. This was considered vital for restoring the senses to the dead person so he or she could be reborn into the Afterlife, and so the body could become the vessel for the *ka* (spirit) of the deceased. This rite was also performed on any statues of the deceased, as well as the cult statues placed in shrines and temples throughout Egypt, thereby animating the statues as vessels for the divine presence of the various deities. It was originally the eldest son's responsibility to carry out this act so that his parent could live

on after death, which explains why the ancient Egyptians considered infertility such a desperate problem. However, during the New Kingdom a new priestly function developed – that of the *sem*-priest, who is depicted in the tomb paintings and vignettes from the Book of the Dead wearing a leopardskin, and performing the Opening of the Mouth ceremony. In the tomb of the Eighteenth-Dynasty king Tutankhamun (c.1336–c.1327 BC) there is a depiction on the wall of the Opening of the Mouth of the deceased pharaoh. It is being performed by his chief official, the vizier Ay, who had himself portrayed in the role of the king's heir in order to legitimize his unlawful claim to the throne. Ay did indeed succeed to the throne and ruled Egypt for about four years (c.1327–c.1323 BC).

It is known that during the New Kingdom this ceremony consisted of 75 separate acts, involving the touching of the mouth, eyes, ears, nose and other parts of the body with a variety of different ritual implements. These included a *pesesh-kaf* (a fishtail-shaped flint knife), a chisel, an adze, a *netjeri*-blade (usually made of meteoric iron), a

rod ending in a snake's head, and the right leg of an ox which would have been specially butchered for the occasion.

Interring the body

All stages of the funeral were accompanied by recitation from the funerary texts (especially the Book of the Dead) by a Lector Priest (who would also have recited the spells during the embalming and mummification of the body). The gist of these utterances was the successful rebirth of the dead person and his or her continued and comfortable existence in the Afterlife. The final offerings made to the spirit of the deceased included natron, incense, eye-paint (malachite or galena), linen, food and drink, as well as the foreleg and heart of a bull.

The mummy was placed inside its coffin, often part of a nest of coffins, which was deposited in the burial chamber together with the canopic chest, food supplies for the deceased and other funerary equipment. Magic bricks (see *Funerary Equipment*) were positioned around the coffin or sarcophagus, and after these extensive and elaborate proceedings the body was left in peace as the tomb was sealed. The waste material from the embalming process was not considered pure enough to bury with the body, but it was still thought to be important to the deceased's existence in the Afterlife, so it was buried nearby.

After the burial, the family and guests sat down at portable tables set up outside the tomb to enjoy a feast of all kinds of food, wine and beer.

Tombs

The ancient Egyptian tomb, whether a pyramid or a shallow pit, was considered the eternal resting-place for the body and funerary goods, both of which were believed vital for rebirth and survival in the Afterlife.

Because towns and villages were built of mudbrick and were situated within the floodplain, very few have survived. Our understanding of ancient Egypt thus relies heavily on the information gleaned from tombs, which were built to last for eternity. Wherever possible they were built of stone or were cut into the natural rock, and they were located on the desert fringes, where they avoided the ravages of the Nile flood. In this hot, dry setting they have survived to this day, and often the painted decoration on their walls still looks fresh and vibrant.

The most splendid monuments were luxuries that only the king, his family and officials, and the wealthiest members of society could afford. Each tomb had a burial chamber, but of equal if not greater importance was the associated 'offering chapel', where it was hoped food offerings would continue to be left for the deceased to ensure a continued existence in the Afterlife. By the New Kingdom (c.1550 BC), the tombs of the pharaohs in the Valley of the Kings each had a mortuary temple as grand as any of the temples dedicated to the most eminent of Egyptian deities.

◀ *The Step Pyramid Complex of King Djoser is Egypt's earliest monumental stone structure.*

Mastabas

Important early royal tombs have been discovered at the cemetery sites of Abydos and Saqqara. These were the burials of the rulers of the First and Second Dynasties (c.3100–c.2686 BC), and those of members of their family and administration. The size and complexity of some of these tombs indicates the increased wealth, control of manpower and organization of the Early Dynastic kings and their governments. They provide us with evidence for the initial stages of building on a monumental scale, and the emergence of a distinct architectural symbolism, especially regarding funerary beliefs and kingship.

Because of their shape, these early tombs are called mastabas, from the Arabic word for 'bench'. They consisted of brick chambers (the central one being the burial chamber) in pits dug in the desert or – by the end of the Second Dynasty – excavated out of the actual bedrock. The pit was covered by a simple superstructure in the form of a plain square or rectangular enclosure, its outer wall often recessed in imitation of a palace façade. This enclosure was filled with sand and gravel, or

Osiris's burial place

Later in Egyptian history Abydos became the chief cult centre of Osiris, the deity most associated with the dead and the Afterlife, and according to legend it was his burial place. The early dynastic cemetery at Abydos was situated in the desert at a site now known as Umm el Qa'ab or 'Mother of Pots'. It is so-called because of the vast quantity of pots and sherds that have been found there. These are the remains of offerings made mainly during the New Kingdom (c.1550– c.1069 BC).

sometimes contained storage chambers or magazines, covering an area of up to 340sq m (410sq yd).

The evidence concerning exactly which of the kings was buried at which of the two sites is a little shaky, and disagreement continues. But it is generally held today that all the kings of the First Dynasty and the last two of the Second Dynasty (Peribsen and Khasekhemwy) were laid to rest at Abydos. Their tombs were marked by pairs of free-standing stone stelae similar to gravestones, bearing the name of the king in a *serekh* design, usually surmounted by the image of the god Horus in falcon form. The other Second Dynasty rulers were buried at Saqqara, on the northern spur of the desert plateau there. This was the cemetery of the administrative capital, Memphis, and so it makes sense that the great administrators were also buried there, in a manner similar to that of the kings.

Funerary palaces

The subterranean chambers of these early tombs were often lined with wooden panelling – a clear indication of long-distance trade, because the ancient Egyptians had no native timber suitable for such a purpose. From the mid-First Dynasty (c.2950 BC), a stairway paved with blocks of granite led to the burial chamber, providing evidence for quarrying in the region of Aswan in the far south of Egypt. At the same time, fine quality limestone was being used in the tombs at Saqqara, quarried across the river at Tura. The threat of tomb robbers was obviously already a concern, even at this very early stage of Egyptian history, because security measures such as portcullises were already in place.

At Abydos each tomb was associated with a separate building, sometimes referred to as a funerary palace, which was situated closer to the cultivation and

▲ *While the* serekh *of King Djet (shown here on a stela from his tomb at Abydos) was surmounted by the falcon Horus, the* serekh *of Peribsen was surmounted by the Seth animal, and that of Khasekhemwy by both Horus and Seth. Early Dynastic Period.*

water supplies. It is very likely that these buildings served a purpose similar to that of the later mortuary chapels and temples. They housed the *ka* of the deceased in a statue and were the focus of the dead person's funerary cult. As such, offerings and votive material such as stelae inscribed with offering formulae (see *Tomb Scenes and Models*) were placed in them. The best-preserved of these structures belonged to the last ruler of the Second Dynasty, Khasekhemwy (c.2686 BC). It is now called Shunet ez-Zebib ('Storehouse of Raisins'), so it has obviously served a more secular function in its time. It appears to have been enormous: its outer

▲ *Djoser's Step Pyramid began life as an almost square mastaba (the outline of which is still visible). This was extended to provide a superstructure for a further eleven burial shafts. A four-stepped pyramid and then a final six steps were added over this structure.*

enclosure measured 54 x 113m (177 x 370 ft) and the inner wall still stands 11m (36ft) high in places and is 5.5m (18ft) thick.

At Saqqara, by the end of the First Dynasty (c.2890 BC), the architects chose to combine the two elements of a tomb and a funerary palace in a single structure, with a mortuary chapel on the north side. This feature continued into the Third Dynasty (c.2686–c.2613 BC) on the north face of the earliest pyramid, the Step Pyramid of King Djoser (c.2667–c.2648 BC).

Both the royal tombs and the funerary palaces were surrounded by rows of simple graves. These were marked by stelae, which tell us that these dead people had been members of the royal entourage. Many were women, but there were also minor palace staff, craftsmen, court dwarfs and the king's favourite dogs. It is impossible to be absolutely certain, but it does seem that some of these retainers died just before the royal tomb was closed, raising the question of human sacrifice. In the case of the First Dynasty king Djer, as many as 580 retainers were buried around his tomb. Were these people killed to accompany and serve the king after his death? If so, this custom did not survive into the Old Kingdom (c.2686–c.2181 BC), when the royal entourage was replaced by models of servants performing tasks, and later by *shabti* figures.

Boat burials and bulls' heads

The mastabas at Saqqara have survived much better than those at Abydos, and they display some interesting features. Three of the tombs had an associated mudbrick boat burial on their north side (see *Boats in Egyptian Religion*). One of these tombs also had an estate modelled in mud-covered rubble on its north side.

Another tomb had a tree plantation on its east side, the purpose of which was probably to provide cool shade for the *ba* of the deceased. A particularly fascinating feature was a raised platform with bulls' heads sitting on it, which ran around some of the mastabas. The heads were modelled out of mud but the horns were real, and it has been estimated that a tomb might be surrounded by up to three hundred of them. Throughout Egyptian history the bull was closely associated with kingship. The pharaoh was referred to as 'Mighty Bull', in the belief that he could assimilate the strength and virility of the animal.

Towards the end of the Early Dynastic Period, the mound-like superstructures of the mastabas at Saqqara were being constructed in the shape of a low stepped pyramid, and so it is possible to trace the development of the early royal tomb from the mastaba to the pyramid. By the Old Kingdom (c.2686 BC), the king was no longer buried in a mastaba, but his high officials continued to be buried in them.

▼ *A recessed outer wall like a palace façade and bulls horns on a surrounding platform have been excavated at tomb 3504 at Saqqara.*

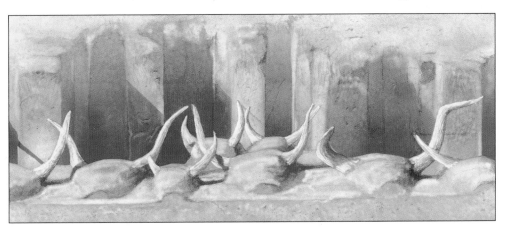

Pyramids

The word 'pyramid' (ancient Egyptian mer) comes from the Greek word pyramis meaning 'wheat cake' (presumably because such a cake resembled a pyramid in shape). The humble origin of the name belies the sheer magnificence of many of the ancient Egyptian pyramids, some of which, many would argue, are the most stupendous structures ever built.

Djoser's Step Pyramid

The earliest pyramid was not quite the type we usually picture, but rather a large stepped structure – hence its name, the Step Pyramid. It was built at Saqqara to house the burial of the Third-Dynasty king, Djoser (c.2667–c.2648 BC), and it is the earliest known monumental stone building. The idea of a stepped superstructure for a tomb was not new, (see *Mastabas*), but much about the Step Pyramid and its surrounding complex of courts, temples and other buildings was truly innovative.

The later Pyramid Texts emphasized the ascent of the dead king to the heavens, so perhaps the concept behind the Step Pyramid was to provide a giant ladder for the king to reach his heavenly destination. It has also been suggested that the pyramid might have represented the primordial mound that was believed to have risen out of the waters of chaos at the time of creation (an image also closely associated with the solar deity). Djoser's pyramid was the masterpiece of his great vizier and architect, Imhotep. The structure developed in stages. It began as an almost square mastaba tomb; it was then extended on all four sides; next a four-stepped pyramid was added over this structure; and finally it was converted into a six-stepped pyramid. It was built out of local

▲ *Djoser's Step Pyramid complex at Saqqara measures over 500 x 250m (547 x 273yd).*

limestone and cased in the better quality Tura limestone from the quarries across the river. The shaft to the burial chamber beneath the pyramid was plugged with a granite boulder weighing three tons.

The architects and builders of the time were experimenters – they made use of smaller and more easily portable stone blocks than were used in the later pyramids. The columns they built were engaged rather than free-standing, and they were built up from segments of stone rather than being carved from single blocks. The builders worked the stone in a way that imitated earlier, more organic building materials. The ceiling blocks and columns in the processional way, for example, were carved to look like bundles of reeds. If the tomb itself imitated a ladder to the Afterlife, perhaps the entrance colonnade was designed to symbolize the Field of Reeds – the place of purification for both the sun and the dead king.

The Meidum Pyramid

The next great achievement in the development of tomb building was the pyramid at Meidum. This was the earliest occurrence of a stepped pyramid with the steps filled in and cased to form a smooth-sided, geometrically true pyramid. The monument may well have been begun by Huni (c.2637–c.2613 BC), the last ruler of the Third Dynasty, and it was completed by Sneferu (c.2613–c.2589 BC), the first ruler of the Fourth Dynasty. It began life as a seven-stepped pyramid, which was cased in Tura limestone. It was later enlarged to become an eight-stepped structure and the steps were cased again. Finally the steps were filled in and cased a final time. It is possible that the smooth sides of the pyramid were thought to symbolize the rays of the sun.

▶ *Today the pyramid at Meidum stands as a three-step tower rising from a mound of debris, probably the result of collapse and quarrying.*

Khufu's Great Pyramid

The pyramid was an icon of the cult of the sun god Re, which increased in importance during the Fourth Dynasty (c.2613–c.2494 BC). It was the most magnificent of status symbols – an unmistakable expression of the might of kingship and the success of the particular ruler buried in it. The most enormous of these structures was the Great Pyramid of the Fourth-Dynasty king Khufu (c.2589–c.2566 BC), built on the desert plateau at Giza. Its complete height would originally have been 146m (479ft). One of its greatest architectural features and feats of engineering is the 'Grand Gallery', which leads to the burial chamber. This is 46m (150ft) long and over 8m (26ft) high, with a huge corbelled vault constructed with its

▼ *The 'Bent Pyramid' at Dahshur was built, together with the neighbouring 'Red Pyramid' by King Sneferu.*

roofing slabs laid at an angle steeper than the slope of the gallery, in order to prevent a build-up of pressure at any one point. Similar precautions were taken in the granite burial chamber, where five compartments were built above the flat ceiling to minimize any risk of collapse.

The sun and the stars

The construction of the pyramids shows that the ancient Egyptians were incredibly successful engineers. They were also very much concerned with the rituals and beliefs surrounding death. It is clear from the Pyramid Texts that there was a fundamental solar element to their funerary religion, but there was also an important stellar one. In the Great Pyramid, two shafts running from the burial chamber were aligned with various stars, including the constellation of Orion (divinely personified by the Egyptians as the god Sah). Orion was possibly intended as the destination of

the king's *ba* when he ascended to take his place among the circumpolar stars. In this and similar ways the ancient Egyptians incorporated the stars into their religious beliefs as well as using a certain amount of astronomical observation in the building of the pyramids, especially in the precise alignment of the tomb with the four cardinal points.

It was not until the reign of King Unas (c.2375–c.2345 BC) at the end of the Fifth Dynasty that the ancient Egyptians began to inscribe funerary texts on the interior walls of their kings' pyramids (see *Pyramid Texts*). From these we can begin to get a clearer idea of how the ancient Egyptians envisaged the rebirth of the king and his survival in the Afterlife. Rulers continued to be buried in pyramids right up until the Second Intermediate Period (c.1650–c.1550 BC). After this, Thebes became the royal burial site, where tombs were cut into the desert cliffs. Meanwhile, non-royals could choose to incorporate a small mudbrick or stone model of a pyramid, known as a pyramidion, into the design of their tombs. This ties in with the notion of the democratization of funerary religion.

Benben Stones and Obelisks

Each of the pyramids would originally have sported a gilded pyramidion (a mini-pyramid) at its pinnacle, which would have glinted strikingly in the sunlight. This feature, together with the sloping sides of the entire structure resembling the rays of the sun as they are seen to jut through the clouds, would have made the pyramid an appropriate icon of solar religion. This was also an important aspect of funerary religion, especially of the king, and especially during the Old Kingdom (c.2686–c.2181 BC).

The sun cult at Heliopolis

The heyday of the pyramid was during the Old Kingdom, a time when the cult of the sun god Re at Heliopolis rose to the forefront of Egyptian state religion, and one of the king's five names came to be introduced by the title 'Son of Re'. The prototype for the true pyramid may well have been the focal point of the cult at Heliopolis. This was a squat standing stone, pointed at its apex, known as a *benben* (from the verb *weben*, 'to rise', which also provides the origins of the ancient Egyptian word for the cap-stone or pyramidion at the top of a pyramid – a *benbenet*). This monument, the original and most sacred of the *benbens*, was erected at Heliopolis at least as early as the First Dynasty. It may well have symbolized the primordial mound that appeared out of the watery chaos of Nun, whence the sun rose for the first time and creation began. It was certainly believed to have been the first point hit by the rays of the rising sun. It is also possible that this stone symbolized the petrified semen of Atum, the creator god of Heliopolis, whose act of masturbation played a key role in the creation of the divine personifications of air and moisture, Shu and Tefnut.

During the Fifth Dynasty, the structure was imitated in sun temples, which were associated with royal pyramid burials, but were also clearly dedicated to the sun god Re. The sun temple of Niuserre

▼ *The obelisks of Tuthmosis I and Hatshepsut at Karnak temple. There is a description of the quarrying and transport of two granite obelisks to Karnak on the walls of Hatshepsut's mortuary temple at Deir el-Bahri.*

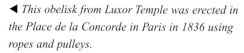

◄ *This obelisk from Luxor Temple was erected in the Place de la Concorde in Paris in 1836 using ropes and pulleys.*

(c.2445–c.2421 BC) at Abu Gurab, north of Abusir (part of the necropolis of the ancient capital at Memphis), was named 'Delight of Re'. It would originally have been dominated by an enormous limestone *benben*, 36m (118ft) in height.

▼ *If the 'unfinished obelisk' in the Aswan granite quarries had been successfully removed from the rock it would have been 42m (138ft) tall and weighed 1197 tons.*

This sacred stone would have stood on a pedestal in the form of a limestone truncated pyramid, 20m (66ft) high, with red granite around the base.

Gold-tipped obelisks

Throughout history, the ancient Egyptians also incorporated a more tapering, needle-like version of the *benben* into the design of their tombs and temple complexes. Today we call these sacred stones obelisks. The ancient Egyptians called them *tekhen*, a word that might also relate to the verb *weben*. They too would originally have had gilded tips, which were also referred to as *benbenet*, and would have reflected the sun's rays majestically. The solar imagery was often extended to the designs carved on the obelisks, such as figures of baboons. These animals were observed to greet the rising sun with great excitement each morning, and to sit on their hind legs, their front paws raised at dawn in order to warm their undersides (hence the ancient Egyptian posture for worship and adoration). The splendour and elegance of the obelisk has continued to command respect, not only in Egypt but throughout the world, and obelisks have been removed from Egypt and re-erected in cities such as Rome, Paris, London and New York.

The *benu*

Like the Greek phoenix, the Egyptian *benu*-bird was connected with the sun and rebirth. As a sacred bird of Heliopolis, the benu was closely associated with the solar deities Re and Atum, and with the obelisk and *benben* stone.

In the Pyramid Texts, the *benu*-bird appears as a yellow wagtail, but by the advent of the Book of the Dead, it was being represented as a kind of grey heron with a long, straight beak, and a two-feathered crest.

Chapter 83 of the Book of the Dead was the 'spell for being transformed into a *benu*-bird'.

The Great Sphinx

When we speak of the Sphinx, we are referring to the earliest colossal statue in Egypt. It is 73m (240ft) long, with a maximum height of 20m (66ft), and is probably a statue of the Fourth-Dynasty king Khafre (c.2558–c.2532 BC). His head, wearing a pleated linen *nemes*-headdress and a *uraeus*, is superimposed on the body of a lion – an animal closely associated with kingship due to its great power and might. In connection with the solar iconography of the pyramid, benben stone and obelisk, the lion was also regarded as a solar symbol in ancient Near Eastern cultures.

The word 'sphinx' comes from the Greek and means 'the strangler', but this implies that the statue had a terrifying aspect, and this was not an idea shared by the ancient Egyptians. It is possible that 'sphinx' was a distortion of the Egyptian *shesep ankh*, meaning 'living image'. Vast numbers of considerably smaller sphinxes have also survived from ancient Egypt. These include not only statues of rulers in sphinx form, but also gods, such as the avenue of ram-headed sphinxes (manifestations of the god Amun) that run between Karnak and Luxor temples.

Khafre's temples

The Sphinx was carved out of a natural outcrop of the limestone rock alongside Khafre's valley temple at Giza. The valley temple was the king's funerary temple, built on a quay at the edge of the Nile Valley and linked by means of a causeway to the smaller mortuary temple adjoining the eastern face of the pyramid. It is possible that the sphinx was intended to serve as a guardian for Khafre's splendid valley temple. But there was another temple, more closely associated with the great statue, located beneath its front paws. Referred to as the Sphinx temple, it appears to have been specifically dedicated to the

Sphinx. It is impossible to be certain about the architectural symbolism and functioning of this temple, because no Old Kingdom texts have survived that refer to it, and none of the Old Kingdom

▲ *The head of the Sphinx was carved from a much better building stone than the soft layers of the body, which have been severely eroded, while the base is carved from a petrified hard shoal and coral reef.*

be known as the Dream Stela. It recounts the tale of Tuthmosis as a young prince on a hunting expedition at Giza. He fell asleep under the Sphinx and, as he slept, the Sphinx, as the solar and creator deity Khepri-Re-Atum, appeared to him in a dream. He promised Tuthmosis the throne of Egypt if he would repair the giant body of the statue and clear the windswept sand that had accumulated up to its neck. Tuthmosis did just this – he restored the lion body with stone cladding and built an open-air chapel between the paws of the Sphinx, with the stela as its centrepiece.

▲ *Several New Kingdom stelae commemorating visits made to the restored Sphinx show a royal statue behind the Dream Stela.*

tombs at Giza belonged to priests or priestesses of its cult. Much about the temple remains a mystery, but it does seem that there was an important solar element to it. It has been suggested that its eastern and western sanctuaries were associated with the rising and setting sun, and that the Sphinx symbolized Khafre in the role of making offerings to the sun god in the court of the temple. However, it is also possible that the Sphinx was originally viewed as an image of the sun god himself, because this certainly appears to have been the case over 1,000 years later during the New Kingdom (c.1550– c.1069 BC), when the Sphinx came to be known as Horemakhet, or 'Horus-in-the-Horizon'.

Tuthmosis IV's dream

The Eighteenth-Dynasty king Tuthmosis IV (c.1400–c.1390 BC) was instrumental in restoring the Sphinx and reactivating its cult. He erected a granite stela, weighing 15 tons and 3.6m (12ft) high, made out of a lintel from one of the doorways of Khafre's mortuary temple, between the paws of the Sphinx. The upper part of this stela depicts the king making offerings to the Sphinx, which the hieroglyphs identify as Horus-in-the-Horizon.

It is because of its detailed inscription that the stela has come to

▶ *The head of a king on the body of a lion, this bronze example depicting Tuthmosis III, was the most common type of sphinx, but sometimes they were ram-headed (criosphinxes) or hawk-headed (hierakosphinxes). 18th Dynasty.*

Boats in Egyptian Funerary Religion

◀ Khufu's boat is 43m (142ft) long and 6m (19ft) wide; it has a maximum draft of 1.5m (5ft) and a displacement of 45 tons.

been found in each. The boats were obviously intended to be dismantled because the pits are not large enough to have contained them when assembled. One of them has been pieced together and is on display in a specially built museum near the pyramid. Its 1,224 individual pieces were painstakingly 'stitched' together using vegetable fibre rope, and joined using mortise and tenon joints, to bring to life a breathtaking vessel measuring a magnificent 43m (142ft) long. Its prow and stern are in the form of papyrus stalks, and its design is based on that of a papyrus reed boat. The boat in the other pit has been photographed using a tiny camera inserted through a hole into the pit, but it has not yet been excavated.

Why boat pits?

Because the River Nile was the main thoroughfare through Egypt, boats were essential in Egyptian daily life. They were the only means of transport across the river, and were by far the most sensible means of travelling up and down the country. For this reason, it is not surprising that the boat should be so highly valued and that it was incorporated into the rituals of death and beliefs concerning the Afterlife.

There are several possible reasons for the occurrence of boat-shaped pits and buried boats in the vicinity of the Great Pyramid. The boatless pits must have been purely symbolic, and were presumably connected with the journeying of the king to the heavens after his death. It was believed that he needed to join the circumpolar stars in the northern sky, but he was also thought to voyage with the sun, and according to much mythology the sun god Re passed through the solar cycle

Boat-shaped pits have been excavated alongside royal mastaba and pyramid burials of the Early Dynastic Period and Old Kingdom (c.3100–c.2181 BC), but the most impressive are those associated with the Great Pyramid of Khufu at Giza. Close to the mortuary temple and three subsidiary pyramids just to the east of the Great Pyramid, five boat-shaped pits were found that appear never to have actually housed boats, and were in fact symbolic.

However, just to the south of the pyramid, two more interesting pits were discovered. They are long, narrow and rectangular, but unlike the boat-shaped pits, they were actually intended for the burial of boats. Indeed, the disassembled parts of a real cedar-wood boat have

▲ *The hieroglyph for 'follower' (*shemset*) – a crook or staff with a knife and some sort of package lashed to it – is often depicted in representations of the solar barque, such as this one from the Book of the Dead of Heruben. 21st Dynasty.*

▲ *A boat pit to the south of the mortuary temple on the east face of Djedefre's pyramid at Abu Roash, recalls the one just outside the entrance to Khufu's temple alongside the Great Pyramid.*

by boat. A boat pit might also have been deemed necessary to symbolize the transportation of the king's *ka* statue.

The significance of the real boats is likely to have been somewhat different. The fact that they were deliberately dismantled when they could have been buried whole, and the fact that their

burials would have lain just outside the original enclosure wall of the pyramid complex, indicates that they are less likely to have had a symbolic role in the funerary complex. They were probably used in the funeral cortege of the dead king, and having performed their function, they were ritually disposed of close to the royal burial.

Model boats
Throughout Egyptian history boats were depicted on the walls of non-royal tombs, and during the Middle Kingdom (c.2055–c.1650 BC) it was popular to place wooden models of them

in the tombs. Because the ancient Egyptians travelled by boat while alive, they expected to do so in the Afterlife. An actual journey that might be depicted in painted or model form was the transport of the dead body from the realm of the living on the east bank to that of the dead on the west bank. A symbolic journey that might also have been represented was the pilgrimage made by the deceased to the cult centre and legendary burial place of Osiris at Abydos.

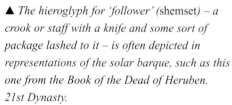

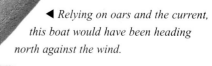

◄ *Relying on oars and the current, this boat would have been heading north against the wind.*

Rock-cut Tombs

Throughout Egyptian history, tombs were cut into the desert rock. Both mastabas and pyramids often had subterranean burial chambers excavated into the rock, but the term 'rock-cut tomb' tends to be used to describe a tomb that has been cut into the desert cliffs, with no superstructure, but very often with a separate funerary chapel or temple.

The best-known rock-cut tombs in Egypt are those located in the area known as the Valley of the Kings, on the west bank of the Nile at Thebes (modern Luxor). It is home to undoubtedly the most famous of the tombs, that of the Eighteenth-Dynasty king Tutankhamun (c.1336–c.1327 BC), which was discovered by the British archaeologist Howard Carter in 1922. The world continues to marvel at the treasure it yielded. Tutankhamun was actually a relatively minor ruler of the New Kingdom (c.1550–c.1069 BC) but, together with the Twenty-first and Twenty-second Dynasty burials excavated at Tanis by the French archaeologist Pierre Montet in 1939, his tomb was by far the best preserved of any royal tomb.

Contrary to popular belief, Tutankhamun's tomb was not intact on discovery – it had been entered, partly robbed, and resealed in antiquity – but the quality and quantity of the funerary equipment found in it were quite stupendous. Many of the objects are made of gold, lapis lazuli, turquoise, amethyst and other precious materials. They include wonderful examples of ancient Egyptian craftsmanship, such as Tutankhamun's mummy mask, coffins, jewellery and shrines, which are now on display in the Egyptian Museum, Cairo.

Despite the richness of its contents, Tutankhamun's tomb was far less grand than others in the Valley of the Kings. It consisted of only four small rooms rather than the usual long corridor-style

▲ There are 62 tombs in the Valley of the Kings, the most famous being that of the young king Tutankhamun.

▼ This was the view of the antechamber of Tutankhamun's tomb that greeted Howard Carter when he first looked into it in 1922.

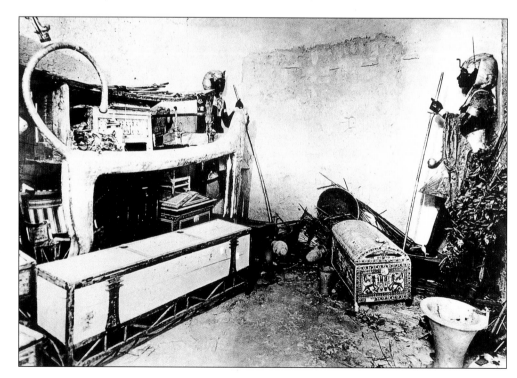

tomb, and as such was probably originally intended as a private burial place (perhaps that of his vizier Ay). On Tutankhamun's death, this tomb may have been hastily enlarged to receive a royal burial, but only one of the rooms was ever decorated.

Design features of the tombs
The first king to choose to have his tomb cut in the Valley of the Kings was probably Tuthmosis I (c.1504–c.1492 BC), the third ruler of the Eighteenth Dynasty. The character of the rock is likely to have dictated the somewhat meandering approach corridor to his squarish burial chamber. The tomb of his successor, Tuthmosis II (c.1492–c.1479 BC), appears to have been more carefully planned. It introduced two interesting new features – a bent axis to the approach corridor and an oval burial chamber. The sudden sharp left turn to the corridor may well have been devised to fool any prospective tomb robbers into believing that the blocked corridor continued straight onwards when in fact, behind another blocked wall, it headed off at a right angle. The oval burial

▼ *The four canopic coffins containing Tutankhamun's internal organs are miniature replicas of the second of the king's three coffins.*

▶ *The lotiform chalice found in Tutankhamun's tomb is carved of a single piece of calcite and inlaid with blue pigment.*

chamber reminds us of the cartouche used to surround the king's name, and in a similar way the walls of the chamber would have surrounded and protected the dead body of the king.

Tomb robbery and flooding
The ancient Egyptians had obviously learned by experience that the burial chambers needed to be safeguarded against both robbery and flooding. The unique survival of Tutankhamun's tomb reveals the lack of success the Egyptians had in protecting their dead and the material buried with them. The plunder of tombs continues to be a problem to the present day, as does the disastrous effect caused by occasional torrential rain that results in destructive flash floods racing through desert wadis such as the Valley of the Kings.

Tuthmosis III's architects introduced a deep 'well' into his tomb, perhaps to protect it against flooding or robbers. They also built a pillared antechamber between the well and the burial chamber, and four small rooms were cut into the two long sides of the burial chamber for the storage of funerary equipment.

Innovation also crept into the tomb of Amenhotep II (c.1427–c.1400 BC), which had a rectangular, columned burial chamber with a sunken crypt at the far end. Horemheb's reign (c.1323–c.1295 BC) heralded the use of a tomb with a straight axis. Unique to the tomb of the Nineteenth-Dynasty king Seti I (c.1294–c.1279 BC) was a passage more than 136m (149yd) long below the burial chamber. Its end cannot be reached, but it seems to be approaching the level of the water table, and the idea behind it might have been the linking of the burial chamber to the primordial waters of creation. The last tomb to be cut in the Valley of the Kings was that of the last ruler of the New Kingdom, Ramesses XI, who died c.1069 BC.

Wall decoration
Like most rock-cut tombs throughout Egypt belonging to men of high status from viziers to craftsmen, the tombs in the Valley of the Kings were elaborately decorated. The walls of the royal rock-cut tombs were covered in paintings of detailed funerary scenes relating to the king's Afterlife, and his interaction with the gods and goddesses of the Egyptian pantheon.

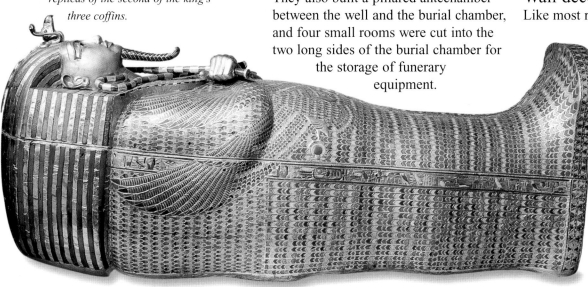

Tomb-builders' Towns and Villages

A great deal concerning the construction of the tombs of ancient Egypt, especially the pyramids, remains a mystery. But archaeologists have unearthed texts that refer to towns, and the towns that housed the tomb builders and craftsmen, or the priests, officials, guards and other personnel involved in the daily running of the funerary cults and complexes of the dead kings. The remains of such settlements have been discovered at Giza, Il-Lahun, Tell el-Amarna and Deir el-Medina on the Theban west bank.

The Giza settlements

At Giza, home to the magnificent Fourth-Dynasty pyramids of Khufu, Khafre and Menkaure, the names of two settlements are known. They are the southern Tjeniu ('boundary mark' or 'cultivation edge') of Khafre, which was probably to the south of the king's valley temple, and the northern Gerget ('settlement') of Khufu, which may have been situated around this king's valley temple. Mudbrick buildings, broken pottery, bread moulds, cooking pots,

animal bones, grinding stones, charcoal and ash have all been discovered in this area. Unfortunately, the ancient settlement appears to extend beneath the modern, ever-growing city of Cairo and its sewers, so further excavation is just about impossible. A community of small mud huts, with

storage bins and grain silos, has also been excavated in front of Menkaure's valley temple. This was a random arrangement of slum housing which eventually overtook the front of the valley temple.

The town of Kahun

The pyramid town of Kahun at Il-Lahun, at the eastern edge of the Faiyum some 100km (62 miles) south-east of Cairo, was specially built to house the men (and their families) who built the pyramid of the Twelfth-Dynasty king Senusret II (c.1880–c.1874 BC). It later provided homes for the priests, officials and their families who served the dead king's funerary cult. It was carefully planned and laid out on a grid system.

▼ *Research into the genealogies of the builders at Deir el-Medina has shown that about 25 interrelated families lived in the village.*

Altogether, 220 small houses have been excavated in the western and southern parts of the town. The north-eastern area was the site of nine or ten sizeable urban estates, each with a large house, garden and granary – presumably the occupants of these were the king's highest officials.

Deir el-Medina

The settlement site that has yielded more written and archaeo-logical evidence of daily life than any other is Deir el-Medina. During the New Kingdom (c.1550–c.1069 BC) it was home to the workmen (and their families) who quarried and decorated the rock-cut tombs in the Valley of the Kings on the west bank at Thebes. The small village was specially planned and constructed to serve this purpose. It was situated in a sheltered spot in the desert, between the Ramesseum and Medinet Habu, with relatively easy access to the Valley of the Kings. We know that the original outer enclosure wall of the village was built during the reign of the early Eighteenth-Dynasty king Tuthmosis I (c.1504–c.1492 BC) (probably the first king to be buried in the Valley of the Kings) because his cartouche has been found stamped on some of the bricks. However, throughout the village's lifetime (that is, for the duration of the New Kingdom, while kings were being buried in tombs in the Valley of the Kings), its founding father and patron deity was considered to be Tuthmosis I's father Amenhotep I (c.1525–c.1504 BC). At the end of the Eighteenth Dynasty,

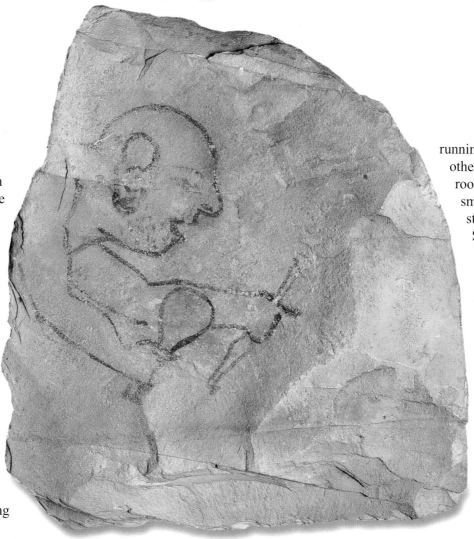

▲ *In addition to their work in the Valley of the Kings, the Deir el-Medina tomb builders such as this stonemason, might take commissions from the wealthy folk of Thebes to quarry and decorate their rock-cut tombs. 19th Dynasty.*

with the return to Thebes following the Amarna period (when the ruler Akhenaten overshadowed Thebes by building a new religious and political capital named Akhetaten in Middle Egypt), the village of Deir el-Medina was enlarged to include about 12 new houses.

The community was divided into an eastern and western section by a narrow street, which was probably originally roofed over. The 70 or so houses were all similar in design, built in a combination of the usual domestic building material, mudbrick, and rough limestone set in mortar. There were also certain architectural features of stone, such as doorways, and whitewashed walls to reflect the sun. The houses were 5–6m (16–20ft) wide, with four rooms

running one behind the other, two large family rooms, followed by a smaller kitchen and storage room.

Staircases led to the flat roofs that served as extra living space, and cellars were often cut from the desert rock for cool storage. It has been suggested that at any one time the village housed about 25 interrelated families.

Excavation beyond the confines of the village has revealed shrines – smaller versions of the huge stone temples of state deities such as Hathor – just to the north, stables for cows and donkeys, and a rubbish dump to the south. Most excitingly, on the desert hillside to the west, is the main cemetery, with beautifully decorated tombs of the village's inhabitants. There are tomb shafts, small mudbrick chapels, and miniature pyramids.

During the reign of Akhenaten (c.1352–c.1336 BC), the inhabitants of Deir el-Medina probably moved to the site today known as Tell el-Amarna in order to quarry out and decorate the tombs of the élite and royal family of the new city of Akhetaten. Here, in the desert about 1.2km (³/4 mile) from the main city of Akhetaten, a village has been excavated. It was roughly 70m (77yd) square, with a thick enclosure wall surrounding 73 identically sized houses and one larger one. The whole settlement was divided into two unequal parts by a thick wall. In its environs were buildings such as chapels, pigsties and storehouses.

Tomb Robbery

◄ *Upon death the king was identified with Osiris. Ramesses II's presence in his mortuary temple, the Ramesseum, includes semi-mummiform figures of him as Osiris attached to the columns.*

external threats (especially from the Libyans to the west and the Nubians to the south). Compared with these, tomb robbery might have been regarded as a minor trouble, but in fact it was taken extremely seriously. After all, to enter a sealed tomb and remove its contents, destroying – or at least endangering – the mummified body in the process (robbers often burned mummies) would have been considered a threat to the existence of the deceased in the Afterlife. In the case of the king it was even a threat to the stability and well-being of Egypt and its people, since the ancient Egyptians believed that the dead were able to affect the lives of the living.

The plunder of Egyptian tombs is by no means a modern phenomenon. At all periods of ancient Egyptian history the possible threat of tomb robbery had to be guarded against, and precautions – such as stone portcullises, confusing corridors and deep pits – were incorporated into all types of tombs. The prolific ancient evidence for disturbance, destruction and theft from tombs reveals just how unsuccessful these measures tended to be. Of most interest to tomb robbers were goods that could be disposed of easily, such as textiles, perfumes and cosmetics, precious woods and ivory. Also valued were objects made from materials that could be recycled, such as gold and silver.

The most detailed and extensive documentation about tomb (and temple) robbery dates to the end of the New Kingdom, during the reigns of Ramesses IX (c.1126–c.1108 BC) and Ramesses XI (c.1099–c.1069 BC). This was a time of various problems, such as ineffectual

rulers, corruption and bribery throughout officialdom, a possible civil war, agricultural failure, inflation and

▼ *In this illustration from Olfert Dapper's* Description de l'Afrique *(1686) the tomb robbers are huddled around an Egyptian mummy.*

▲ *The hypostyle hall at Medinet Habu provided a barrier between the outer courts of the mortuary temple and the mysterious inner sanctuaries.*

The tomb robbery papyri

A number of judicial papyri, known as the 'tomb robbery papyri', tell us how the tomb robbers were dealt with. As they concerned the plunder of royal tombs in the Valley of the Kings, it is not surprising that the king seems to have been personally responsible for setting up a commission to investigate the robberies. A court (*kenbet*) was set up to hear the proceedings at Ramesses III's mortuary temple at Medinet Habu,

and scribes were present at all times to record the trials and the confessions. The court records appear to have been hidden for safekeeping in the mortuary temple of Medinet Habu.

The document known as Papyrus Mayer B of Ramesses IX's reign is a detailed account of the theft of bronze and copper vessels, utensils, clothes and textiles from the tomb of Ramesses IX in the Valley of the Kings. Other documents contain references to the theft of objects by the foreman Paneb from the tomb of Seti II, and an attempted entry into the tomb of Ramesses II and his children's tomb in

the twenty-ninth year of Ramesses III's reign. (This is the same year as the earliest strike in recorded history, staged by the workman of Deir el-Medina when they did not receive their usual pay.)

The Abbott and Amherst Papyri are dated to the sixteenth year of Ramesses IX's reign. They recount the inspection of both royal and non-royal tombs that it was claimed had been violated, and the beatings and confessions of certain thieves. Other papyri contain accounts of thefts by priests from temple buildings (including Ramesses III's temple at Medinet Habu), and the recovery of gold, silver and copper from tomb thieves, all of whom turned out to be members of the necropolis staff.

Punishment for theft

There is evidence of the guilty being imprisoned in the Temple of Maat at Thebes, threats of mutilation, including having the nose and ears cut off, and of being sent to Ethiopia. But the ultimate punishment for tomb robbery must have been death. Seven men were put to death on the stake following a trial described in three separate papyri.

Royal mummy caches

The tomb robberies in the Valley of the Kings at the end of the New Kingdom seriously threatened the survival of the royal mummies. In about 1000 BC the worried priests made the important decision to transfer the bodies of 56 dead kings and queens to safer hiding places. Forty of these mummies were discovered in a tomb near Deir el-Bahri in 1881. The other 16 were unearthed 17 years later in the tomb of Amenhotep II in the Valley of the Kings.

Popular Religion

Ancient Egyptian life was beset by trials and tribulations. These included dangerous animals such as scorpions, snakes, hippopotami, crocodiles, lions and hyenas; the loss of livestock and crops; famine; infertility; infant mortality and illness. All these had to be contended with, and religious beliefs were often the best way to explain otherwise inexplicable calamities. Rituals could help to solve everyday problems and maintain stability and well being.

'Popular religion' is the term used to describe this day-to-day religion of the people, but the evidence is so biased towards the literate, wealthy minority that it requires careful detective work to glean any information about the ideas and practices of the ordinary person. We can, however, learn about the private aspects of folk religion from finds such as a desperate, childless woman's votive offering of a fertility figurine at the local shrine of Hathor, the cow goddess of fertility; and the more public ones, such as a community's celebration of a divine festival at the local cult temple.

Magic and superstition played a crucial part in daily life, and were by no means considered unorthodox or an alternative to the religion of the state temples. A priest used to performing rituals in the cult of a state deity could also be called upon to carry out what we would term magic or sorcery. State and popular religion were clearly interrelated.

◀ *Crocodiles and hippopotami were among the perils of daily life that needed to be safeguarded against. This Nilotic scene appears on the wall of Meremka's 6th dynasty tomb at Saqqara.*

Magic

Clement of Alexandria, writing in the third century AD, observed that 'Egypt was the mother of magicians', and right up to the present day, Egypt has been viewed by those outside it as a place of magic and mysticism. The ancient Egyptians had a word, *heka*, which we translate as 'magic'. But we must not corrupt its meaning with the modern associations of magic – the idea of magic as non-establishment, or as an alternative to the generally accepted religious norm, would not have applied in ancient Egypt.

Heka, for the ancient Egyptians, conveyed a sense of the catalyst or energy that made creation possible. So every time a ritual was performed involving *heka*, it was as if a further development was thought to have been made in the process of creation. In the mythology of creation, *heka* was associated with *sia*, 'divine knowledge', and *hu*, 'divine utterance'. *Heka* itself was considered to be neither good or bad, but as an energy or power it could be channelled in either direction. The recorded incidents of what might be called antisocial magic in ancient Egypt tend to be fairly rare before the Roman Period, and any instances of unacceptable magic were usually attributed to foreign sorcerers. Similar to *heka* was *akhu*, which tends to be translated as 'sorcery', 'enchantments' or 'spells'. Again, *akhu* was in itself neither a negative nor a positive phenomenon and it could be worked in either direction.

There would have been certain members of each local community

◄ *Seneb, an achondroplastic dwarf, was Chief of all Palace Dwarves, in charge of the royal wardrobe and a priest of the mortuary cults of kings Khufu and Djedefre, so he was clearly highly respected and by no means ostracized.*

Magical cures

Magic aided the search for an answer to the perennial question 'Why me?' If a woman was suffering from a headache and convulsions, she might be visited by a respected member of the community (see *Who Performed Magic?*). He or she might trace the source of the disease to the anger of a particular deity, the magic of a foreign sorcerer, the malevolence of a demon or the ghost of a dead relative (see *The Negative Influence of the Dead*). The solution might then have been the performance of a ritual, including the recitation of a spell, in order to cure the woman. Deities and the dead tended to cause particular problems for the living when their temples or funerary chapels fell into disrepair or their offerings were forgotten.

who were credited with the ability to perform rituals using *heka*. There were also people who were believed to have an intrinsic possession of the force – either having been born with it, as dwarves were thought to be, or gaining it during certain periods of their life, as was the case with breast-feeding women. All kings, deities and the dead, by their very nature, were thought to have a certain degree of *heka*.

God of magic

The ancient Egyptians chose to personify divinely all that was crucial to them, including abstract concepts and natural phenomena. In this way they could pay their respects and make offerings to them, in order to ensure their continued and benevolent existence. The magical force of *heka* was divinely personified as the god Heka, who was represented in human form, holding snakes crossed in front of him. Like the household gods and goddesses, no major cult centres dedicated to Heka, or temples built in honour of him. He was worshipped as a secondary deity at Heliopolis, Memphis and Esna, and his

presence would have been ubiquitous in the temples throughout the country dedicated to other deities. We can discover something of the nature and characteristics of Heka by reading a range of ancient texts from different periods of Egyptian history. The Coffin Texts of the Middle Kingdom (c.2055–c.1650 BC) describe him as 'the unique lord made before duality had yet come into being', while he is referred to as 'Lord of Oracles, Lord of Miracles, who predicts what will happen' in an inscription found on the Graeco-Roman temple at Esna.

We also know of a goddess called Weret Hekau, meaning 'Great of Magic'. She took the form of a cobra, and it is possible that the snake-shaped wands used by those skilled in magic were crafted in this way in order to represent this goddess. The rearing cobra, known as a *uraeus*, on the front of the royal headdress, which was poised ready to spit venom at the king's enemies, was also sometimes described as *weret hekau*.

Wands and spells

A variety of wands and other paraphernalia of popular ritual have survived from ancient Egypt, as have collections of magic spells recorded on papyrus. The aim of these spells tended to be to ward off danger, such as the threats posed by snakes and scorpions, and to prevent or cure illness and particularly problems relating to fertility, pregnancy and birth. As in funerary religion, there was clearly a strongly held belief in the creative power of the words and images used in Egyptian magic. Knowledge of the relevant names was essential for the magic to prove effective.

Another important aspect of ancient Egyptian magic was sympathetic magic.

The mythology told that as a young boy, Horus had survived the threat of snakes and scorpions in the marshes of the Delta, and so if children were identified with the young god, they too could be protected from harm. Similarly, the goddess Isis (or Hathor, depending on the text) had successfully given birth to Horus, and so a woman having a difficult labour might transfer the pain by identifying herself with that goddess (see *Rites of Passage*).

▲ *The deity Heka was represented anthropomorphically, sometimes holding two crossed snakes.*

▲ *This wooden female figurine, found in a tomb under the Ramesseum in western Thebes, holds metal snake wands. It is uncertain whether the figure represents a goddess with a leonine head (perhaps Beset) or a woman wearing a mask,*

Who Performed Magic?

Every community in Egypt must have had at least one wise person to whom the local people turned in times of need. This person was trusted and believed able to offer advice and perform rituals, using *heka*, or magic, to solve people's problems. Various titles have survived indicating the particular areas of expertise of these people. As was usual with Egyptian professions, it is likely that a father would have handed down his skills and secret knowledge to his son (or a mother to her daughter), and so one family would probably have become well known for practising magic over many generations.

Chiefs of mysteries

The word *hekau* (sometimes translated 'magician') existed as a general term for anyone who used magic, and a title that was obviously associated with magic was that of *Hery Seshta*, 'Chief of Mysteries or Secrets'. This title was found on the lid of a wooden box in a tomb of the late Middle Kingdom found under the Ramesseum in western Thebes. The box was among a selection of objects that had evidently been used for magical purposes. They included spells and religious papyri, a bronze snake wand, a wooden female figure wearing a mask of Beset (the female form of the protective spirit-deity Bes) and holding metal snake wands, a female fertility figurine, an ivory clapper and part of a magic rod.

The owner of this equipment for performing magical rituals was a priest, who would presumably have played an important role in the life of the local temple and that of the community. It may have been the figure known as the Lector Priest, whose job was also an extramural one. It was the Lector Priest who was responsible for reciting the spells in the temple, and during the embalming process and funerals. Among their other special skills, Lector

Priests were believed to be able to interpret dreams.

Other temple titles associated with the performance of magical rites were '*Hekau* of the House of Life' and 'Scribe of the House of Life'. There would have been a House of Life in most temple complexes. It was a place of copying, reading and research, rather like a library, scriptorium, school and university rolled into one.

Another important man was the *Sau*. It is uncertain exactly what he did, but the word *sa* is the word for both 'protection' and 'amulet', and so *Sau*

▲ *The lioness goddess Sekhmet, who was feared as the bringer of disease, paradoxically became associated with healing because of the need to appease her wrath. The title 'Priest of Sekhmet' became synonymous with 'doctor'.*

tends to be given the rather ambiguous translation, 'amulet man'. Perhaps he was responsible for making the amulets required by the local villagers or townspeople. Or perhaps, once a craftsman had manufactured the amulets, he was able to perform the ritual that would imbue the amulets with magical significance and supernatural

▲ *Selket appears as a protective deity together with Isis, Nephthys and Neith on the four corners of Tutankhamun's golden shrine.*

Scorpion charmers

Someone whose skills would have been much sought after was the *Kherep Selket*, literally, 'the one who has power over the scorpion goddess' – or, the local scorpion charmer (who no doubt also charmed snakes). The enormous numbers of spells to ward off snakes and scorpions, and to cure their bites, indicate the extent of the problem, and one that is still common in Egypt today. Modern snake charmers use practical techniques to ensnare their prey, but they also rely on magical chanting.

In ancient Egypt, a Lector Priest and a doctor could also hold the title *Kherep Selket*. The title *Sunu*, 'doctor' or 'physician', was held by people who prescribed both medical and magical remedies (see *Medicine*). The priests of the lioness goddess Sekhmet specialized in medicine and were closely associated with magic. Because this goddess was feared as the bringer of plague and other disease, magical rituals had to be performed in order to appease her and dissuade her from doing harm.

powers. The records show that the *Sau* could be a woman, especially if she was also a midwife or a nurse.

A more specifically female title was *Rekhet* (literally 'knowing one'), which can probably best be translated 'wise woman'. The *Rekhet* appears to have been a medium, so if someone believed he was suffering because of the anger of one of his deceased relatives, he would consult a Rekhet. She would then liaise with the spirit world to find out which relative required appeasing (see *The Negative Influence of the Dead*).

▲ *Animal figurines (usually turtles, lions and crocodiles) were often attached to the top side of decorated hollow 'magic rods' which were probably used to establish the magician's authority over these various animals.*

Medicine

As far as the ancient Egyptians were concerned, there was no clear distinction between magic and medicine, and the two were fundamentally interrelated. About ten papyri have survived containing texts that today we call magico-medical texts because they combine the use of various remedies (to be taken internally, applied externally, or administered by fumigation), together with spells to be recited as part of magical rituals incorporating amulets and other such devices. It was crucial that the seemingly rational cures, which clearly influenced Greek medicine, were used in conjunction with spells. A woman suffering from irregular periods, for example, was advised to take a herbal remedy while reciting an incantation.

As already noted, the title *Sunu*, which means 'doctor' or 'physician', was held by people who practised both practical medical and magical techniques. The priests of the goddess Sekhmet would have been involved in temple rituals, but they also specialized in medicine.

Magico-medical papyri

During the third century AD, Clement of Alexandria observed that of the 42 books that comprised the sum total of all Egyptian knowledge, six were devoted to medicine, covering the topics of anatomy, illnesses, surgical instruments, drugs, eye ailments and gynaecology. These books have never been discovered, but various papyri do provide us with interesting information on all these subjects. Diagnosis was clearly based on both clinical examination and empirical knowledge. Pregnancy, for example, was diagnosed by pulse rate, propensity to vomit and internal gas, together with the appearance of the eyes, breasts and skin pigmentation. It appears that the Egyptian approach to medicine was perhaps more 'scientific' than in Babylonia and Assyria, where illness

tended to be more readily attributed to possession by demons. The ancient Egyptians accepted that some illnesses were incurable and so did not attempt to treat them. They also realized, for example, the effect of diet on a person's health (a Roman Period papyrus, Papyrus Insinger, blames ailments in the limbs on overeating).

▲ *This wooden statue represents a doctor who was practising his medical skills as early as the 5th Dynasty.*

Many of the ingredients for the prescriptions in the magico-medical texts are decidedly unappealing. For example, at least 19 different types of excrement are mentioned, including that

▶ *The medicinal use of onion appears frequently in the magico-medical papyri, for example in remedies for snake bites. This wall painting in the Theban tomb of Nakht shows them being carried. 18th Dynasty.*

of the fly and the ostrich. The logic behind such a peculiar choice of medicine appears to have been the principle of treating like with like. Rotting food trapped in the body was thought to cause a range of problems, and remedies containing faeces were thought to encourage these residues to travel out of the body.

Useful drugs

The Egyptians were the first people to use a number of drugs that modern studies have proved would have been medicinally effective. Honey, for example, was used both for magical and ritual purposes (see *Demons* and *Rites of Passage*), and for medical ones. It is now known to be resistant to bacterial growth, to act as a hypertonic – drawing water from bacterial cells, causing them to shrivel and die – and to exhibit antibiotic action due to a bacterial enzyme called inhibine which is secreted by the pharyngeal glands of the bee. It has proved to be efficacious against staphylococcus, salmonella and candida bacteria, and has been used to treat surgical wounds, ulcers and burns. In the Nineteenth-Dynasty Papyrus Leiden 1,348, the first of the spells prescribed for the cure of burns was to be said over a dressing of honey.

Onion occurs in the ancient texts, and it is now known that onion juice is an antibiotic, a diuretic and an expectorant.

▶ *Only the lower portion survives of this statue of the kneeling figure of the physician Horkheb. Beneath his offering of* hes-*jars is an inscribed 'Appeal to the Living' that priests should make offerings to his spirit now that he is dead, with a curse on those who fail to do so. 26th Dynasty.*

▲ *A number of implements are depicted on an offering table on this wall relief in the temple of Kom Ombo. There is much uncertainty as to their use, but they are probably Roman surgical instruments (the relief dates to the latter half of the 2nd century AD).*

Garlic was also used for medicinal purposes, and its healing properties are generally accepted today. It is said to contain an amino-acid derivative called allium, which releases the enzyme allinase. Its antibacterial qualities (it is an antibiotic exhibiting 1% of the strength of penicillin) are useful for treating wounds, and it is antifungal against candida. Thanks to the presence of methyl allyl trisulphide, which works to dilate the blood-vessel walls, it thins blood, lowers blood pressure and helps to prevent heart attack. It also lowers cholesterol levels, aids digestion and stimulates the immune system.

Ox liver or its juice was employed in ancient Egypt for night blindness, and we now know that animal liver is high in vitamin A and may indeed be effective against some forms of night blindness.

The various prescriptions did not necessarily have to be taken internally, but might be applied to parts of the body – for instance, raw meat used on wounds is very good for stopping bleeding.

The mouse cure

Some outlandish remedies, which we would not expect to find anywhere but in ancient sources, do actually occur much closer to home and almost to the present day. For example, according to the Nineteenth-Dynasty papyrus now known as Berlin 3027, which deals with the illnesses of young children and their mothers, the cure for an uncertain illness called *sesmi* was to eat a cooked mouse. This remedy can be found used in a very similar way in the works of Dioscorides, Pliny, the Algerian physician 'Abd er-Razzak at the end of the seventh century AD, and the Arabic physician Ibn el-Betar in the thirteenth century AD. Mouse also figures in Culpeper's *Pharmacopoeia Londinensis* (1653), and in the *Pharmacopoeia Universalis* (1831). It has been said that in England during the 1920s, mouse was flayed, fried, boiled or made into pie and given to children in order to cure incontinence, dribbling and whooping cough.

Because it was usual for the ingestion of remedies to be accompanied by magic rites, Papyrus Berlin 3027 states that the bones of the mouse should be wrapped in a linen cloth (often stipulated for amuletic devices), knotted with seven knots (a magic number) and worn around the neck. A similar practice has been found among the Tlokwa of Botswana. The magical potency of the mouse may relate to a belief expressed by Pliny, and found in medieval bestiaries, that the mouse spontaneously emerged from the Nile mud after inundation.

Demons

The ancient Egyptians used magic to guard against the possible threat of demons and other malevolent forces, such as evil spirits, ghosts and hostile manifestations of deities. Demons were believed to be able to cause a variety of problems, especially illness. It has already been noted that the ancient Egyptians did not regard magic and medicine as distinct entities, but as very much interrelated (see *Medicine*). Demons were particularly associated with the goddess Sekhmet, who was regarded as the bringer of plague and other serious illness. In fact, there was a class of demon known as the 'Messengers of Sekhmet'. Sekhmet was also associated with fire and heat, so a fever might be blamed on her demons. Headaches and stomach problems were often said to be caused by demons contaminating the ill person's body, and so an emetic might be prescribed in an attempt to rid the person of the demon.

The desert and the netherworld

Demons were thought either to live in the desert, which was barren and associated with Seth, the god of chaos and infertility, or in an inverted netherworld. This meant that they lived upside down, so their mouths were where their anuses should have been, and they were said to eat their own faeces. In direct contrast to humans, for whom honey was sweet and delicious, demons were believed to find it bitter, and even to fear it. For this reason, honey was ideal for use in rituals to ward off demons and evil spirits. After giving birth, a woman might eat a cake made of honey, presumably to give her energy, but also to keep demons at bay at this particularly vulnerable time in her and her newborn baby's life. Garlic was also believed to have an apotropaic effect on demons. It was said to harm them, and so it was used in spells and rituals to protect young children against malevolent spirits.

▲ *In ancient Egyptian religion the knife was considered a magic weapon.*

▼ *An important aim of funerary spells was to help the dead person deal with demons in the underworld. The donkey was identified with the demon par excellence, Seth: in the Book of the Dead of Chensumose, it is depicted trussed as a way of controlling its malevolence. 21st Dynasty.*

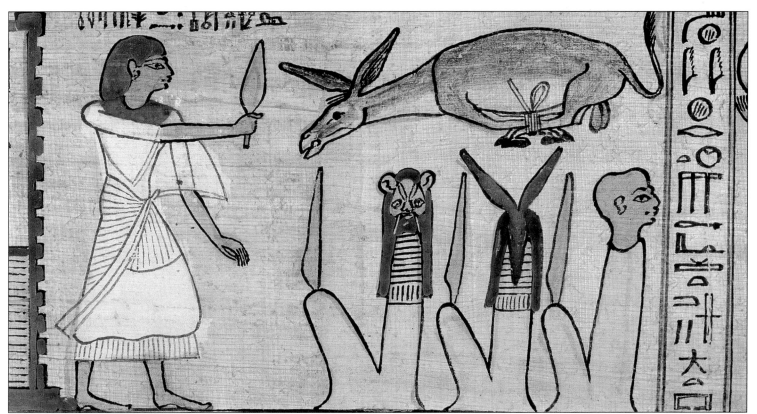

Household Deities

The two deities most closely associated with protection of the household and family life, especially women and children, were Bes and Taweret. They must have been close to the hearts of the ancient Egyptians, as they feature heavily in the various spells associated with illness and the hazards of everyday life. Like Heka (see *Magic*), no cult temple was dedicated to either of these deities, but their presence was ubiquitous in family life. Although they were associated with the relatively peaceful environment of the household, they could certainly be forces to be reckoned with. It was important to stay on the right side of these deities, by invoking them and making offerings to them. Both deities could be depicted looking surprisingly fierce, with teeth bared and tongue sticking out. It is thought that this may well have been for apotropaic reasons – that their aggressive expressions would scare away evil influences – and so their presence at particularly vulnerable times, such as childbirth and childhood, would have been deemed valuable. Bes was also thought to be able to ward off snakes from the house.

Bes the spirit-deity

It would probably be more correct to refer to Bes as a spirit or a benevolent demon than as a fully fledged deity. In fact, Bes may well have been a generic term for a number of protective demons. He was represented as a rather strange bandy-legged dwarf, with a lion's ears and mane, and a tail. He often wore a feathered headdress and an animal pelt over his back, and held a *sa* amulet of protection. His appearance ranged from jovial to really quite ferocious. He was often depicted playing musical instruments and hopping about, especially in the context of childbirth. His head appears in a protective capacity above the naked figure of the child Horus on the stelae known as *cippi* of Horus (see *Paraphernalia of Ritual*).

◀ *Taweret's name means 'the Great One'. In the magical texts she is sometimes referred to as 'sow' (*reret*).*

▲ *The female musician playing the lute on this faience dish has the image of the protective spirit Bes tattooed on her thigh. 18th Dynasty.*

The hippopotamus goddess

Taweret was portrayed as a hippopotamus standing on her hind legs, with a large stomach and pendulous breasts, so there was a clear visual association with pregnant women, and she could be called on to help every woman, whether royal or commoner, in childbirth. To heighten her apotropaic, or protective, capacity she was made to look more terrifying by having a crocodile tail on her back and a leonine muzzle, arms and legs. The most terrifying guise the ancient Egyptians could give a deity was as a composite animal incorporating elements of dangerous creatures, the prime example of which was the funerary demon Ammit (see *The Weighing of the Heart*). Taweret was often portrayed wearing a headdress composed of a low *modius* (a cylindrical headdress) surmounted by two plumes, sometimes with horns and a disc. She usually clutched a *sa*, *ankh* or *tyet*-amulet (see *Amulets*).

◄ Cosmetic spoons and dishes were often decorated with the image of a duck, which appears to have had erotic connotations. Bes was also a common motif on toilet objects and other personal possessions.

particularly vulnerable time, not only to actual threats such as scorpions but also to ghosts and nightmares. In keeping with their apotropaic presence, Bes and Taweret were often depicted brandishing knives. The figure of Bes was also used as a tattoo, usually on the upper thigh of female singers and musicians.

The persistence of tradition

The archaeological record at the site of Tell el-Amarna reveals that however radically the Eighteenth-Dynasty 'revolutionary' King Akhenaten (c.1352–c.1336 BC) attempted to change the state religion, there was no way that he was going to succeed in stamping out the traditional popular beliefs of the ancient Egyptian people. The presence of numerous amulets in the form of these domestic deities, and a stela depicting a mother and child worshipping Taweret (found under the stairs in one of the houses in the Main City) are good evidence for the continued reliance of the average person on the deities of most immediate importance in their lives. In the walled village at Tell el-Amarna, as well as in the tomb builders' village at Deir el-Medina, fragments of wall painting have been discovered in the main living rooms of some of the houses, which include Bes and Taweret in their design. Both deities were ever-present in the lives of most ordinary ancient Egyptian people.

Amulets and furniture

An incredible number of amulets in the miniature form of these deities have survived, so their popularity is evident. They were also incorporated into the design of furniture (especially beds), musical instruments, pottery and other vessels. Faience vessels have been found in the form of Taweret with a pouring hole in place of one of her nipples, and it is assumed that these would originally have contained milk. Images of Bes and Taweret on headrests would have been popular because sleep was considered a

Paraphernalia of Ritual

A variety of unusual objects have been discovered whose definite use and symbolic value will probably always remain uncertain. But this leaves us exciting scope for speculation. Rituals pertaining to the trials, tribulations and celebrations of everyday life would have been performed in the home, at shrines and at tombs or graves (especially those of relatives). The 'equipment' of popular ritual and belief included wands, amulets, votive objects, ceremonial vessels and a range of other artefacts, both inscribed and uninscribed.

Figurines

In the early twentieth century, the female figurines that today are called 'fertility figurines' were regarded as symbolic 'concubine figures' placed in tombs to service the sexual needs of the deceased male tomb owner. Closer scrutiny of the archaeological contexts of these objects has revealed that a larger number have actually been found in temple and domestic contexts than in tombs, so they were more frequently a ritual object of the living rather than of the dead.

Most are likely to have been votive offerings to deities such as the goddess of fertility, Hathor, and spirits of the dead particularly fathers, see *The Positive Influence of the Dead*. They may have been offerings from women who were unable to conceive, and who were seeking help from the divine or spirit world to solve their desperate problem. They tended to be made out of clay, wood or faience, and the emphasis in the fashioning of them was quite clearly on the pubic region and, to a lesser extent, the breasts. Sometimes the head was merely a 'pinch' of the clay, and the feet were rarely modelled. It has been suggested that this was a deliberate device to prevent the figurine from

▶ *The patterns on some female fertility figurines are thought to represent tattoos. Middle Kingdom.*

◀ *Over a dozen feminoform vessels have been found, all dating to the Eighteenth and Nineteenth Dynasties, and perhaps made to contain milk. They range from 11–17cm (4½–6½in) in height.*

▲ *By depicting the enemies of Egypt in a subdued state, it was believed this would magically become reality. Tutankhamun's ceremonial stool shows Syrians and Libyans on the top surface, and Nubians and Sudanese on its underside.*

leaving the place where it was deposited, since the ancient Egyptians believed in the magical creative properties of their religious imagery. We can be more certain of the purpose of these figurines when they were inscribed, usually with a woman's plea for a child (infertility was always regarded as a woman's problem).

There is evidence for private fertility cults that would have made use of a selection of ritual paraphernalia. A cache of votive material was discovered under the stairs of a house at the site of Tell el-Amarna, the ancient capital city of Akhetaten. The stash included a stela showing a woman and child worshipping the household goddess Taweret, two broken female figurines, and two model beds. It is impossible to tell whether these objects had been hidden here, were placed here for safekeeping, or whether this was in fact the location of a household shrine.

Another magical type of figurine was the execration figurine – a rough clay figure of a bound captive, often inscribed with a curse against a named foreign ruler, a group of people, or a particular place. The knowledge of a name was of magical significance and allowed the exercise of magical control over the possible threat of the foreigner. Often such a figure would be smashed in an execration ritual to destroy the power of the foreign ruler. Such execration texts were also sometimes inscribed on pottery bowls, which might be similarly ritually smashed and buried.

Ritual vessels

Various types of vessel clearly had a ritual significance, for example those in the form of pregnant and breast feeding women, and the deities Bes and Taweret. Pots have been discovered in the form of pregnant women with their hands rubbing their distended stomachs. These pots often date to the Eighteenth Dynasty (c.1550–c.1295 BC) and tend to be made of calcite (although there is a particularly

fine pottery example from Abydos in the Cairo Museum). The oil they contained would have been used to ease stretch marks and may have had some aromatherapeutic value, but the pots themselves would have also had a sympathetic magical significance. Several pots have been discovered with tampons painted on them. These were used to prevent miscarriage, and so a woman who possessed a feminoform vessel protected in this way would have hoped that she would benefit from the magical security it offered.

Pots dating to the Eighteenth and Nineteenth Dynasties (c.1550–c.1186 BC) have also been found in the form of breast-feeding women, sometimes with a spout in place of a nipple. Breast milk may have been stored in these vessels. Lactating women's milk was an important ingredient in several spells and remedies, indicating belief in its magical potency. It is possible that whatever the type of milk stored in a feminoform jar, it was believed to magically 'become' women's milk, and so might be used for magical purposes.

Cippi of Horus

Spells were often recorded on ritual objects, such as a type of stela known as a *cippus* of Horus. Examples that have survived tend to be made of stone or wood, and range in date from 1400 BC to the second century AD. The focus of each *cippus* was an image of the god Horus as a child (depicted naked and wearing the characteristic hairstyle of childhood, the 'sidelock of youth') triumphing over a selection of dangerous animals such as crocodiles, snakes and

◀ *The protective influence of the spirit-deity Bes was harnessed on the stelae called* cippi *of Horus used in the later period of Egyptian history, and held here by a healing statue inscribed with magical texts. Ptolemaic Period.*

scorpions. A representation of the head of the protective spirit-deity Bes tends to figure over Horus. Much of the rest of each *cippus* is covered in spells relating to dangers such as snakes and scorpions. The idea seems to have been that water (perhaps ideally rainwater) was poured over the *cippus* so that it would become magically imbued with the potency of the spells. The water could then be drunk or applied externally as a cure, antidote or preventative against hazards such as scorpion bites. Like breast milk, rainwater was considered to be of particular magical and medicinal effectiveness. For some reason we shall probably never know, it was thought to be especially effective in the healing of leg ailments.

Identical in purpose to the *cippi* were 'healing statues', of which a particularly fine example is that of Djedhor now in the Cairo Museum. He holds a *cippus*, but all the available surfaces of Djedhor, himself, together with the plinth on which he kneels, are also covered in spells. Water was obviously meant to run over the statue because it sits in a collecting trough, and there is at least one channel for draining off the water.

Wands

The most treasured possession of a practitioner of magic, such as a *Hery Seshta* ('Chief of Mysteries or Secrets'), would probably have been his wand. Three types have survived from ancient Egypt: the snake-shaped wand, the apotropaic (or protective wand) and the magic rod.

Snake-shaped wands were usually made of bronze. They could either be elongated, such as the Eighteenth-Dynasty example in the British Museum, London, or more coiled, such as the one dating to the First Intermediate Period (c.2181–c.2055 BC) in the Fitzwilliam Museum in Cambridge. It is possible that these wands were believed to represent the cobra-form goddess Weret Hekau ('Great of Magic'). Depictions of the divine personification of magic, Heka, show him holding two crossed snakes, and wooden and ivory figures masked like Bes or Beset, and connected with magic, hold metal snake wands. The Old Testament Book of Exodus records that the magicians attending Pharaoh performed the miracle of turning their wands into serpents.

Apotropaic wands

About 150 curved apotropaic wands have been found, mainly dating to the First Intermediate Period and Middle Kingdom (c.2181– c.1650

BC). They could be made of calcite, faience or ebony, but were usually of hippopotamus ivory. It is therefore possible that a deliberate association was being made with Taweret, the hippopotamus goddess. All manner of weird and wonderful magical imagery decorate these wands, including dancing baboons, snake-breathing lions, winged quadrupeds, human-headed winged snakes and sun discs on legs. More conventional representations of vultures, hippopotami, frogs and crocodiles also appear, as do depictions of protective *sa* and *udjat*-eye amulets and Seth, the god of chaos and infertility, as well as the apotropaic household deities Bes and Taweret, who are often shown wielding knives in a rather threatening fashion. Sometimes the terminal of the wand is adorned with the head of a leopard. When the wands are inscribed, the brief inscriptions are concerned with protection.

The inscriptions and imagery imply that these wands were used to benefit women and children, particularly at times of birth and early childhood. Their exact ritual purpose is uncertain. Perhaps they were placed or touched upon the pregnant woman or newborn child, or used to mark out a magic space in which the pregnant woman or mother and child would be protected from misfortune.

Magic rods

Similar imagery can be found on the magic rods that have survived from the Middle Kingdom and Second Intermediate periods of ancient

It is possible that the break in this ivory apotropaic wand was done deliberately before it was placed in a tomb. On its other side this wand is inscribed with a promise of protection for the Lady of the House, Seneb.

Egyptian history (c.2055–c.1550 BC). Glazed steatite examples incorporate representations of frogs, turtles, baboons, crocodiles and felines, as well as lamps and amuletic symbols such as *sa*s and *udjat*-eyes. These rods would have had miniature models of the animals attached to them using tiny pegs. We are not certain how they were employed, but they were presumably used to dominate the animals depicted on them, and turn their power into a protective rather than a malignant force. Some magical spells refer to the brandishing of a stick or a branch (the poor man's bronze or ivory wand), particularly in the commanding of malevolent spirits and demons.

◄ *This coiled serpent wand was found in a tomb under the Ramesseum in western Thebes, tangled in a mass of hair.*

Amulets

Amulets were miniature devices believed to endow the owner or wearer with powers or magical protection. The ancient Egyptian words for 'amulet' – *sa*, *meket* and *nehet* – all derived from verbs meaning 'to guard' or 'to protect', while a fourth term – *wedja* – had the same sound as the word meaning 'well being'.

The earliest recognizable amulets date back to the Badarian phase of the Predynastic Period (c.5500–c.4000 BC). They have been found in graves, but it is likely that they were also considered useful to the owners during their lifetimes. We have no texts for the Predynastic Period, so cannot know the significance of these amulets. An amulet of an antelope's or gazelle's head, for example, might have been considered to be able to turn the owner into a successful hunter of the animal; it might have blessed the owner with the swiftness attributed to the animal; or if the animal was associated with evil, as it was later in Pharaonic history, it might have served an apotropaic purpose.

Stringing and knotting

Most amulets had a loop attached so that they could be suspended. Some rare examples of the original stringing have survived – intricately twisted and knotted thread made from flax fibres. The ancient Egyptians may have worn their amulets beautifully strung around their necks for all to see, but the evidence appears to indicate that they were probably knotted and bundled together and secreted somewhere safe on the person. We know that the tying and untying of knots were certainly very important in ancient Egyptian magic. The magico-medical texts record that

▶ *The decoration on Tutankhamun's chest includes the alternation of the* ankh *and the* was- *sceptre (symbolizing power) above the hieroglyphic sign of a basket meaning 'all'.*

amuletic images were sometimes painted or drawn on linen placed on the patient's body. Or they could be drawn directly on the patient's hand and then licked off. We also learn from the texts that certain spells were to be recited over very specific amulets. Spell 30 of the magical text on Papyrus Leiden 1,348, had to be recited four times over a 'dwarf of clay' placed on the forehead of a woman suffering from a difficult labour. This would probably have been an amulet of the dwarf spirit-deity Bes.

Miniature representations of deities such as Bes, Taweret and Hathor were acquired to ensure the protection and influences of the divine world. Other popular amulets were the scarab, with its creative and solar associations, the protective *udjat* or Eye of Horus, associated with wholeness and healing, and the *tyet* (see *Funerary Amulets*).

The *tyet*-amulet was particularly important for the protection of women during pregnancy and childbirth, because it was associated with Isis and,

▲ *The best known of all ancient Egyptian amulets is the scarab, examples of which have been found made of every material known to the Egyptians.*

more specifically, with her blood. We cannot be certain of its meaning but it is knot shaped. It possibly represented the knotted girdle of the goddess, or it has also been suggested that it represented a tampon inserted into Isis when she was pregnant so that she would not miscarry

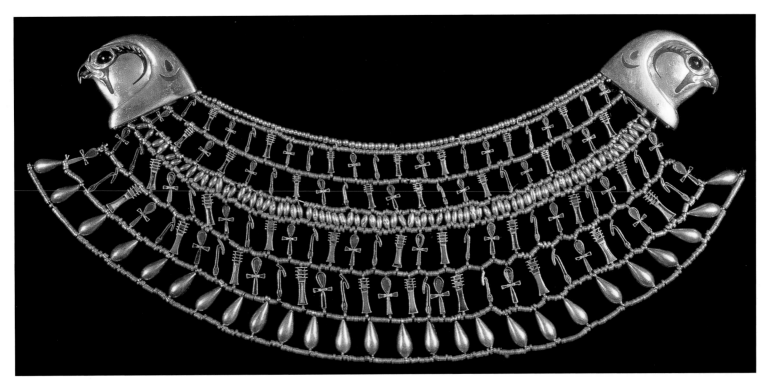

▲ *The* ankh, djed, *and* was *amuletic signs are often found together, with the symbolic meaning of 'life, stability and power'. This collar belonged to Khnumit, daughter of the 12th-Dynasty king Amenemhat II.*

or so that her wicked brother Seth could not harm the son she was carrying. It would therefore have been hoped that by sympathetic magic, the owner or wearer of the amulet would also be protected against miscarriage.

Two other amulets that would have been particularly meaningful in popular religion were the *ankh* and the *sa*. The *ankh* was the hieroglyphic symbol for 'life' (or perhaps, more specifically, the life-giving elements of air and water), and may have represented a sandal strap, or perhaps a more elaborate knot or bow. The *sa* was an amulet of protection, and may have represented a mobile papyrus shelter, tied up for transportation – vital protection against the sun for anyone who worked out in the fields or desert. The household deities Bes and Taweret were often depicted standing, resting their front paws on *sa* amulets.

As might be expected, these amulets were included in the decoration of magical implements such as apotropaic wands and magic rods (see *Wands*), and ceremonial devices such as the sistrum (see *Music and Dance in Religion*).

They were also included in the design of more secular objects, such as furniture, musical instruments, vessels, cosmetic spoons and mirrors. Other amulets included cowrie shells (either the actual shells or imitations of them made from other materials), which were often strung to make girdles, worn by women to protect their fertility; parts of animals such as claws and hairs from a cat; and models of parts of the human body, plants or animals.

Oracular amuletic decrees

During the late New Kingdom and Third Intermediate Period (c.1100–c.747 BC), amulets also took the form of short spells written on tiny pieces of papyrus rolled up inside cylindrical tubes, designed so that they could be worn around the neck. The text usually read as if it were a proclamation by a deity or the gods in general, promising to protect the wearer and threatening divine retribution to those who endangered him or

▶ *The frog was a symbol of creation, fertility, birth and regeneration. This amulet dates to the 1st Dynasty, but much later on, the Christianized Egyptians adopted the frog as a symbol of the resurrection.*

her. One Twenty-second Dynasty example of an oracular amuletic decree in the British Museum, London, declares:

We shall fill her womb with male and female children. We shall save her...from miscarrying, and from giving birth to twins.

Often it is obvious that the wearers were children, whose fates were decreed by the gods at birth. They were promised long life, good health, lots of possessions, and protection against demons, foreign sorcerers, the Evil Eye and harmful manifestations of the gods and goddesses.

Rites of Passage

Women in society

The primary role of ancient Egyptian women was to have children and to run the household. Ordinary women did their share of hard physical work, such as gathering in the harvest and grinding the corn. They tended to be responsible for food production and were employed as musicians, dancers, acrobats and mourners, among other jobs. Women did not hold public office and it is unlikely than many of them were literate. A woman's status largely depended on that of her husband, but we do know that women of the higher social class were able to sit on local tribunals; witness documents, execute their own last testament; inherit, buy, administer and sell property; free slaves; adopt children; and sue.

I n all cultures, the transitional stages of the human life cycle are vulnerable times, coinciding with the fundamental changes from non-pregnant to pregnant, from foetus to child, and from child to adult. The ancient Egyptians believed that rituals were necessary to help them through the precarious phases of pregnancy, childbirth, early childhood and puberty. All of these, if attained without mishap, were marked by celebrations that involved giving thanks to the gods.

Fertility rituals

A woman's ability to conceive was of paramount importance to the security of her marriage, her social standing, and the comfort of her spirit after death. She would not have fulfilled her expected role in society if she died before bearing children. For this reason it is hardly surprising that childless women should turn to the divine or spirit world for a solution to their problem. There is much evidence of fertility rituals, both within the house – involving imagery of Bes and Taweret (see *Household Deities*) – and at sacred places such as tombs, temples and shrines, involving votive offerings such as fertility figurines (see *Paraphernalia of Ritual*).

Both household deities and great state gods and goddesses, such as the cow goddess Hathor and the ithyphallic god Min, were closely associated with fertility (both of the Egyptian people and of the land). During the Graeco-Roman period, if not earlier, women seem to have exposed their genitals before the cult statue of Hathor in an attempt to assimilate the goddess's fertility. Various amulets were worn, or made as votive offerings, to ensure fertility. These included tiny representations of the deities Bes, Taweret and Hathor, as well as model penises, breasts and female genitals.

An absence of menstruation was clearly linked to pregnancy. Both menstrual and birth blood must have been considered to be impure because women were expected to perform purification rituals after both of these events. Pregnant women were thought to be particularly susceptible to the ill effects caused by harmful spirits and demons. Spells were devised to prevent the demon personification of death from having sexual intercourse with a pregnant woman – a violation that would have had adverse effects on the unborn child.

Ensuring a trouble-free birth

Rituals were performed to ensure that the expectant mother had a trouble-free pregnancy and

▼ *In addition to free-standing fertility figurines, examples exist of limestone or terracotta figures of naked women lying on model beds (sometimes decorated with convolvulus), often with a child (usually male) beside her thigh or being suckled.*

birth, to speed up the labour, to safeguard the newborn baby, and to guarantee the mother an adequate supply of milk. These often involved reciting a particular spell at the appropriate time. Associated with the significance of knots in ancient Egyptian magic, the woman probably bound up her hair very tightly when the baby was due, so that it could be loosened during labour, thereby sympathetically releasing the baby from the womb. Certain props were also used in the popular ritual at birth, such as amulets and apotropaic wands.

Women had their babies squatting on bricks or sitting on a wooden birthing stool. Like all that was of greatest importance in the lives of the ancient Egyptians, the birth brick was divinely personified as the goddess Meskhent. She was depicted as a brick with a human head, or as a woman wearing a headdress consisting of a brick or a peculiar emblem. This may have represented the forked uterus of a cow (or perhaps two long palm shoots with curved tips), or a *peshesh-kaf* knife (a flint fishtailed knife that was used to cut the umbilical cord). It was thought that the goddess predetermined the lives of newborn babies, and their fates were ritually inscribed or recited over the bricks.

Sympathetic magic was also used during childbirth. Spell 28 of the magical text written on Papyrus Leiden 1,348 declares: 'Hathor, the Lady of Dendera is the one giving birth.' This meant that Hathor would give birth, and in so doing suffer on behalf of the woman who was actually in labour; a transfer of pain was believed to take place. The playing of musical instruments, singing and dancing also appear to have been important at the time of childbirth.

It may be that the fragments of wall painting found in houses at Deir el-Medina and the workmen's village at

Tell el-Amarna portray the period of confinement and celebration following a successful birth. The scenes include parts of figures of the household spirit-deity Bes; a dancing female flute player with a Bes tattoo on her thigh and the convolvulus plant (which was associated with fertility) around her; a child; the lower part of a naked kneeling woman with convolvulus and a servant girl. The

▲ *Hathor, Lady of Dendera, retains a reputation for helping women who have fertility problems to this very day. Egyptian women who want children still visit the crypts of her temple.*

paintings decorated mudbrick platforms, today referred to as 'box-beds'. It has been suggested that these beds were where women gave birth or nursed their newborn babies, but they may well have

▲ *Rectangular mudbrick 'box-bed' structures (which would originally have been plastered and painted or whitewashed) have been found in the corner of the front room of 28 of the 68 houses excavated at Deir el-Medina.*

▼ *The mother and child on this ostracon have been drawn in a 'confinement pavilion' surrounded by convolvulus.*

been ordinary beds, or altars (or neither). The subjects of the paintings are similar to those found on *ostraca* (inscribed pieces of pottery or limestone flakes) from Deir el-Medina.

We know from one of the *Tales of Wonder*, a collection of stories composed during the Middle Kingdom (c.2055–c.1650 BC) and found on Papyrus Westcar, that beer-drinking was considered to be obligatory after childbirth. But first the mother and child had to undergo a period of confinement or separation from the outside world. The end of this period of 14 days was marked by ritual cleansing and by eating a honey cake that was thought to keep demons at bay and to stabilize and strengthen the mother.

Breast feeding provided essential nourishment for the newborn baby. A lactating woman could ensure or stimulate her milk supply by wearing an amulet in the form of the rising moon. Amulets in the shape of breasts have also been found. Lactating women were credited with *heka* (see *Magic*), and breast milk (especially that of a woman who had given birth to a male child) was considered to be a potent ingredient in a number of the magico-medical texts (especially in remedies for colds, eye problems and burns).

Vulnerability in early childhood

In addition to the predictions made about a baby at his or her birth, it was believed that a baby's viability was indicated by its first utterance. If it was '*ny*' it would live, and if it was '*embi*' it was bound to die. Infant mortality was indeed high in ancient Egypt, and early childhood was a vulnerable time. The texts known as the *Incantations for Mother and Child*, found on Papyrus Berlin 3027, consist of two books of spells and prescriptions for the treatment of infant illnesses, and for the protection of children against demons and the dead. It was feared that female spirits might try to snatch the infant from his or her mother (see *The Negative Influence of the Dead*). One of the spells is intended to cure a child of a fever. It is entitled 'Spell for a Knot' and was to be recited:

> *...over the pellet of gold, the forty bread pellets, and the cornelian sealstone, with the crocodile and the hand. To be strung on a strip of fine linen; made into an amulet; placed on the neck of the child.*

A child's name was vital to his or her personal identity. The names given at birth could reflect several popular religious practices, including the

celebration of festivals of particular deities, such as *Hathoremheb* ('Hathor is in festival'), and the consultation of oracles during pregnancy, for example *DjedDjehutyiwefankh* ('Thoth says he will live'). Others were devised to protect the child from harm, for instance *Amunhedebirtbint*, which means 'Amun kills the evil eye'.

Rituals of puberty

The ability to produce offspring was presumably the deciding factor in the transition from childhood to adulthood. Rituals probably accompanied a girl's first menstruation, but very little is known about ancient Egyptian puberty rituals. Any symbolic or ritual recognition of attaining adulthood quite possibly involved the cutting off of the 'sidelock' – the hairstyle often worn by young children. There is also some evidence for the circumcision of pubescent boys. The Sixth-Dynasty tomb of Ankhmahor, the 'royal architect', at Saqqara contains what appears to be a scene of a young boy (aged about ten or twelve) being circumcised. The inscription on a stela from Naga ed-Deir, now in the Oriental Institute in Chicago, claims that the owner was circumcised together with 120 others. Another First Intermediate Period inscription (c.2181–c.2055 BC), this time in the tomb of Mereri in Dendera, tells us that Mereri was proud of having circumcised the youths of the town. Certainly by the Twenty-fifth Dynasty (c.747 BC), circumcision was associated with purity.

Marriage would have formalized adulthood because it meant that women could begin to produce children. Consequently marriage, at least for a woman, probably took place in her early teens, so that she could conceive as soon after her first menstruation as possible.

▲ *The man performing this ritual circumcision operation is identified as a* ka-*priest, but this may well have been an honorary title for élite men of various occupations or official positions.*

As far as we know there was no religious marriage ceremony, but no doubt a celebration would have accompanied the initiation of a new household, and the first step towards the formation of a new family unit (the basis of the ancient Egyptian social structure). Marriage – at least for those with property and disposable wealth – was marked by the drawing up of a contract, which supplied the woman with a surprising number of rights and benefits. The surviving agreements show that divorce was socially acceptable, that women remained in possession of their dowries, and that divorced women could expect compensation from their ex-husbands.

Taboos

We know of various taboos in ancient Egyptian society, but it would probably be wrong to assume that each one applied to all classes of people living throughout Egypt during all of Pharaonic history. It is more likely that particular taboos corresponded to a certain type of person (for example the priesthood) in a particular geographical area, during a certain period of Egyptian history.

Taboos were particularly associated with ritual cleanliness. For this reason, for example, sexual intercourse was taboo for several days before entry into sacred places such as temples. The eating of certain foods also appears to have been considered taboo (identified as they were as *bwt*, the ancient Egyptian word used to refer to the concept of taboo), especially those relating to demons, specific deities or to a state of purity.

Food

The Calendars of Lucky and Unlucky Days prohibited the eating of certain foods on certain days. The food most frequently prohibited in the most detailed surviving example of such a

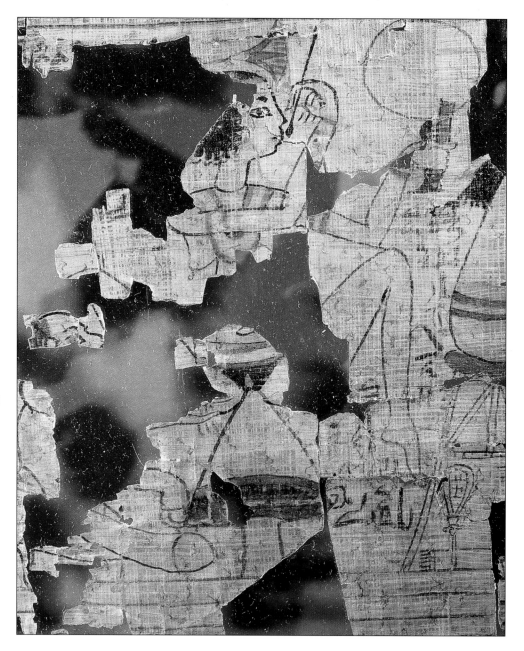

▲ *The Turin Erotic Papyrus contains relatively rare examples of depictions of sexual intercourse. Dating from the 19th Dynasty, it seems to portray the adventures of a comic character on a visit to a brothel.*

Epagomenal days

Certain days of the year were considered taboo for performing activities of any consequence. These were especially the 'epagomenal' days, which had been added on to the original calendar of 360 days. According to mythology these five extra days were created in order that the five children of Geb and Nut (Osiris, Isis, Seth, Nephthys and Horus the Elder) could be born. The day of Seth's birth had a particularly evil reputation, but all five were known as 'the days of the demons'.

calendar, called the Cairo Calendar, is fish. Fish appears to have been considered unclean, and it has been suggested that eating fish may have been considered unsuitable for a state of religious purity because it caused the breath to smell. The word for a 'stink' (*henes*) was written with the hieroglyphic sign of a *Petrocephalus bane* fish. The ancient Egyptians also made use of the *Barbus bynni* fish to write the word *bwt*, ('abomination'), and the *Mormyrus kannume* oxyrhynchus fish was used to write the word *hat*, ('corpse'). According to Plutarch's version of the myth of Osiris in the first century AD, Osiris's penis ended up in the river Nile and was eaten by three types of fish: the Nile carp (*Lepidotus*),

the oxyrynchus (*Mormyrus*), and the phragus. This did not, however, stop the oxyrynchus fish from being regarded as sacred in the town of that name in the Faiyum region.

Another negative aspect of fish might have been its association with the sea, which was regarded as a place of chaos. The king and priests appear not to have been allowed to eat fish because of its association with Seth, the god of chaos and barrenness. The Twenty-fifth-Dynasty Victory Stela of Piye, now in

▶ *The status of the pig was somewhat ambiguous but in the tomb of Kagemni a swineherd is depicted giving milk to a piglet from his own mouth. Saqqara*

the Cairo Museum, tells us that most of the Delta princes were forbidden from entering the palace because they had not been circumcised and because they ate fish, which, according to the inscription, was an 'abomination to the palace'. There is, however, considerable evidence for the consumption of fish in ancient Egypt, so that a fish that was taboo in one area may have been eaten in another. Archaeology has shown that the most numerous of all the food remains found in floor deposits in the main chapel of the Walled Village at Tell el-Amarna are fish bones, so fish was obviously at least prepared in this sacred environment.

Some foods certainly seem to have been considered impure, as is evident from this threat found in a tomb:

> *All who enter my grave in their impurity and who have eaten what an eminent spirit detests…I/shall seize his neck like that of a bird…*

So it was considered blasphemous, or at least disrespectful, to enter a tomb after having eaten certain foods. Inscriptions in the Graeco-Roman temple at Esna inform us that abstinence from certain foods was necessary for a period of

▶ *The bulti fish* (Tilapia nilotica) *was observed to incubate and hatch its eggs in its mouth, so it came to symbolize the concept of rebirth.*

about four days before entering the temple or celebrating religious festivals. These might have included certain kinds of fish, pork, beans, salt and onions, all of which were taboo (although by no means universally so).

It may be that any avoidance of pork was due to the association of the pig with the god Seth. The lengthy record of temple offerings written on Papyrus Harris, which dates from the reign of the Nineteenth-Dynasty king Ramesses II (c.1279–c.1213 BC), does not mention pork, but it has been found in other offering lists. Before the Eighteenth Dynasty, pictorial representation of domestic pigs or reference to them in the magico-medical texts was very rare, but pork was clearly eaten throughout Egyptian history (although probably less so than beef, lamb or mutton, and goat, and to a greater extent by the poorer classes). Pig bones have been excavated with butchery marks on them; pigsties and accompanying butchery facilities have been excavated alongside the Workmen's Village at Tell el-Amarna; and pigs are listed among farm products in such texts as *The Tale*

of the Eloquent Peasant. A pork taboo might have originated from the severe illness caused by the consumption of pork if it was not eaten or preserved immediately after slaughter.

Aphrodisiacs and alcohol

The aphrodisiac properties credited to a particular foodstuff could have been a reason for prohibiting it to certain members of society. Plutarch, writing in the first century AD, supposed any abstinence from salt in Egypt to be for this reason. According to Herodotus and other classical writers, Egyptian priests did not eat beans. Diodorus Siculus, in the first century BC, explained the bean and lentil taboo of the Egyptian priests by the supposition that if everyone was allowed to eat everything, something would run out. However beans must have been a staple of the Egyptian diet, and it is likely that the classical writers did not always fully understand the circumstances in Egypt. Pliny and Plutarch are unlikely to have been correct, for example, when they wrote that libations of wine were prohibited at the temple of Heliopolis. If a taboo concerning wine did exist at this temple it is more likely to have been one forbidding the priests from drinking it in the sacred enclosure. There may have been rules regulating the daily alcohol consumption of priests, and again it is the classical writers who suggest that similar limits were set for the king.

Maat

Maat was the principle that held ancient Egyptian society together and underpinned religious belief. The word is usually translated as 'truth', 'order', 'justice' or 'balance'. To recognize abstract concepts in their system of beliefs, the ancient Egyptians felt a need to divinely personify them and this they did with *maat*, which was represented as the goddess Maat, a woman with an ostrich feather on her head.

The idea of *maat* as universal order or harmony corresponds with the most

Wisdom literature

There is a body of surviving literature from ancient Egypt, known today as Instructive or Wisdom Literature. It tended to be written as if by a father for his son, or by a tutor for his pupil, and it tells us how a young boy was expected to lead his life correctly – a code of moral values that would have acted as a check on human behaviour.

The text known as the *Writings of Ptahhotep* was attributed to a vizier of the Fifth Dynasty, but its earliest appearance is in a papyrus dating from the Twelfth Dynasty. It offers a series of maxims to be followed to achieve success in life, based on the ideal of an existence in accordance with the principle of *maat*.

The *Instruction of King Amenemhat I* was written as if the dead king is speaking in a revelation to his son and successor Senusret I. It warns Senusret of disloyalty among the courtiers, and emphasizes the contrast between the divinity of kingship and the limitations of a mortal king, between the ideal – embodied in the concept of *maat* – and the realities of life.

▲ *In a funerary context the goddess Maat was often depicted with large enveloping wings – much associated with protective female deities – as here in the tomb of the 19th-Dynasty king Sethnakhte in west Thebes.*

fundamental role of the reigning king. This was to maintain *maat* on a national level by building temples and making offering to the gods (in fact, the ancient Egyptian deities were said to live off *maat*) and thereby placating them; by exercising control over the potential enemies of Egypt (which basically amounted to all foreigners); and by controlling nature (especially wild animals). Life in Egypt was thought to be characterized by *maat*, whereas outside its borders *isfet* reigned, that is chaos, epitomized by the desert, wild animals, foreign lands and foreign people.

The moral code

The ideal was to lead a life in accordance with *maat*, corresponding to the socially acceptable or ethical way to behave. The texts of the Wisdom Literature reveal that certain crimes were considered crimes against *maat*. These included disorder, rebellion, envy, deceit, greed, laziness, injustice and ingratitude. The Old Kingdom *Writings of Ptahhotep* declare that 'Maat is great and lasting in effect'.

▲ *In the Middle Kingdom Maat, was described as being at the nostrils of Re, while by the 18th Dynasty she was being called 'daughter of Re'. This tomb scene at Deir el-Medina dates to the 19th Dynasty.*

The emphasis was very much on how people should listen as opposed to being deaf to *maat*, and on the idea that greed destroys social relations. In the Middle Kingdom *Tale of the Eloquent Peasant*, the lazy and the greedy are said to be deaf to *maat*.

If, when he died, a man wanted it known that he had spoken truthfully and had acted in accordance with justice, thus maintaining social harmony, he would have a recurring formula inscribed on his tomb: 'I have spoken *maat*, I have accomplished *maat*.'

The concept of *maat* and the importance of living a just life was central to the beliefs about judgment after death – when the dead person's heart was weighed in the balance against *maat*, symbolized by the feather worn on the head of the goddess Maat.

Justice for all?

The concept of justice for all is apparent in the textual evidence from ancient Egypt and in theory everyone in Egypt had access to a fair hearing. The author of the *Instruction for Merikare,* written during the Middle Kingdom (c.2055–c.1650 BC) advised the new king to 'make no difference between a man of position and a commoner'. Later on, in the New Kingdom (c.1550–c.1069 BC), the viziers were being instructed, 'See equally the man you know and the man you don't know, the man who is near you and the man who is far away.' As overseer of the courts of Egypt, the vizier held the title, 'Priest of Maat'.

Of course, in practice it would be very surprising to find a society in which position, influence and wealth did not count for anything. Bribery was probably common practice, because in another piece of instructive literature dating to the Ramesside period, the author Amenemope felt it necessary to write: 'Do not accept the reward of the powerful man, and persecute the weak for him.'

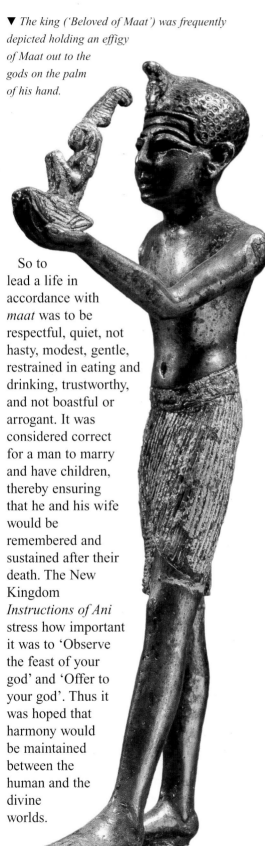

▼ *The king ('Beloved of Maat') was frequently depicted holding an effigy of Maat out to the gods on the palm of his hand.*

So to lead a life in accordance with *maat* was to be respectful, quiet, not hasty, modest, gentle, restrained in eating and drinking, trustworthy, and not boastful or arrogant. It was considered correct for a man to marry and have children, thereby ensuring that he and his wife would be remembered and sustained after their death. The New Kingdom *Instructions of Ani* stress how important it was to 'Observe the feast of your god' and 'Offer to your god'. Thus it was hoped that harmony would be maintained between the human and the divine worlds.

Purification

We know that everyone who entered the temples of ancient Egypt was expected to be ritually pure. Most priests were called *wab*, meaning 'purified'. Their daily rituals involved washing themselves and the cult statues of the gods, hence the importance of the sacred lake within each temple complex. Our best evidence for ritual purity dates to the later periods of ancient Egyptian history. Inscriptions tell us that those entering temples were expected to cut their nails, shave the hair on their head and remove other body hair, wash their hands in natron (a naturally occurring salt), dress in a certain kind of linen (they were forbidden from wearing wool), not to have recently had sexual intercourse, and to have abstained from certain foods for about four days.

However, we can assume that similar criteria would have applied throughout Pharaonic history. At the end of the New Kingdom (c.1069 BC), a *wab*-priest of the ram-headed creator god Khnum at Elephantine, having sworn an oath not to enter the temple until he had spent ten days drinking natron, entered after only seven days, and was consequently considered ritually impure. A papyrus document records the charges of ritual impurity and perjury brought against this priest.

Washing facilities

T-shaped and rectangular limestone purification troughs, together with sunken mudbrick plastered basins and rectangular limestone lustration slabs, have been found near the shrines close to the Workmen's Village at Tell el-Amarna. Similar facilities were discovered during excavations in the shrine area to the north of the Ptolemaic temple dedicated to the goddess Hathor at Deir el-Medina. Ritual purity would have been closely linked to the concept of taboo (*bwt*). The ideal state of ritual

purity during the New Kingdom is described in Chapter 125 of the Book of the Dead as:

> ...*pure, clean, dressed in fresh clothes, shod in white sandals, painted with eye-paint, anointed with the finest oil of myrrh.*

And the image corresponding to the spell was to be drawn:

> ...*on a clean surface in red paint mixed with soil on which pigs and goats have not trodden.*

▲ *Opinion differs as to whether the nine large calcite basins in Niuserre's solar temple at Abu Gurab were used in the slaughter of animals or the ritual purification of offerings.*

Obligatory ritual purity also applied to entry into tombs, visitors to which were liable to be punished if they caused any damage or did not comply with the conventions of purity.

Purification rituals were also important on a more popular level, for ensuring social acceptance and thus a harmonious, ordered household or community. Within the life cycle of the family, sexual intercourse, menstruation and birth were all considered unclean, requiring subsequent purification rituals in order to allow the individual(s) concerned to be reintegrated into society, especially after a period of confinement or seclusion, for example following childbirth.

The ancient Egyptian word used euphemistically for 'menstruation' and 'to menstruate' is *hesmen*, the same as that for the verb 'to purify oneself', and the purifying agent natron. In the tale of Setne-Khaemwese and Naneferkaptah, written in demotic on a papyrus of the Ptolemaic period, now in the Cairo Museum, a woman named Ahwere reveals her pregnancy by announcing the absence of her menstruation with the words: 'When my time of purification came, I made no purification.'

Cleansing rituals

Bodily fluids, and particularly menstrual and birth blood, do appear to have been considered to be impure. The fear seems to have been that the pollutive blood might attract demons. These demons were thought to be scared of honey, so it was considered sensible for women to eat cakes made of

▼ The blade of this razor from Deir el-Medina is bronze, and the handle is wooden.

honey after having given birth. In the tale entitled *The Birth of the Royal Children* on the Middle Kingdom Papyrus Westcar, now in the Egyptian Museum, Berlin, we are told that following Ruddedet's giving birth to triplets, she '...cleansed herself in a cleansing of 14 days'. Purification rituals of this kind involved washing and the burning of incense. Scenes of the confinement period, when the mother and baby were kept separate from the rest of society, were illustrated on ostraca (flakes of limestone) and on paintings on the brick platforms in the living rooms of houses at Deir el-Medina and in the Workmen's Village at Tell el-Amarna. These include female serving girls holding mirrors, basins and cosmetic tubes, as well as musical instruments. The required purification was usually followed by celebration. Following Ruddedet's 'cleansing' in Papyrus Westcar, she sends her maid to fetch beer and then '…they sat down to a day of feasting'.

Texts have survived from the tomb-builders' village at Deir el-Medina that reveal that one of the reasons for a man's absence from work in the Valley of the Kings might have been because he was 'making himself pure for Taweret' (or 'Taweret was making him pure'). Taweret was the household goddess associated with pregnancy and childbirth. It may have been expected that a man should

◄ From the Middle Kingdom onwards, mirrors took the form of a sun disc of polished bronze or copper, with the handle often in the form of a papyrus stalk and/or the goddess Hathor.

miss work and perform a purification ritual if a female member of his family was menstruating or had given birth.

The circumcision of children also seems to have related to purity. Herodotus made this association in the fifth century BC, when he commented that the Egyptians were circumcised as they 'preferred purity above fresh air'. The inscription on the Twenty-fifth-Dynasty Victory Stela of Piye tells us that three local rulers were not granted an audience with the king because they were 'uncircumcised and ate fish'. In contrast Namart, the prince of Hermopolis, was allowed entry because he was 'pure and did not eat fish'.

In the magical texts, such as the Demotic Magical Papyrus of London and Leiden which dates to the beginning of the third century BC, it is made clear that a state of purity is deemed necessary for the efficacy of the particular spell or ritual. The only specified requisite for purification was an abstinence from sexual intercourse (seemingly for three days beforehand), and it was considered ideal to include a young boy in the ritual, specifically because he was a virgin.

The ancient Egyptians also appear to have associated the condition of impurity with the period of mourning, as temple access was denied to people in this state.

Lucky and Unlucky Days

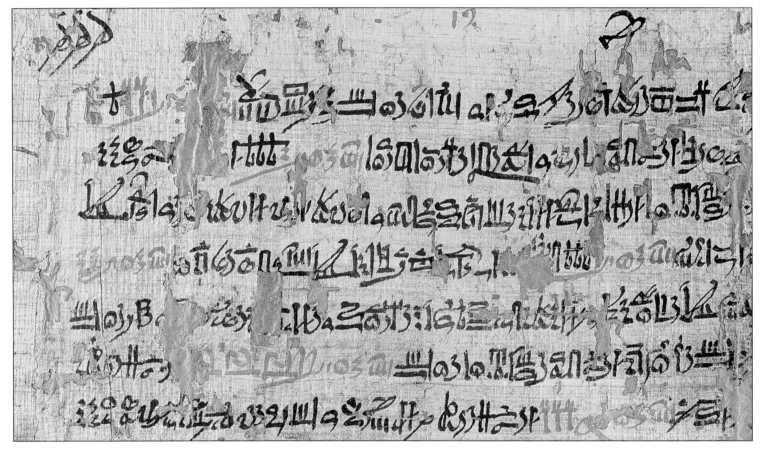

▲ *On this calendar, days described as lucky are written in black, and those described as unlucky in red. 19th Dynasty.*

Calendars that have survived from ancient Egypt categorize each day of the year as either lucky or unlucky. The best known of these is the one known as the Cairo Calendar, which is said to have come from Thebes and to date to the reign of the Nineteenth-Dynasty king Ramesses II (c.1279–c.1213 BC). But the language in it seems earlier than Ramesside, and the text does not mention the Theban triad of deities, Amun, Mut and Khonsu, so the original contents of the calendar were probably earlier in date.

Days seem to have been categorized according to the mythical events that were said to have happened on them. For example, a day on which two gods had fought was considered unlucky, whereas a day on which a god had made a successful journey was regarded as fortunate. By consulting a Calendar of Lucky and Unlucky Days, an ancient

Egyptian would know whether or not it would be sensible to carry out a certain activity on a certain day. For example, some days were deemed to be suitable for performing certain rituals in the home, for pacifying the spirits of dead relatives (see *Ancestor Worship*), or for making a votive offering at a local shrine or temple, inscribed or accompanied by an oral request. These calendars may have been consulted to determine the most auspicious day for a magician to work a spell for someone.

Rituals carried out in temples were tied in with the calendar of religious festivals. The basis for the reasoning found in the Calendars of Lucky and Unlucky days seems to have been a religious calendar of the festivals of the various gods and goddesses.

It is possible that the Calendars of Lucky and Unlucky Days were the result of amassing a body of recorded

incidents, which were then listed in a calendrical order according to experience. Private individuals must have been able to own their own version of such a calendar, because the scribe Qenherkhepshef, who lived at the tomb-builders' village of Deir el-Medina in the late thirteenth and early twelfth centuries BC, certainly possessed his own copy, which is now in the British Museum, London.

The epagomenal days

The calendars made it clear that nothing of any consequence should be done during the five-day period added on to the original year of 360 days. According to the mythology these five extra days were created in order that the five

▲ *According to Egyptian mythology, Seth and Nephthys were two of Nut's children, and were also thought to be consorts.*

children of Geb and Nut – Osiris, Isis, Seth, Nephthys and Horus the Elder – could be born, and it was considered to be an extremely dangerous period. The day on which Seth was supposed to be born had a particularly evil reputation, but all five were known as 'the days of the demons'.

Directions and predictions

The calendars specified certain activities to be carried out on certain days. For example, it is advised that on the nineteenth day of the second month of the season of *Akhet* ('Inundation'), when, according to myth, the embalming

oil was prepared for Osiris, wine should be drunk until sundown instead of beer, the more usual daily drink. The calendars were also used to predict the cause of death if someone died on a certain day. For example, if someone died on the sixth day of the second month of *Akhet*, it was likely to be as a result of intoxication. This must have been considered a favourable way to meet one's end because it coincided with a day of revelry in the divine world.

The calendars were used to predict a child's future, depending on the day on which he or she was born. The fifth day of the second month of *Akhet*, for example, was described as a day of offerings to the deities Montu and Hedjhotep, and it was predicted that a child born on this day would have his or her death caused by copulation. A child born on the tenth day of the fourth month of *Akhet* was destined to die of old age with an offering of beer poured on his face – this may well have been

considered an ideal way to end one's life. Herodotus, writing in the fifth century BC, noted:

The Egyptians have ascertained the god to whom each month and day is sacred and they can therefore tell, according to the date of the child's birth, what fate is in store for him, how he will end his days, and what sort of person he will become

The idea of a Calendar of Lucky and Unlucky days persisted in medieval Europe. In the thirteenth century AD astrological calendars were produced in which some days were designated as 'Egyptian Days'. These were considered to be unpropitious for anything except the working of black magic. The observance of such 'Egyptian Days' was one of the charges made against French heretics at the inquisitorial courts in the thirteenth century AD.

▼ *An enormous quantity of written evidence, both on papyrus and on ostraca (flakes of limestone and potsherds), has been discovered at the tomb-builders' village of Deir el-Medina.*

Dreams

The ancient Egyptians believed that what they dreamed had a bearing on their daily lives, and that the interpretation of dreams was a valid means of predicting the future. A collection of texts has survived from ancient Egypt, which are known today as 'Dream Books'. They consist of lists of possible dream scenarios and what the dreams indicate will happen in the life of the dreamer. For example, if

▶ *Hatshepsut's mortuary temple at Deir el-Bahri is set in a deep bay in the desert cliffs which were in turn at the foot of the pyramidal peak sacred to the goddesses Hathor and Mertseger.*

A dream directory

The Dream Book of qenherkhepshef discovered at Deir el-Medina is written in tabular form, with the dreams described in one column of text and interpretation in another:

If a man sees himself in a dream...

...submerging in the river: good: this means purification from all evils.

...eating crocodile: good: this means acting as an official among his people.

...burying an old man: good: this means flourishing.

...seeing his face in a mirror: bad: this means another wife.

...shod with white sandals: bad: this means roaming the earth.

...copulating with a woman: bad: this means mourning.

...his bed catching fire: bad: this means driving away his wife.

someone dreamt that he was drinking warm beer, it was thought to forewarn that the dreamer would soon suffer harm. A careful reading of the texts in the original shows that many of the correlations between the content of the dream and the prophecy are based on the use of puns (a potent form of magic). For instance, to dream about a harp meant that something evil would surely happen to the person in question; whereas to dream about a donkey indicated that the dreamer was soon to be promoted. To get a sense of the magical use of language in these predictions we have to know that the ancient Egyptian word for 'harp' was *benet*, and the word for 'evil' was *bint*; that the word for 'donkey' was *aa* and the word for 'to be promoted' was *saa*.

Who would actually have been in possession of these books? Did certain priests and magicians own them? Or might a family have had its own copy of such a manual in their home, ready to consult whenever they felt the need? We know that the scribe Qenherkhepshef, who was in charge of the administration of Deir el-Medina in the late thirteenth and early twelfth centuries BC, owned one. Today it is known as Papyrus Chester Beatty III. It is written in

▶ *From at least the beginning of the Old Kingdom, the ancient Egyptians used headrests to support their heads while they slept. The presence of the protective spirit-deity Bes in the design of Tutankhamun's headrest is apotropaic.*

the hieratic script and is now in the British Museum in London. Although it dates to the Ramesside Period, it has been noticed that the language used is very Middle Kingdom in style, and so perhaps it is a copy of a text originally compiled in the Eleventh or Twelfth Dynasty. The library of this particular scribe was pretty impressive, including as it did, examples of poetry, literature,

▲ *As 'Lady of the West', Hathor was protectress of the west Theban necropolis. She was depicted on stelae and funerary papyri as a cow leaving the desert to come down into the papyrus marshes and she acted as a link between the tombs and life in the Nile Valley.*

history, magical spells and a Calendar of Lucky and Unlucky Days.

The Lector Priests would have acted as the link between the temples and the local communities. Their role in the temple was associated with the written and spoken word in the form of spells and incantations, and they were closely associated with magic throughout Egyptian history. Apart from their ritual duties, they had a reputation as interpreters of dreams. They presumably consulted these 'Dream Books'.

▶ *Tuthmosis IV recorded his dream in which the Great Sphinx appeared to him in all its aspects – Khepri-Re-Atum – on the stela he set up between the paws of the Sphinx.*

Fear of nightmares

Because dreams were believed to be of such great significance, it becomes clear why the Egyptians were so concerned about nightmares and attempted to guard against them with spells and apotropaic headrests. Papyrus Chester Beatty III suggests using protective spells on waking from a nightmare, and examples of headrests have been found decorated with images of the protective household deities Bes and Taweret (sometimes brandishing knives against any possible threat to the sleeper).

The magical papyri of the Ptolemaic Period explained to people how they could go about directing the anger of the god Seth against their enemies, causing them nightmares or even death. It was thought possible to cause someone much upset and trauma by sending them dreams of ill omen.

Incubation

During the first millennium BC, a practice known as 'incubation' became popular. People went to sleep in structures known as sanatoria or healing sanctuaries, built specifically for this purpose inside the precincts of temples, in order to have healing or helpful

◀ *Imhotep, the architect of the Step Pyramid at Saqqara, was deified during the Late Period and was one of the patron deities of the healing sanctuary in Hatshepsut's mortuary temple.*

dreams, particularly to help to solve infertility problems. Part of the Eighteenth-Dynasty ruler Hatshepsut's mortuary temple at Deir el-Bahri was converted into one such sanatorium. It was dedicated to the two deified sages Imhotep (the vizier and chief royal architect during the reign of the Third-Dynasty king Djoser (c.2667–c.2648 BC)) and Amenhotep, son of Hapu, a high official during the reign of the Eighteenth-Dynasty king Amenhotep III (c.1390–c.1352 BC).

In the story of Setne Khaemwese and Si-Osire, written in demotic on papyrus and dating to the Roman Period, Mehusekhe, the wife of Setne, seeks a solution to her inability to conceive. She spends a night in a sanctuary where she has a dream in which she is advised to concoct and take a remedy made from the crushed gourds of a melon vine. This she does, but it is also clearly stated that she must have sexual intercourse with her husband and, as a result, she becomes pregnant.

There were some occasions on which gods were said to have appeared to people in dreams and in this way to have affected or sanctioned a particular decision (a form of oracular consultation). During the New Kingdom (c.1550–c.1069 BC), one Theban official was said to have been inspired by the goddess Hathor in a dream to build his tomb in a certain place.

Oracles

The earliest unambiguous evidence that the ancient Egyptians consulted oracles dates from the New Kingdom (c.1550–c.1069 BC). It takes the form of papyri, and – more often – ostraca, the pieces of pottery or limestone on which scribes took notes, from the tomb-builders' village of Deir el-Medina on the west bank of the River Nile at Thebes. At Deir el-Medina it was usually the oracle of the tomb-builders' royal patron deity Amenhotep I that was consulted. His shrine was located just outside the village, to the north.

Oracles tended to be consulted on certain festival days, when the cult statue of the god was carried in procession out of his or her shrine or temple on the shoulders of a number of priests. An expression that regularly occurs in the records as an introduction to a description of the consultation with the deity is the phrase 'As I stood before (him)'. However, although the ordinary person might have come closer to a cult statue during this festival procession than at any time (it was usually in the temple), it was still always concealed from view, often in a barque shrine.

Ostraca now in the British Museum, London, reveal that oracles were used mainly in disputes over property (especially houses and tombs). They might also be consulted to end a disagreement between a buyer and a seller. On Ostracon 576 from Deir el-Medina, it is recorded that the buyer asked the oracle to specify the amount of grain he ought to receive because a certain tradesman had the reputation of sneakily reducing it. Sometimes advice or questions were asked of the oracle. Ostracon 562 records the specific question: 'Should I go North?' In this way we are able to learn something of the mundane problems and indecisions of ordinary life, and the comfort to be gained from having the gods endorse everyday decision-making.

Oracular judgement

Oracles were also considered useful for helping to solve crimes, and for bringing the guilty to justice. In the case of a robbery, a list of suspects might be named before the god, and he then had to indicate the guilty suspect. Ostracon 4 from Deir el-Medina records that two articles of clothing had been stolen from a man. The houses of the possible thieves were named in front of the cult statue of Amenhotep I, and when that of the scribe Amen-nakht was named the god made a sign of affirmation. The scribe was summoned to a tribunal (*kenbet*) with his daughter, who was in fact found to be the thief. So the local oracle and the court would have strengthened each other's decision-making in the judicial process.

The ancient texts are ambiguous about the way the oracles gave their answers, but there were various ways in which a god might have made his decisions known: by the priests speaking; by mechanical manipulation inside the statue, such as the movement of the head; by the statue carried by the priests moving forwards or backwards; or by the god approaching an affirmative or negative piece of writing placed on

▲ *On festival days the barque shrine of Amun was processed on the shoulders of priests, as shown here in a relief from Hatshepsut's chapel at Karnak. It was on these occasions that the oracle of the god might be consulted.*

either side of the processional way. In the previously mentioned case of the names of the houses possibly sheltering the thief, the names may have been written on reed strips, with the god then somehow guiding the decision as to which one was drawn.

The word of the oracle does not seem to have necessarily been final (it was obviously not automatically accepted as law). Two separate papyri exist that each refer to the same dispute, with a lapse of three years between them, indicating that it was still being debated. If the response given by one oracle was not what the petitioner wanted to hear, it appears to have been possible for him to go on to consult other deities. Even so, it seems to have been usual for those consulting oracles to be called upon to swear oaths binding them to the oracle's decision: in view of this it may be that the ancient Egyptians were not quite so fearful of their gods as we often assume them to have been.

Oaths

The ancient Egyptian words for 'oath' (*wah* and *ankh*) and 'to swear' (*ankh* and *ark*) were the same as those for 'to endure', 'to live' and 'to wrap or bind'. Oaths tended to be sworn on the life or reign of the ruler, beginning, 'As the Ruler who lives forever endures…' Others were sworn by a god, in which case it could be a specific deity such as Re, Re-Horakhty, Amun or Ptah in his specific role as 'Lord of Truth'; or by the *ka* (or spirit) of a particular deity, such as Thoth; or by the idea of *netjer* – the divine – or gods in general. The Eighteenth-Dynasty ruler Akhenaten (c.1352–c.1336 BC) chose to revolutionize the state religion of ancient Egypt, so that all gods were

▼ *The donkey was the principal load-bearer of the ancient Egyptians, whose word for 'donkey' was the onomatopoeic* aa. *20th century copy of a wall painting from a Theban tomb by Nina de Garis Davies.*

abolished except for the solar deity Aten, whom he elevated to a supreme position together with himself and his family. In tombs at Tell el-Amarna, the site of Akhenaten's capital city, the inscriptions of oaths begin, 'As the Aten endures and as the Ruler endures...'

The Oath of the Lord

One particular oath was especially used for legal purposes, and that was the *ankh n neb* or 'Oath of the Lord'. It was a royal oath, because the lord in question was the ruling pharaoh. It is possible that the Egyptians did not want

◄ *The crocodile (*Crocodilus niloticus*) was common and dangerous in the Egyptian environment. Being thrown to the crocodiles was sometimes threatened as an extreme penalty for the breaking of an oath.*

suspected criminals speaking the actual name of the king. Ancient texts inform us of lawsuits, and provide us with lists of witnesses who were called upon to swear an oath such as, 'As Amun endures and as the Ruler endures, we speak in truth.' One of the papyri that deal specifically with the extensive tomb robbery that took place at the end of the Twentieth Dynasty states that, 'The Oath of the Lord was given to him [the foreigner Pai-Kamen] not to speak falsely.' It appears that the defendant or witness might be beaten before even taking the oath; for example, Papyrus Mayer A tells us that, 'The citizeness lneri was examined by beating with a stick. The Oath of the Lord was given to her not to speak falsely.'

Instances of people swearing falsely are, however, recorded. We learn from Papyrus Salt 124 that a man named Paneb was charged with having stolen a goose, and that 'He took the oath of the Lord about it, saying "I do not have it" (but) they found it in his house.' We know of the penalties threatened for perjury, but there is much less evidence

of punishments actually being carried out. Papyrus Mayer A informs us that 'Examination was made of the herdsman of the House of Amun, the thief Pai-Kamen. An oath on penalty of mutilation, not to speak falsely.' On another occasion, outlined in Papyrus Abbott, a coppersmith was taken to the scene of a confessed crime and 'He took the Oath of the Lord on penalty of beating and having his nose and ears cut off, and of being put upon the stake.' Punishments for the breaking of an oath that are referred to in other accounts include being sent to Ethiopia or being thrown to crocodiles.

Oaths might accompany sale contracts. The presence of registered witnesses to an oath seems to have made it legally binding. Sometimes oaths were taken several times to emphasize them. Oaths also accompanied promises, such as the promise to repay borrowed money (a failure to repay could be treated as theft). Oaths were also used in marriage contracts, for example, the marriage agreement in Papyrus Berlin 304, dating from the Twenty-second Dynasty, includes the words, 'He said, "As Amun lives and as Pharaoh lives and as the chief priest of [Amun] lives... If I wish to divorce her and I love another woman, I am the one who must give her the things recorded above".'

▲ *Each plume of Amun's headdress was divided into two, reflecting the duality of the Egyptian world view, and each feather was divided into seven horizontal segments (seven being a ritually significant number). 20th Dynasty.*

Breaking an oath

It seems unlikely that the ancient Egyptians would have taken an oath sworn in the name of a deity lightly but, just as the pronouncements of the oracles were not necessarily accepted, oaths do not appear to have carried absolute authority. In a case of sexual misconduct said to have taken place at Deir el-Medina, a man called Mery Sekhmet was found to have broken the oath he had been made to swear. He was not punished for this misdemeanour, however; he was just instructed to swear another one.

A promise and a threat

Sometimes an oath was coupled with a curse. A woman named Rennefer wanted to make her slave foster-children freemen, so they might inherit her property, and she said: 'As Amun endures and as the Ruler endures, may a donkey copulate with him, and a female donkey copulate with his wife, he who shall call one of them slave.'

Festivals and Pilgrimages

Festivals were occasions of celebration – of music, dancing, eating and drinking. They were also times when ordinary people might benefit from a closer encounter with the cult statue of a deity than was usually possible. For most of the time, the cult statue resided in a shrine in the dimly lit inner sanctuary of a temple – a place forbidden to the impure and uninitiated. But on festival days, the statue was carried in procession out of the temple, accompanied by musicians, singers, dancers, acrobats and incense burners. People might have come close to the statue, but still would not have seen it because it was carefully hidden from the masses. During a festival they might be given the opportunity to commune with the deity by consulting its oracle. This gave them a chance to consult the god for his wisdom on an issue that was important to their daily lives, such as whether it was a good time to make a long and difficult journey. The divine go-ahead was sought. A god might also be asked to settle a dispute or indicate the person responsible for a crime.

Calendars of festivals

The Hour Priests working in the House of Life in each of the temples worked out the annual calendar of festivals around which the temple's year revolved. Some of the calendars have survived; for example, in the Festival Hall of the Eighteenth-Dynasty king Tuthmosis III (c.l479–c.l425 BC) at Karnak temple, 54 feast days are

▶ Bread and beer were the staples of the Egyptian diet, and wooden models such as this one were intended to ensure their production for eternity. Middle Kingdom.

listed for one year. And at Ramesses III's mortuary temple at Medinet Habu, 60 festivals are listed. We learn from this 'calendar of feasts and offerings' that 84 loaves of bread were required for a monthly festival, and almost 4,000 for the national Festival of Sokar, the Memphite funerary deity.

The focus of some festivals was the visitation by one deity on another. The cow goddess Hathor, for example, left her main cult centre at Dendera each year to journey by boat to Edfu, where she was united with the

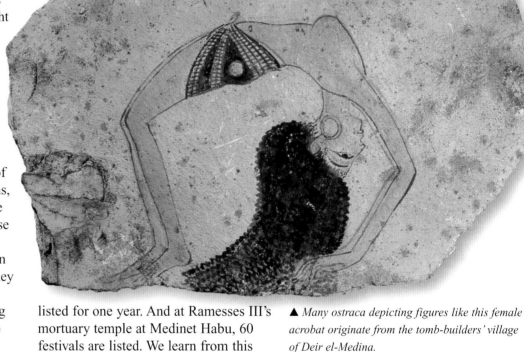

▲ Many ostraca depicting figures like this female acrobat originate from the tomb-builders' village of Deir el-Medina.

falcon deity Horus. Another annual festival, held from the early Eighteenth Dynasty onwards, was the Festival of Opet, which lasted from two to four weeks. The cult statues of Amun, his consort Mut, and their child Khonsu were carried in procession in barque shrines from their temple complex at Karnak to Luxor temple, along a route lined with ram-headed sphinxes. In the late Eighteenth Dynasty they began to make this journey in ceremonial boats on the River Nile. At Luxor, Amun was

▲ In this tomb painting the cones balanced on the heavy black wigs of these women revellers at a banquet symbolize sweet-smelling ointments. They also wear jewellery and fine clothing.

believed to have sexual intercourse with the mother of the reigning king so that she would give birth to the royal *ka*. The king was then united with his *ka* in the sanctuary of the temple, and he was believed to emerge as a god.

The dead were also involved in important festivals such as the Beautiful Festival of the Valley, which lasted 12 days and was celebrated from the early Eighteenth Dynasty onwards. The divine family of Karnak left their east-bank temple and crossed the river to visit Deir el-Bahri, and later, another mortuary temple as well. Ordinary people celebrated this festival at their family burial place by sharing a meal with the spirits of their dead relatives.

Revelry at Bubastis

People made pilgrimages to the more important festivals. Writing in the mid fifth century BC, Herodotus recorded the journeying of pilgrims to the cult site of Bubastis in the eastern Delta, to celebrate the festival of the cat goddess Bastet. He described the trip to Bubastis by boat, during which the women on the river hurled abuse at women on the banks, danced, hitched up their skirts, and exposed their genitals to the world

around them. This bawdy behaviour was probably meant to pass fertility from the women to the land (or vice versa). We know that on other occasions women exposed themselves before a statue of the goddess Hathor, hoping to benefit from the goddess's close association with fertility.

Herodotus wrote that 700,000 people (excluding children) attended the festival of Bastet. People sang and musical instruments such as the flute and castanets were played. Sacrifices were made, and more wine was drunk than during all the rest of the year.

Probably the cult centre most commonly

▶ A married couple are depicted on this limestone stela from Abydos. The man holds a sekhem *sceptre in his right hand, denoting 'power' and 'might'.*

visited by pilgrims was Abydos, the legendary burial place and chief temple of Osiris, the god of the dead, the Afterlife, rebirth and vegetation. During the Middle Kingdom (c.2055–c.1650 BC), thousands of people went to Abydos and set up private stelae in cenotaphs and tombs around the temple of Osiris, thereby hoping to ensure a never-ending participation in the festivals of the god. These stelae also functioned as family monuments, and for this reason repeated pilgrimages were made, both to the temple of Osiris and to these memorials to the deceased. Scenes on the walls of New Kingdom private tombs often depict a symbolic pilgrimage being made by the dead person to Abydos.

Music and Dance in Egyptian Religion

Singers, dancers and musicians were an important part of temple life. People believed that the gods enjoyed, and were pacified by, singing, music and dance. In the New Kingdom *Teachings of Ani*, song, dance and incense are described as the food of the gods. These activities accompanied the daily temple rites, figured highly at festivals and formed a part of more personal religious rituals – during funerals and at childbirth, for example. No musical notation has survived from ancient Egypt, but we do have the words of songs; illustrations of musicians, singers and dancers; the titles of people in these professions; and ancient musical instruments such as the harp, lute, lyre, flute, double reed-pipe, drum, cymbals, tambourine, bells and a form of guitar.

Temple musicians

If temple musicians played before the cult statues of the gods, we can assume that they would not have been allowed to lay their eyes upon the statues (because only the king and High Priest were in a position to do this). It has therefore been suggested that any musicians allowed into the inner sanctuary were quite likely to have been blind. Male harpists depicted on the walls of tombs do occasionally appear to be blind, and disability does not seem to have been considered a bar to purity; there is no reason to believe that people with physical disabilities were ostracized by ancient Egyptian society.

At festivals, musicians, singers and dancers walked in procession out of the temple with the shrine housing the cult statue. Often the point was not to produce pleasing music, but a rhythmic sound to create a state of religious ecstasy – or simply a loud noise to scare away harmful spirits, for example at birth. Clappers and *sistra* were the two instruments most useful for these purposes. Clappers were usually made of

ivory, which meant that they were curved like apotropaic wands. They often had a design carved into them, such as a shrine, a woman's head or the head of Hathor (some texts describe this goddess as 'Lady of Dance'). *Sistra* were ceremonial rattles, which were

▲ *The double reed-pipe was played by female musicians accompanying dancers at festive occasions. 18th Dynasty.*

▼ *Hathor was 'Lady of the Vulva' and the 'Hand of Atum': the combination in these clappers probably had sexual connotations.*

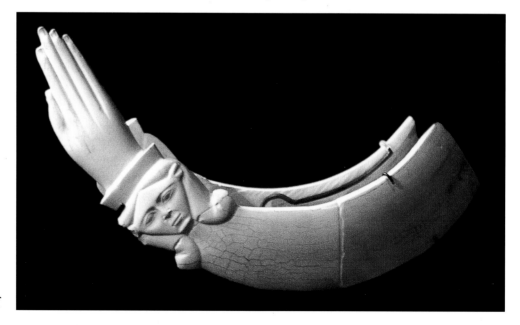

most frequently made of bronze. They were very much associated with the goddess Hathor, whose priestesses shook them as part of the rituals they performed. They often had the head of this goddess incorporated in their design, and they may have been thought to stimulate fertility. In her manifestation as Nebethetepet, or 'Lady of the Vulva', Hathor was represented as a *naos sistrum* (a *sistrum* with the design of a shrine incorporated into it). *Menat-* necklaces were also carried and shaken by the priestesses.

The household spirit-deity, Bes, was often depicted playing various musical instruments, especially a drum or tambourine. Bes was closely associated with pregnancy and childbirth, and music was important in the celebration following a successful birth. Several of the fragments of wall painting found in houses at Deir el-Medina show Bes

▲ *Men and women were never shown dancing together. Here men dance on a relief in the tomb of Kagemni at Saqqara.*

dancing and making music. One fragment reveals a naked, dancing female playing the flute. According to the mythology, Bes appeased the enraged Hathor when she was sulking at Philae by playing the tambourine and harp to her, and he is depicted dancing and playing a tambourine and harp on columns in the Temple of Hathor at Philae.

Births and deaths

In the tale of *The Birth of the Royal Children* on the Middle-Kingdom Papyrus Westcar, the midwives who arrive at the house of the woman in labour are disguised as dancing girls (they also happen to be goddesses). It may well have been common for female dancers to play a part at the time of birth. A scene in the Sixth-Dynasty tomb of Mereruka at Saqqara depicts a female dancing troupe (a *khener*) before his wife Watekhethor, and the hieroglyphic text reads: 'But see the secret of birth! Oh pull!'

Dancers were also present at funerals to elate the spirit of the dead, and to scare away evil spirits. These were the *muu*-dancers who wore kilts and tall, white reed headdresses. From as early as the Fifth Dynasty (c.2490 BC), lion-masked dwarves appear to have been linked to groups of women employed to sing and dance on religious occasions.

Agricultural rites

Singing was a key element of the rites associated with agriculture. Harvesters might chant a lament, accompanied by a flute, in order to express their sorrow at the first cutting of the crops, which was thought to symbolize the wounding of Osiris, the god of vegetation. Dancing was also related to agricultural rites, both as a means of stimulating growth and

▲ *The ancient Egyptians appear to have made little distinction between dancing and what we would describe as acrobatics, shown in this relief from Hatshepsut's chapel at Karnak.*

and as a form of thanksgiving. A particularly good example of agricultural dances at the time of the harvest can be found in the Theban tomb of Antefoker dating from the Middle Kingdom (c.2055–1650 BC). The dances appear to be measured and fairly sedate. The *keskes*-dance, associated with Hathor, involved holding mirrors and what appear to be wooden or ivory sticks, carved in the shape of a hand at one end; they were probably clappers. The hand-shaped implements may be linked to Hathor in her aspect of Djeritef, 'his hand', that is the hand of Atum, said in the Heliopolitan creation myth, to have created Shu and Tefnut by masturbating.

A limestone relief of c.1400 BC, now in the British Museum, London, includes a male figure with a lion's head (possibly a Bes mask), carrying a staff with a human hand at the tip, in a register labelled 'dancing by children'.

Beer and Wine in Egyptian Religion

Beer and wine – distillation for making spirit drinks was unknown in ancient Egypt – were important in both temple and popular rituals. They were presented as offerings to the gods in the temples and shrines, and to the spirits of the dead in the tombs, funerary chapels and temples. They were also drunk at festivals and other celebrations, and were used in magical rituals and medicine. Together with bread, beer was a staple of the Egyptian diet, and the Wisdom Literature tells us that it was a mother's responsibility to provide these two sources of nutrition for her children. The gods were thought to be pacified and humoured by alcohol. In the myth of *The Destruction of Mankind*, the ferocious lioness goddess Sekhmet is prevented from wiping out humankind altogether by being made drunk on beer dyed red to resemble human blood.

From lists of offerings to the gods compiled during the New Kingdom (c.1550–c.1069 BC), we can learn about the variety, source and quantity of alcohol arriving at the temples. Libation with alcohol played a well-attested role in ancient Egyptian ritual, whether at annual festivals such as the Festival of the Nile and Drunkenness, or at occasional ceremonies, such as the foundation of a new building.

In the Afterlife

Beer- and wine-making depended on successful agriculture and abundant harvests, for which the ancient Egyptians believed they needed the beneficence of certain deities, in honour of whom they held festivals and made offerings. The fundamental need for constant supplies

▶ *Wine and beer figure largely on New Kingdom offering lists. This granite statue of Tuthmosis III holds jars of wine: such offerings were a means of appeasing supernatural forces – both deities and spirits of the dead.*

of agricultural produce was of crucial importance to the ancient Egyptians, not only on earth but also in the Afterlife. This explains the private tomb scenes of harvesting, brewing, viticulture and winemaking, which represent the hope of having eternal supplies not only for the deceased but also for everyone in Egypt. The practise of depicting particular actions and events was to the Egyptians a means of magically ensuring they would happen in the Afterlife. Thus, by illustrating such scenes of daily life (captioned in hieroglyphs), the basic fundamentals of existence were being recognized and, with hope, laid down for eternity. This preparation for the future ensured the continued smooth running of the natural order of the cosmos, encapsulated in the concept of *maat*.

The patron deity of wine presses was male, Shezmu, but on the whole the female-oriented nature of brewing, from early in Pharaonic history, was closely reflected in the divine world. The presiding deities of beer were the goddesses Menqet and Tenemyt, whose names probably derived from the terms for a type of beer jar and beer, respectively. The equivalent deity of vineyards and wine-making was Renenutet, a cobra-form goddess of harvest and abundance. A number of private New Kingdom Theban tombs contain scenes of viticulture, with the presence of small shrines dedicated to this snake goddess.

Wine had a special significance in the cults of the goddesses Bastet, Sekhmet, Tefnut and particularly Hathor, the goddess most closely associated with alcohol and drunkenness. A song inscribed on a wall of the hypostyle hall of the Temple of Hathor at Philae, tells of a 'festival of intoxication' celebrated in honour of the goddess, and we learn that a perfect year was believed to have its beginnings in drunkenness.

Dance and alcohol were particularly closely related in the cult of Hathor. The spirit-deity Bes, who was associated with music, dance, fertility, sexuality and the protection of the family, was also connected with alcohol. Wine and beer jars were specially made in his form.

Attendance records have survived from the New Kingdom tomb-builders' village of Deir el-Medina in western Thebes. They tell us that it was not unheard of for men to take days off work specially to brew beer for a particular occasion, which was usually religious in nature. An ostracon, or inscribed potsherd, from Deir el-Medina, now in the Cairo Museum, describes the celebration of a festival of the deified king Amenhotep I, who was the patron deity of the tomb builders:

The crew [necropolis workers] *were in jubilation before him* [Amenhotep I] *for four whole days of drinking with their children and their wives.*

Communing with the gods

Drunkenness appears to have gone hand in hand with celebration (inscriptions in the early Eighteenth-Dynasty tomb of Ahmose at El-Kab include the words 'drinking into intoxication and celebrating a festive day'), but it appears also to have been considered beneficial for communing with the gods. Three visiting scribes left a graffito at Abusir, in the fiftieth year of the Nineteenth-Dynasty ruler Ramesses II's reign. It reads: '...It is as we stand drunk before (you) [Sekhmet of Sahure], that we utter our petition.'

The various 'Dream Books' that survive indicate that if an Egyptian dreamt that he or she was drinking beer or wine it was a good omen. Depending on the type of beer being drunk, the dreamer would rejoice, live or be healed. However, if the beer was warm, then it was thought to predict suffering.

Beer and wine figure frequently in the remedies in the magico-medical texts. In

▲ One of the Delta vineyards belonging to the estate of Amun is said to have produced 'wine like drawing water without measure'. Workers tread grapes in this painting from the tomb of Nakht in Thebes. 18th Dynasty.

Wine- and beer-making

Vineyards existed in the Delta and in large desert oases such as Kharga and Dakhla. Wine was produced both for ritual use and for consumption in the wealthier households. The juice was extracted by treading the grapes, and tomb paintings show the technique used for wringing the last of the juice from the skins by putting them in a sack tied to two poles and forcing the poles apart. The primary fermentation was in large, unstoppered jars. The wine was then decanted into sealed jars and left on racks to ferment a second time. These wine jars were labelled with the date, the place of origin and the maker's name. Both red and white wines were made.

Beer, the staple drink of the ancient Egyptians, used the same ingredients and similar processes to those involved in bread-making, and these two basic commodities might be produced in the same place. Modern microscopy analysis of dried residues of beer has revealed that it was made by mixing together two parts: one of malted, ground emmer wheat or barley in cool water, with another part of the same in hot water and well heated. The resulting mash was sieved and fermented.

many cases, they may well have served only as vehicles for the prescribed ingredients, to improve the taste and consistency. Because beer was probably cheaper and more easily accessible than wine, it is not surprising that it was prescribed more often than the latter. Spell 24 of Papyrus Leiden I, 348 was to be recited while drinking beer, in order to cure stomach troubles. By sympathetic magic, the sufferer was identified with the divine personification of intoxication, Seth, 'in that name of his, "beer",' who '...confuses a heart in order to bear away the heart of the enemy, friend, dead male, dead female...' Other papyri also contain 'spells of the beer', which were similarly intended to

drive away the demons thought to be tormenting the patient – a method of exorcism by intoxication. According to Papyrus Berlin 8,278, by drinking wine and beer Seth gained the courage and power to 'take away the heart' of the enemies. For the ancient Egyptians, to remove the heart was to eradicate the being, because this organ was considered the seat of wisdom, emotion and indeed consciousness. In this way, alcohol was deemed capable of the expulsion of a demon from the body.

◀ It was usual to label wine jars, so we know much about the circulation of wine and that most of it was produced in Lower Egypt. This jar was found in the tomb of Tutankhamun.

Ancestor Worship

The ancient Egyptians were keen to remember and placate their dead relatives, because of their belief in the effects that the dead could have on their lives (see *The Positive Influence of the Dead* and *The Negative Influence of the Dead*). They worshipped their ancestors on special occasions. These included the annual Beautiful Festival of the Valley, when people visited the tombs of their relatives and commemorated the dead, eating a communal meal with them, and the festivals of Osiris at Abydos, when people visited family memorials erected there in the form of stelae (see *Festivals and Pilgrimages*).

The ancestors were also revered on a more daily basis in family homes. People had shrines to their ancestors in niches in their main living rooms, with special stelae and anthropoid busts providing the focus for worship – the point of contact between the living and their dead relatives. The Calendars of Lucky and Unlucky Days inform us that certain days were considered suitable for 'pacifying your *akhu* [the spirits of the ancestors]', and several texts state specifically that this must take place 'in your house'.

Excellent Spirits of Re

A particular type of ancestor stela has been discovered, mainly at the tomb-builders' village of Deir el-Medina (although six have been discovered elsewhere in the Theban region, and two at Abydos). These are known as *akh iker n Re* stelae ('Excellent Spirits of Re' stelae), 47 of which have been discovered dating to the New Kingdom, but especially to the Nineteenth Dynasty (c.1295–c.1186 BC). The *akhu* to which these stelae were dedicated could be either male or female, and were presumably the spirits of people who had been particularly respected during their lifetime, and after death were

▶ *Most of the surviving 'ancestor busts' are made of limestone or sandstone.*

believed to have particular influence in the divine world. Families seem to have appealed to these ancestors to ensure the continuity of the family line, asking them to act as intermediaries for them in the realm of the gods.

The stelae were fairly standardized, although variations have been found. The dead ancestor tended to be depicted seated before an offering table, smelling a lotus blossom. He or she was often shown holding a cloth, sceptre or *ankh*-sign. Offerings were probably made – and prayers said – before the stela.

Ancestor busts

About 140 'anthropoid busts' are also known from ancient Egypt. They have been found mainly in domestic contexts throughout the country, but again especially at Deir el-Medina. Their significance is uncertain but it is possible that they symbolized a family's ancestors. They range from just over 1cm ($^1/_2$in) to 28cm (11in) in height, and are made of clay, limestone, sandstone, faience or wood, usually painted. They tend to be a single bust, although about five double busts have been discovered.

The bust consists of a human head on a rounded support or base that resembles shoulders. But there is no modelling of the human chest and it is difficult to determine which sex they are meant to

be, although the remains of red paint indicates the conventional colour of men's skin in the art of the period. In most cases they wear a collar, some of which have pendant lotus blossoms and buds on the front. Most wear tripartite wigs, but some are bareheaded.

It was always supposed that these objects were associated with ancestor worship in the household, but depictions of them in scenes from the Book of the Dead imply that they served a purpose in a funerary context. The fact that most of them bear no inscriptions makes their interpretation much more difficult.

The Positive Influence of the Dead

The Ancient Egyptians believed that the dead (especially spouses and relatives) possessed supernatural powers that might be called upon to solve various problems in the lives of those still living. The best evidence for this belief comes from the fascinating letters that have survived, written from a living person to a dead one. Today these letters are referred to as Letters to the Dead. The 20 or so that we know of range in date from c.3100–c.1200 BC, but a corresponding oral practice may have been common throughout Egyptian history.

Letters to the Dead

The letters were placed in the tombs of the people to whom they were addressed, probably at the time of the funeral or when the tomb was reopened for later burials. Some were written on pottery dishes, and it is possible that they were left at the tomb full of food offerings, so that as the spirit of the deceased symbolically ate the food the

▶ A continuous supply of food offerings helped ensure the beneficence of the spirits of the deceased. This wooden model of a female offering bearer is from the tomb of Assiut. Middle Kingdom.

text would reveal itself. One such letter, written in ink in hieratic, can be seen on a shallow pottery dish in the Petrie Museum of Egyptian Archaeology in London. It dates to the First Inter-mediate Period (c.2181–c.2055 BC) and was discovered at Diospolis in Upper Egypt. The letter is to the dead man Nefersekhi from his 'sister' (probably his widow making use of a term of affection). She tells him that a trustee of the dead man's property is defrauding their daughter of her share of the inheritance, and she is desperately appealing for his intervention.

The content of this letter is typical – it is addressed to a man (usually it was a deceased husband or father who was appealed to in this way), it deals with legal problems (and especially wrangles over inheritance), and it supposes that now that the man is dead he is closer to the divine world – making it easier for him to influence it – and that he himself now has supernatural powers that could be of use to those still alive.

Another similar example, dating to the Old Kingdom (c.2686–c.2181 BC), can be found on a piece of linen in the Cairo Museum. It is addressed to the deceased

◀ Jewellery and other personal adornment was by no means restricted to women in ancient Egyptian society, as exemplified here by Sennefer's large gold earrings and bracelets in a painting on the wall of his tomb.

head of the family by his widow and son. They are distressed because, against their wishes, relatives have come and removed pottery and servants or slaves from their house. The widow is particularly upset and she says that she would rather that either she or her son died (it is not quite clear which one) than she should see her son subordinated to this rogue branch of the family. The letter begins with the widow reminding the dead husband and father that he himself had spoken out against these thieving members of the family on his deathbed. She and her son quote him on the importance of inheritance and of solidarity between the generations.

It is difficult to be certain exactly how the dead man was expected to help the situation. Perhaps the widow had decided to seek help from her husband after her case had failed in the local court. It seems that the widow thought that her husband might be able to pursue the case in a kind of parallel divine court. It is possible that the piece of linen was originally wrapped around some kind of votive offering to the spirit of the dead man.

A cure for infertility

In addition to helping out with legal problems, deceased relatives were also appealed to when a woman was having difficulties conceiving a child. Because there were no practical measures to cure infertility, and because a woman's ability to have children was so important to her status and well being, both in this life and the next, childless women would seek help from the divine or spirit world. An Old Kingdom Letter to the Dead on a pot now in the Haskell Oriental Museum of Chicago is a plea to a deceased father from his daughter. It reads: 'Cause now that there be born to me a healthy male child. (For) you are an *akh iker* [excellent spirit].'

Fertility figurines have also survived inscribed with a request to a father to grant his daughter a child. These female figurines, with their exaggerated pubic regions, clearly symbolized fertility and sexuality. There seems little reason to attempt a distinction between the possible erotic and procreative connotations of these figures, for as far as the ancient Egyptians were concerned both concepts united to ensure the continued existence of the people of Egypt. The figurines themselves would have served as votive offerings to the dead. One Middle Kingdom example in the Berlin Museum has a child on the left hip, and an inscription on the right thigh reads: 'May a birth be granted to your daughter Seh.' The ancient Egyptians' belief in the creative and magical potency of the written word was profound. In the inscription on this

▲ *In a painting on the wall of his tomb in Aswan, Sarenput sits before a table laden with offerings.*

particular figurine, the quail chick used to write the letter 'w' has been written without legs. Could this have been to safeguard against this hieroglyphic sign coming to life and disappearing? Or perhaps it was intended to reduce the danger such a chick could pose to the crops.

A cure for an illness

The dead were sometimes called upon to help cure illness. The 'Cairo Bowl', which dates to the early Twelfth Dynasty (c.1900 BC), has a letter on it from a woman named Dedi, addressed to her dead husband. It tells him that their servant-girl is ill, and appeals to him to help her to get better.

Ritual objects used in everyday magic, such as apotropaic wands, have been

discovered in the accessible outer areas of tombs. They may have been placed there to benefit from the supernatural powers of the dead person. In recent times, village magicians in Egypt and the Sudan are known to have given added power to their magic charms by temporarily burying them in the vicinity of tombs (the most popular tombs being those of people particularly respected in life for their wisdom or piety). Execration figurines have also been found buried near tombs (see *Paraphernalia of Ritual*), perhaps with the intention that the dead would continue the punishment of the enemies of Egypt into the Afterlife.

The Negative Influence of the Dead

The ancient Egyptians believed that unsettled dead people could haunt them and cause them all kinds of distress. These were the spirits of people who had died violently or too young or without a proper burial, or they might have failed to achieve what was expected of them in life, such as the production of children. If an inexplicable disaster struck an Egyptian family, such as a severe illness or the sudden loss of livestock, then a dead person's spirit might be behind it. To forestall such losses and afflictions at the hands of the dead, it was thought a sensible precaution to propitiate their spirits with regular offerings, and to do nothing that might offend them. At all times it was considered that the dead required respect from their families and descendants.

In one story that is partly preserved on several ostraca of the late second millennium BC, the High Priest of Amun-Re confronts an *akh* ('spirit')

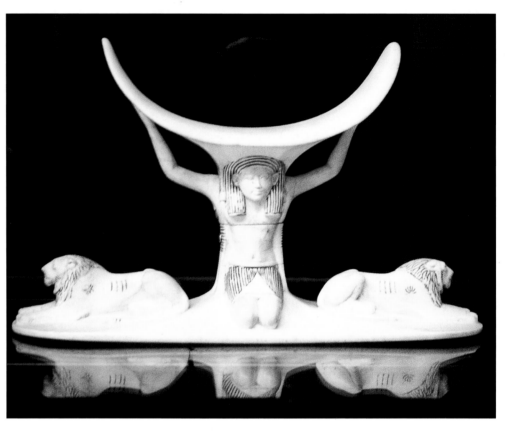

▲ *The recumbent lions on Tutankhamun's headrest were intended to protect the sleeper. Funerary art often shows the crouching lion serving a defensive role.*

Exorcism

The curses known as the Execration Texts were mainly aimed at the destruction of Egypt's enemies, but some were written to exorcise the malignant ghosts of those who had rebelled against the state. By destroying the names of these people, their spirits were considered to have been vanquished, thereby extending their punishment into the Afterlife.

The defacement of images of the dead person also amounted to an attack on his or her spirit in the Afterlife. If the tomb was destroyed, it followed that the spirit would no longer be able to receive sustaining offerings and its power would be correspondingly diminished or eliminated.

who has been causing trouble in the Theban necropolis. The ghost admits that it is unhappy because its tomb has fallen into disrepair. In an attempt to settle and appease this restless spirit, the High Priest promises an endowment for cult offerings and a whole new tomb. The ancient Egyptians believed that food offerings and the preservation of the body were crucial for a contented existence in the Afterlife.

Troublesome women

Whereas it was usual to invoke dead husbands and fathers for help and guidance, it tended to be the spirits of dead women who were regarded as troublemakers. In a Letter to the Dead on papyrus which is now in the Rijksmuseum van Oudheden in Leiden, a widowed husband living in Memphis during the Nineteenth Dynasty writes to his wife, who seems to have been dead for about two years. He makes it quite clear that he cared for her during her

lifetime and that he has stayed faithful to her after death, and so he does not think it is fair that she should continue to haunt him. Sadly, the letter does not tell us how the hauntings were manifesting themselves, but the man in question had quite clearly had enough and he threatens his deceased wife with some kind of court case before a divine tribunal. A similar letter was written on an ostracon dating to the end of the Twentieth Dynasty, from the Scribe of the Necropolis, Butehamon, to his dead wife Akhtai.

Protection against ghosts

Female ghosts were considered a particular threat to pregnant women and nursing mothers, and to young children, especially if the ghost's antecedent had

▲ *A small pyramidion marked the tomb chapels of the New Kingdom rock-cut tombs at Deir el-Medina, such as this one belonging to the craftsman of the royal tomb, Amennakht, and his wife Nubemsha.*

died before giving birth successfully herself. Many of the oracular amuletic decrees, and the texts in the Brooklyn Magical Papyrus dating to the first millennium BC, mention female ghosts as a dangerous threat against which precautions must be taken.

Another type of harmful spirit was referred to as *mut*, which is often translated as 'dangerous dead'. The texts sometimes classify executed traitors and prisoners of war as *mut*. But in everyday magic, a *mut* seems to have been a ghost who could or would not pass on to the realm of the dead and therefore continued to plague the living.

The ancient Egyptians also used spells to protect themselves against terrifying night-time apparitions (of both male and female ghosts). It was believed that the dead could cause nightmares, and even inflict sickness on the sleeper. In addition to spells to guard against these, they used headrests decorated with apotropaic figures to ward off evil, such as those of the protective household deities Bes and Taweret.

The magico-medical texts quite often cite the malign influence of the dead as a cause of disease, or as a threat to its cure. Even the shadow of a dead person was regarded as a potential source of harm to the medicine prepared by a doctor. Spells were devised to drive the dead out of the limbs of a patient.

Even otherwise benign spirits were considered to be capable of punishing the living if they were roused. The degree of violence that the dead were credited with is exemplified by those tomb inscriptions that warned anyone thinking of robbing the tomb that the dead person was now capable of exacting revenge by killing the robber and ruining his whole family.

Mythologizing Ancient Egypt

Outsiders have always regarded Egypt as an alien place. Its monuments have inspired awe, and the customs of its people have aroused fascination. The civilization of Pharaonic Egypt is so remote that although much evidence has been unearthed we still know relatively little – the scope for misinterpreting or even inventing Egypt's past is huge.

Until the early nineteenth century scientific archaeology was not practised and hieroglyphic script had not been deciphered, so the ancient texts were unfathomable. It is easy to see how 'Egypt of the Pharaohs' came to be mythologized. Scholars of the Western world based their understanding of ancient Egypt on the works of the classical writers, but we now know that these are far from reliable. The Graeco-Roman perception of Egypt was largely created from the legendary poems of Homer and the often inaccurate writings of Herodotus.

Despite great advances in archaeology and philology, the modern age continues to mythologize Egypt's past. Hollywood has helped to foster absurd ideas such as the 'curse of the mummy', and followers of the New Age movement have looked to Egypt as a fount of mysterious knowledge.

◀ *The Great Sphinx, guardian of Khafre's valley temple, has intrigued travellers to Egypt over the centuries. Illustration from* Views in Egypt *by Luigi Mayer (1801)*

The Legacy of the Classical Writers

Until the early nineteenth century, the West's understanding (or misunderstanding) of ancient Egypt had much to do with the works of classical authors, although the seventeenth century did see the first 'archaeological' visits to Egypt. Men such as the English astronomer John Greaves (1602–52) visited Giza twice, measured and examined the pyramids, made a critical analysis of the classical writings about them, and published *Pyramidographia, or a Discourse on the Pyramids in Aegyt* in 1646. Another was the Frenchman Claude Sicard (1677–1726), who visited Upper Egypt four times and was the first modern traveller to identify the sites of Thebes and to

◄ *Serapis was a Ptolemaic invention: a combination of the Egyptian gods Osiris and Apis, represented as a Hellenistic deity (his attributes were those of Zeus, Helios, Hades, Asklepios and Dionysos). Marble sculpture from Pergamon, 2nd century AD.*

▲ *Herodotus was quite clearly mistaken when he wrote, '...they [the Egyptians] have no need to plough or hoe, or to use any other ordinary methods of cultivating their land.' A wall painting from the tomb of Sennedjem shows him farming with his wife. 18th Dynasty.*

ascribe correctly the Colossi of Memnon and the Valley of the Kings on the basis of classical descriptions.

The father of history

The greatest influence on the classical writers who documented Egypt was Herodotus (c.490–c.420 BC), who is often referred to as the 'Father of History'. He was certainly the best-known tourist in classical times. He was born in Halicarnassus in Caria on the south-western coast of Asia Minor. He wrote a series of nine books called *The Histories*, whose purpose was to trace the events that brought Greece into conflict with Persia. Within this framework, he also recorded all the

information he had been able to collect – and he was undoubtedly an avid collector of information.

Herodotus was probably in Egypt some time between 450 and 430 BC, and it is Book II of his series that describes Egypt. He appears to have gone to some length to collect information in Memphis, which he then sought to have backed up in Thebes and Heliopolis. Wisely, he spoke to priests, who were educated and had access to the nation's archives housed in the temples. But he relied wholly on oral testimony, and he was not familiar with the Egyptian language. He may have misunderstood much of what he was told and, as a foreigner, the Egyptian priests are unlikely to have disclosed much information to him. Quite clearly he did not believe all that he was told, but he chose to record it nonetheless, thereby ensuring the propagation of bizarre stories about ancient Egypt, both via an

▼ *The Palestrina Mosaic formed part of a floor in the Italian town of Praeneste (Palestrina). It probably dates to the early 1st century BC and its subject is a Nilotic landscape, showing the popularity of Egyptian themes in the Roman world.*

oral tradition and a written one. For example, after recounting a tale of a phoenix which was said to fly from Arabia to Heliopolis every 500 years, with his dead father in an egg of myrrh, he added, 'I give the story as it was told me...but I don't believe it.'

Herodotus was particularly interested in religion, medicine, mummification, customs and taboos, architecture (especially that of the pyramids) and astronomy; as well as geography (especially the flooding of the Nile),

transport, flora, fauna, food, clothing, and historical events. He was intrigued by what he learnt, and had enormous respect for the country and its people:

About Egypt I shall have a great deal more to relate because of the number of remarkable things the country contains, and because of the fact that more monuments which beggar description are to be found there than anywhere else in the world.

▲ *The Rosetta Stone records in Greek, demotic and hieroglyphic scripts the religious ceremonies attending the coronation of Ptolemy V in 205 BC.*

He recorded, for instance, that women traded at market while men stayed at home and wove; that women urinated standing up and men sitting down; that they kneaded dough with their feet and clay (and even dung) with their hands. He was fascinated by the Egyptians' relationship with animals, especially the keeping and mummification of sacred animals. His description of their obsession with cats was particularly unreliable:

What happens when a house catches fire is most extraordinary: nobody takes the least trouble to put it out, for it is only the cats that matter: everyone stands in a row, a little distance from his neighbour, trying to protect the cats, which nevertheless slip through the line, or jump over it, and hurl themselves into the flames. This causes the Egyptians deep distress.

Herodotus felt that he was in a position to compare Egypt with other parts of the ancient world, and the Egyptian people with their neighbours. Because of the stable climate, for example, he wrote, '...next to the Libyans, they are the healthiest people in the world'.

He attempted to explain the inundation of the River Nile, and supplied various theories, such as the occurrence of seasonal winds that checked the flow of the river current towards the sea; the melting of snow in the southern mountains; and the supernatural nature of the river. His own explanation was elaborate, involving the sun, evaporation and winds dispersing the vapours, but the cause of the annual flood was basically deemed a mystery.

Unwittingly, Herodotus laid the foundations for a confused picture of life in Pharaonic Egypt. He wrote:

...the Egyptians themselves in their manners and customs seem to have reversed the ordinary practices of mankind.

Herodotus's writings on the actual history of Egypt are confused and his chronology is very jumbled. Even for Herodotus, writing in the fifth century BC, the beginnings of Dynastic Egypt were shrouded in the distant past, and the pyramids were already ancient and mysterious tourist attractions. He was, however, in a position to provide relatively accurate information concerning the Twenty-sixth Dynasty (664–525 BC), and the invasion of Egypt by the Persian ruler Cambyses in 525 BC.

Diodorus Siculus

Both the historian Diodorus Siculus (c.40 BC) and the historian and geographer Strabo (c.63 BC–c.AD 24) imitated Herodotus. Diodorus Siculus was born in Agyrium in Sicily. He visited Egypt between c.60 and 56 BC, and described Egypt in the first book of his *Bibliotheca Historica*, which set out to cover the history of the world up to Julius Caesar's conquest of Gaul. He was clearly amazed by some of the customs he believed to be typically Egyptian and, like Herodotus, he included among these

▶ *Egyptian scribes wrote using a rush brush. The Greeks introduced reed pens, which were adopted by the Egyptians by the 1st century AD. 25th Dynasty.*

Champollion

The ancient Egyptian written sources were unintelligible until Jean François Champollion le Jeune (1790–1832) deciphered hieroglyphs. Working on the replicated hieroglyphic and Greek inscriptions on the Rosetta Stone (a priestly decree issued in 196 BC inscribed on a slab of black granite, now in the British Museum), he just beat the English scholar Thomas Young with the publication of his findings in 1822, though he did not achieve his ambition of visiting Egypt until 1828.

Using his knowledge of Coptic, Champollion was able to deduce not only the meaning of hieroglyphs and hieratic text but the structure of ancient Egyptian grammar.

▲ *By the age of 17, Champollion had already learnt to read Arabic, Syrian, Chaldean, Coptic, Latin, Greek, Sanscrit and Persian. Portrait by Léon Cogniet, 1831.*

mummification and the excessive treatment and worship of animals. He related the revenge of an Alexandrian mob on a Roman ambassador who had accidentally killed a cat (there is no ancient Egyptian evidence for this kind of behaviour). The pyramids and the Nile also fascinated him.

Strabo
Born in Pontus in north-eastern Asia Minor, Strabo spent several years in Alexandria in about 27 BC, and discussed Egypt in the eighth book of his *Geography*, published in c.23 AD.

His descriptions include those of Alexandria, the Faiyum, Theban monuments such as the Colossi of Memnon and the Valley of the Kings, and the Nilometer at Elephantine.

Strabo travelled with the Roman Prefect Aelius Gallus, escorted by priests and guides. In the seventeenth book of *Geography* he claims that tourists continued to be fascinated by the Nile, the monuments, the religion and the funerary customs, the exotic animals and worship of them, and the superior wisdom of the priests. One of his aims seems to have been to verify whether the sites of Egypt were worthy of their reputations. He decided that the following were: the oases; the tombs in the Valley of the Kings; the boating stunts at Philae; the pyramids; and the

stone chips around the pyramids, said to be petrified beans that were eaten by the pyramid builders.

Misinterpreting hieroglyphs
None of the classical writers appears to have made any effort to understand hieroglyphs, and until they were deciphered in the early nineteenth century, they tended to be regarded as esoteric and magical. The Renaissance in Europe heralded a keen interest in ancient Egypt, and one of the first classical texts to resurface and be studied in the fifteenth century was Horapollo's *Hieroglyphica*, dating to the fourth century AD. Rather than the true meaning of the ancient inscriptions, this gave symbolic explanations of hieroglyphs, which were believed to encapsulate profound truths.

In the seventeenth century, the Jesuit scholar Athanasius Kircher (1601–1680) published several volumes of entirely fictitious interpretations of hieroglyphic inscriptions, reflecting the theory that hieroglyphic signs were mystical symbols, which could be used to explain the secrets of the Egyptian cosmos.

Misunderstanding the Pyramids

The breathtakingly enormous size of some of the pyramids, their immense antiquity and the fact that it is impossible to know with certainty how they were built (because no texts have been discovered to inform us), have resulted in some wild, unfounded speculation about them. It was Herodotus who first established the mistaken association between the construction of the Great Pyramid and the employment of slave labour, with no mention made of the corvée system. He also propagated the story that Khufu had forced his daughter to prostitute herself in return for blocks of stone, which were then used to build the middle of the three queens' pyramids to the east of the Great Pyramid.

In the first century AD the slave labour myth was augmented by the Jewish historian Josephus, who stated that the Hebrews were worn out during their sojourn in Egypt by, among other great toils, being forced to build pyramids. In fact the pyramids at Giza were constructed over a millennium before the time of the Hebrews.

Building the pyramids

We still do not know exactly how the Pyramids were built. Theories vary, but often include artificial flooding to provide a level, and the construction of earth ramps up which to drag the stone blocks. The enormous labour force needed to erect the pyramids and other great Egyptian monuments was assembled under a regime of obligatory service to the state, known as the corvée system. Each household had to provide food supplies or manpower for the state building projects. An advantage of becoming a priest was the chance of exemption from this conscription.

Arab legends

When the Arabs conquered Egypt in AD 642, they clearly marvelled at the pyramids and were quick to mythologize them. One popular Arab legend claimed that the great pyramid at Giza was in fact the tomb of Hermes (the Greek deity identified with the Egyptian god of wisdom and the scribal profession, Thoth). The purpose of the pyramid was said to be to conceal the literature and science held within it, well hidden from the eyes of the uninitiated, and to protect them from the flood – seemingly a merging of the catastrophic Biblical flood and the annual inundation of the River Nile. If we were to believe the Yemeni Arabs, the pyramids of Khufu and Khafre on the Giza plateau were actually the tombs of their ancient kings, one of whom was said to have defeated the Egyptians.

According to an early Coptic legend, a certain King Surid was responsible for the construction of the three pyramids at Giza. It tells that he had scientific knowledge recorded on their internal walls; sculptures and treasure placed inside them; and an idol positioned

▲ Europeans were fascinated by pyramids, which they tended to represent with impossibly steep sides. This scene is from a peepshow box of c.1750 depicting the Seven Wonders of the World.

outside each of the pyramids to guard it. Surid was said to have been buried in the 'Eastern Pyramid' (Khufu's), his brother Hujib in the 'Western Pyramid' (Khafre's), and Hujib's son Karuras in the 'Pied Pyramid' (Menkaure's).

Continuing this tradition, the fifteenth-century Arab historian al-Maqrizi recorded that an ancient king named Surid decorated the walls and ceilings of his pyramid chambers with scientific imagery and depictions of stars and planets. He was also supposed to have filled the chambers with hordes of treasure, including miraculous iron weapons that would never rust and glass that could bend without breaking. Al-Maqrizi also stated that when King Surid died, he was buried in the pyramid together with all his possessions. It is possible that the name Surid was a corruption of 'Suphis', the name used by Herodotus in the fifth century BC when referring to Khufu.

The story of the tremendous treasure buried inside the Great Pyramid can also be found in the tale of *The Thousand and One Nights* (also known as *The Arabian Nights*), along with the description of what is said to be the first ever break-in to the pyramid, in about AD 820, by Caliph al-Mamun, the son of Haroun al-Rashid. His men are said to have used iron picks and crowbars, and to have heated the stones with fire and then poured cold vinegar on them. It is, in fact, highly likely that the first forced entry into the Great Pyramid took place in antiquity, and that al-Mamun's men made use of a passage created by ancient thieves. A man named Denys of Telmahre, the Jacobite Patriarch of Antioch, was present when al-Mamun entered the pyramid, and he states that the pyramid had already been opened before their visit. This particular tale of the alleged earliest break-in was indeed rather too fanciful to be true. The same (albeit tamed) story was recorded by Abu Szalt of Spain. Rather than fabulous treasure, he reports that al-Mamun's men discovered only a sarcophagus with some old bones inside it.

Joseph's granaries

The Coptic and Arab myths were certainly closer to the truth than the explanations of medieval Europeans. Pilgrims to the Holy Land also chose to visit Egypt in order to see sites such as the pyramids, which they believed to be

▶ *The Freemasons adopted religious imagery for their secret rites, as shown by this nineteenth century Italian design for a Masonic temple. 19th century.*

the 'granaries of Joseph' (an idea recorded as early as the fifth century AD in the Latin writings of Julius Honorius and Rufinus). The pyramids were also depicted as granaries in, for example, a mosaic dating to the twelfth century in one of the domes of St Mark's in Venice. Many later fifteenth- and sixteenth-century representations of pyramids were just as inaccurate, even when

▲ *The new entrance to the Louvre Museum in Paris is a high-tech glass pyramid.*

executed by people who had actually seen them. They tended to be portrayed with much steeper sides than the real things, thereby mirroring more familiar classical monuments.

Mysteries of the pyramids

The seventeenth century saw the advocating, especially by Athanasius Kircher, of the magical and mystical significance of the pyramids - a belief still held by many people today. Modern theories about the pyramids range from the downright silly, such as their construction by aliens, to the less absurd, such as their alignment with the belt of Orion. The weird and wonderful connections made with the pyramids are endless, including their power to achieve immortality and world peace. Even if the ancient pharaohs had not intended any of these associations, they would no doubt be extremely satisfied to find that their pyramids are still inspiring awe and wonder in the twenty-first century AD.

The Curse of the Pharaohs

Everyone loves a good story. Everyone also loves to be scared witless when they can maintain a safe and comfortable distance from the object of their fear. 'Strange and mysterious Egypt', with its dark tombs and ancient mummies, is the perfect setting for terror and intrigue. It is hardly surprising, therefore, that Hollywood was quick to capitalize on the 'Curse of the Mummy'. This idea was, in fact, a popular theme in literature from the mid-nineteenth century onwards. Authors such as Bram Stoker and Arthur Conan Doyle were keen to write about the awful revenge wrought by mummies whose tombs had been disturbed.

Tutankhamun's tomb

It was the discovery of the almost intact tomb of the Eighteenth-Dynasty ruler Tutankhamun (c.1336–c.1327 BC) that

▼ Tutankhamun's mummy lay in a close-fitting nest of three anthropoid coffins (the innermost of solid gold) inside a quartzite sarcophagus.

▲ Two life-sized black wooden statues of the king guarded the entrance to his burial chamber, seen here just after the door seal had been broken.

resulted in worldwide Egyptomania and an obsession with the ancient curse of the pharaohs. The great discovery was made by the archaeologist Howard Carter (1874–1939) while excavating in the Valley of the Kings, in the employment of the fifth Earl of Carnarvon. On 4th November 1922 he discovered a flight of steps leading down to a blocked door covered in seals bearing the cartouche of Tutankhamun. On entering the tomb on 26th November, 'the day of days', it was found to contain the body of the boy-king and the most incredible quantity of marvellous funerary goods.

Not only was this a discovery of breathtaking gold treasure, but its owner Tutankhamun had been buried in an unusual tomb (see *Rock-cut Tombs*). He had died in his teens, and he was closely connected with the infamous King Akhenaten (c.1352– c.1336 BC), who had made revolutionary changes to the art and religion of Egypt. People's imaginations began to run wild.

▲ *Before removing the contents of Tutankhamun's tomb to Cairo, every object had to be scientifically recorded, photographed and often conserved. The king's body was left in his tomb, inside his outer coffin in the sarcophagus.*

Within six months, on 5th April 1923, Lord Carnarvon died, and in newspapers around the world his unexpected death was instantly blamed on 'the curse'. Conan Doyle declared that it was the result of 'elementals – not souls, not spirits – created by Tutankhamun's priests to guard the tomb'. One newspaper printed the translation of a curse said to be written in hieroglyphs on the door of the second shrine: 'They who enter this sacred tomb shall swift be visited by wings of death.' But this curse was wholly fictitious, as were all the other curses reported to the press, such as the one said by a necromancer to have been found by Carter carved in hieroglyphs on a stone at the entrance of the tomb. It was supposed to have read: 'Let the hand raised against my form be withered! Let them be destroyed who attack my name, my foundation, my effigies, the images like unto me!'

Carnarvon had been a weak man ever since a car accident, and was exhausted by the circumstances surrounding the discovery of Tutankhamun's tomb. He accidentally cut open a mosquito bite while shaving; it became infected, and he ended up with a fever. In this further weakened state, he fell prey to pneumonia. Some of the newspapers suggested that Carnarvon had pricked himself while in the tomb on a sharp object, such as an arrowhead, doctored with a poison so potent that it was still active after 3,000 years. Other articles in the press reported that Carnarvon had become infected by deadly micro-organisms that had laid dormant for millennia.

Rumours spread like wildfire. It was said that at the moment of his death, all the lights went out in Cairo, and his son and heir, Lord Porchester, sixth Earl of Carnarvon, claimed that at their family home in Highclere Castle in England his father's favourite dog howled and dropped down dead at exactly the same moment as the earl passed away.

The newspapers began to report the deaths of anyone who might have had any connection with Carnarvon or the tomb, thereby linking further deaths with 'the curse'. The deaths recorded included those of Carnarvon's younger brother Aubrey Herbert, an X-ray specialist on his way to examine the royal mummy; Carter's right-hand man Arthur Mace (who was in fact already suffering from pleurisy before the tomb was discovered); the American railroad magnate George Jay Gould (who had visited the tomb, but was touring Egypt due to his ill health); an unnamed associate curator in the British Museum (who was said to have been labelling objects from the tomb, although there are no objects from Tutankhamun's tomb in the British Museum); and the French Egyptologist Georges Bénédite (who died as a result of a fall after visiting the tomb). The list of 'victims of the mummy's curse' goes on, but the American Egyptologist Herbert E. Winlock took great pleasure in compiling his own list with the more rational explanations of these people's deaths. Today, the discovery of Tutankhamun's tomb is remembered as much for the 'curse' as for the Egyptological significance of this great archaeological excavation.

▼ *The tombs of Ramesses IX and Tutankhamun at the time of their re-opening in 1922. The Valley of the Kings was known to the ancient Egyptians as* ta set aat *, 'the Great Place', or more informally, as* ta int, *'the Valley'.*

Glossary

The word list below is intended as a quick reference for terms that appear frequently throughout the book.

Abusir Papyri: administrative documents of the mortuary cult of the Fifth-Dynasty king Neferirkare (c.2475–c.2455 BC), whose funerary temple complex was associated with his pyramid at Abusir.

aegis: broad necklace surmounted with the head of a deity.

akh: transfigured spirit.

Akhet: four-month season of Inundation, when the River Nile was in flood.

akhu: enchantments/sorcery/spells.

Ammit: 'the gobbler'; composite beast with the head of a crocodile, the front legs and body of a lion or leopard, and the back legs of a hippopotamus; present at the 'Weighing of the Heart' ceremony held after death in order to eat the heart of anyone who was found to have committed wrong during his or her lifetime.

amulet: charm or protective device, usually worn or carried about the person.

ankh: hieroglyphic and amuletic sign for life; it may represent a sandal strap or an elaborate knot.

Apophis: serpent demon who threatened the sun god travelling through the Netherworld at night, and the dead travelling through the Afterlife.

apotropaic: able to ward off harm.

atef-crown: tall white crown with a plume on each side and a small disc at the top.

ba: personality/motivation; portrayed in art as a human-headed bird.

barque shrine: boat-shaped shrine.

benben: squat stone obelisk.

benbenet: gilded cap-stone or pyramidion at the top of a pyramid or obelisk.

Book of the Dead: 'the formulae for going forth by day'; illustrated funerary spells developed in the New Kingdom (c.1550–c.1069 BC), written mainly on papyrus.

Byblos: port on the Lebanese coast, important for the import of cedarwood.

canopic jars: jars used to store the embalmed internal organs following mummification.

cartonnage: plaster (gesso)-stiffened linen.

cartouche: (Egyptian: *shenu*) oval outline around two of the king's five names: his birth name (nomen) introduced by the title 'Son of Re' *(sa Re),* and his throne name (prenomen) introduced by the title 'He of the Sedge and the Bee' *(nesw bity).*

cippus of Horus: stela engraved with the image of the god Horus as a child overcoming creatures such as crocodiles and snakes, and inscribed with spells against scorpions, snakes and so on.

Coffin Texts: funerary texts inscribed mainly on coffins of the Middle Kingdom period (c.2055–c.1650 BC).

Coptic: use of Greek letters to write the Egyptian language; used throughout the Christian Period in Egypt.

demotic: cursive script derived from hieratic during the Twenty-sixth Dynasty (664–525 BC).

Deshret: (i) 'Red Land'– the desert; (ii) Red Crown of Lower Egypt.

djed-pillar: amulet; symbol of stability; backbone of Osiris.

Duat: the Afterworld, connected with the eastern horizon.

Ennead: (Egyptian: *pesedjet*) group of nine deities associated with Heliopolis.

epagomenal days: 'days upon the year'; five days added to the calendar to make the year up to 365 days.

execration texts: curses naming foreign rulers and places, used to magically destroy the enemies of Egypt, written on bowls, tablets and clay figurines in the form of bound captives, which were then smashed as part of execration rituals.

faience: glazed ceramic material composed primarily of crushed quartz or quartz sand (with added lime and plant ash or natron); usually a blue or green colour.

false door: an inscribed stone or wood architectural feature found in tombs and mortuary temples, in front of which food offerings were placed for the dead.

Fields of *Hetep* *'offering' and 'satisfaction'*: realm of the Afterlife connected with the western horizon.

Fields of *Iaru* *'reeds'*: realm of the Afterlife connected with purification and the eastern horizon.

healing statue: statue covered with spells to protect against snakes, scorpions, and so on.

heart scarab: large scarab amulet wrapped into the mummy bandages over the heart, inscribed with Chapter 30 of the Book of the Dead.

heb sed: royal jubilee festival usually celebrated by the king after 30 years on the throne.

Hedjet: White Crown of Upper Egypt.

heka: magic/divine energy.

heliacal rising: first sighting of the dog star Sirius on the eastern horizon just before dawn, after a 70-day period when it is invisible due to its alignment with the earth and the sun.

Hery Seshta: 'Chief of Mysteries or Secrets'.

hieratic: cursive form of hieroglyphs.

hu: divine utterance.

hypocephalus: bronze or cartonnage disc inscribed with Chapter 162 of the Book of the Dead; placed under the heads of mummies from the Late Period (c.747–c.332 BC).

hypostyle hall/court: roofed, pillared temple court.

Imhet: the Afterworld; connected with the western horizon.

imiut: fetish of the cult of Anubis; made from the inflated or stuffed headless skin of an animal (usually feline) tied to a pole in a pot.

incubation: practice of sleeping in a temple sanatorium in order to receive helpful or healing dreams from a god or goddess.

isfet: chaos.

ka: spirit/vital force/sustenance; represented pictorially as a person's double.

Kemet: 'Black Land'; Egypt (the Nile Valley and Delta).

kenbet: court/tribunal.

kherep Selket: 'the one who has power over the scorpion goddess'; scorpion and snake charmer.

Lector Priest: priest responsible for reciting spells and ritual texts.

maat: order/truth/justice/harmony.

mastaba: Arabic word for 'bench'; a tomb with a mound-shaped superstructure and a subterranean burial chamber.

menat-necklace: broad, beaded necklace with long counterpoise.

Metternich Stela: *cippus* of Horus now in the Metropolitan Museum of Art, New York.

mut: 'dangerous dead'/ghost.

muu-dancers: dancers at funerals, who wore kilts and tall hats.

naos: innermost shrine; home to the cult statue in a temple.

Narmer Palette: mudstone ceremonial palette commemorating the victories of the Protodynastic ruler Narmer (c.3100 BC); found in the 'Main Deposit' at Hierakonpolis; now in the Cairo Museum.

natron: naturally occurring salt; a compound of sodium carbonate and bicarbonate.

Neb Tawy: 'Lord of the Two Lands'; royal title.

Nebty-name: 'Two Ladies name'; one of five royal titles, referring to the cobra goddess Wadjet and the vulture goddess Nekhbet.

nemes: simple, pleated linen headdress worn by the king.

Nenet: undersky.

Nesw Bity: 'He of the Sedge and the Bee' (emblems of the Nile Valley and the Delta respectively); King of Upper and Lower Egypt.

Nilometer: measuring gauge used to record flood levels.

nome: administrative district; 22 in Upper Egypt, 20 in Lower Egypt.

obelisk: more tapering, needle-like version of the *benben*.

Ogdoad: (Egyptian: *Khmun)* group of eight deities associated with Hermopolis.

oracular amuletic decree: short spell, in the form of a divine decree, written on a tiny roll of papyrus placed inside a cylindrical tube during the late New Kingdom and Third Intermediate Period (c.1100–c.747 BC).

ostracon: flake of limestone or potsherd used for notes and sketches.

Per Ankh: House of Life in a temple complex; the place for copying, reading and research.

Peret: season of planting and growth.

peristyle court: open, colonnaded temple court.

phyle: one of four groups of priests working in the temple at any one time (on a rota system).

Pschent: Double Crown of Upper and Lower Egypt.

pylon: monumental temple gateway.

Pyramid Texts: funerary texts inscribed on the internal walls of pyramids from the reign of Unas (c.2375–c.2345 BC) at the end of the Fifth Dynasty to the First Intermediate Period (c.2181–c.2055 BC).

rekhet: wise woman.

Restoration Stela: stela from Karnak, now in the Cairo Museum, inscribed with a decree issued during the reign of Tutankhamun (c.1336–c.1327 BC) declaring the state's return to polytheism.

Rishi: Arabic word for 'feathered'; a style of anthropoid coffin decorated with a feathered effect.

Rosetau: 'passage of dragging', entrance to a tomb; necropoles of Memphis and Abydos.

Rosetta Stone: priestly decree issued in 196 BC, inscribed on a black granite slab, (British Museum, London).

sa: amulet/protection; mobile papyrus shelter.

Sau: 'amulet man'; title borne by wetnurses and midwives.

scarab: dung beetle; amulet of rebirth/creation/new life.

sebakh: Arabic word for ancient mudbrick and remains of organic refuse used in modern times as a fertilizer.

Sekhemty: Double Crown of Upper and Lower Egypt.

sem-priest: funerary priest who officiated at the 'Opening of the Mouth' ceremony.

sema tawy: 'Unification of the Two Lands'.

serdab: Arabic for 'cellar'; a small room in an Old Kingdom tomb, housing a statue of the deceased, often with eye-holes or a narrow slit in the wall.

serekh: niched/recessed palace façade; copied as a decorative feature on tombs, sarcophagi and coffins; used as a surround to the king's name in the Early Dynastic Period (c.3100–c.2686 BC) prior to the advent of the cartouche.

shabti/shawabti/ushabti: human-form funerary figurine thought to perform hard work for the deceased in the Afterlife; often inscribed with Chapter 6 of the Book of the Dead.

Shemau: Upper Egypt: the Nile Valley from the first cataract north to just south of Memphis.

Shomu: season of harvest and low water.

sia: divine knowledge.

side-lock: hairstyle worn by children.

sistrum: ceremonial rattle.

Sons of Horus: the four deities who guarded the internal organs in the four canopic jars.

soul house: pottery house with courtyard modelled with food offerings; placed in tombs.

sphinx: statue (usually of a king) with a lion's body.

stela: slab of wood or stone, bearing inscriptions, reliefs or paintings.

Sunu: doctor/physician.

syncretism: the fusion of two deities into one; for example, Amun-Re.

talata: demolished stone blocks (maybe from the Arabic for 'three hand breadths', describing their dimensions).

Ta-Mehu: Lower Egypt: from just south of Memphis to the north coast of Egypt.

tekenu: human-headed sack-like object of unknown function, depicted drawn by cattle on a sled in funerary processions.

Tura: limestone quarry on the east bank of the Nile, across the river from Memphis.

tyet: protective amulet; girdle or blood of Isis.

udjat-eye: (or *wadjat*-eye or Eye of Horus) protective amulet; symbolizing healing/making whole/strength/perfection.

uraeus: rearing cobra worn on king's forehead as part of his headdress; poised to spit poison at enemies.

vizier: the highest official, the king's right-hand man.

wab-priest: most common priestly title, indicating that the priest was purified (or perhaps a purifier).

wadj: 'green'; papyrus-form amulet symbolizing freshness/flourishing/youth/joy.

was-sceptre: animal-headed sceptre; amulet of power/divinity/well being/prosperity.

wep renpet: 'opening of the year'; New Year festival.

Museums with Egyptian Collections

Many centuries of plunder, exchange, archaeological excavation and universal fascination with Egyptology have resulted in the dispersal of ancient Egyptian artefacts and the accumulation of important collections throughout the world.

Australia
Melbourne National Gallery of Victoria
Sydney Australian Museum, Nicholson Museum of Antiquities, Ancient History Teaching Collection

Austria
Vienna Kunsthistorisches Museum

Belgium
Antwerp Museum Vleeshuis
Brussels Musées Royaux d'Art et d'Histoire
Liège Musée Curtius
Mariemont Musée de Mariemont

Brazil
Rio de Janeiro Museu Nacional

Canada
Montreal McGill University, Ethnological Museum, Museum of Fine Arts
Toronto Royal Ontario Museum

Cuba
Havana Museo Nacional

Czechoslovakia
Prague Náprstkovo Muzeum

Denmark
Copenhagen Nationalmuseet, Ny Carlsberg Glyptotek, Thorwaldsen Museum

Egypt
Alexandria Graeco-Roman Museum
Aswan Museum on the Island of Elephantine
Cairo Egyptian Museum
Luxor Luxor Museum
Mallawi Mallawi Museum
Minya Minya Museum

France
Avignon Musée Calvet
Grenoble Musée de Peinture et de Sculpture

Limoges Musée Municipal
Lyons Musée des Beaux-Arts, Musée Guimet
Marseilles Musée d'Archéologie
Nantes Musée des Arts Décoratifs
Orléans Musée Historique et d'Archéologie de l'Orléanais
Paris Bibliothèque Nationale, Louvre, Musée du Petit Palais, Musée Rodin
Strasbourg Institut d'Egyptologie
Toulouse Musée Georges Labit

Germany
Berlin Staatliche Museen: Ägyptisches Museum, Staatliche Museen: Papyrussammlung, Staatliche Museen: Preussischer Kulturbesitz,
Dresden Albertinum
Essen Folkwang Museum
Frankfurt-am-Main Liebieghaus
Hamburg Museum für Kunst und Gewerbe, Museum für Völkerkunde
Hanover Kestner-Museum
Heidelberg Ägyptologisches Institut der Universität
Hildesheim Roemer-Pelizaeus-Museum
Karlsruhe Badisches Landesmuseum
Leipzig Ägyptisches Museum
Munich Staatliche Sammlung: Ägyptischer Kunst
Tübingen Ägyptologisches Institut der Universität
Würzburg Martin von Wagner Museum der Universität

Greece
Athens National Museum

Hungary
Budapest Szépmüvészeti Múzeum

Ireland
Dublin National Museum of Ireland

Italy
Bologna Museo Civico
Florence Museo Archeologico
Mantua Museo del Palazzo Ducale
Milan Museo Archeologico
Naples Museo Nazionale
Palermo Museo Nazionale
Parma Museo Nazionale di Antichità
Rome Museo Barracco, Museo Capitolino, Museo Nazionale Romano delle Terme Diocleziane
Rovigo Museo dell'Accademia delle Concordi
Trieste Civico Museo di Storta ed Arte
Turin Museo Egizio

Vatican Museo Gregoriano Egizte
Venice Museo Archeologico del Palazze, Reale di Venezia

Japan
Kyoto University Archaeological Museum

Mexico
Mexico City Museo Nacional de Antropologia

Netherlands
Amsterdam Allard Pierson Museum
Leiden Rijksmuseum van Oudheden
Otterlo Rijksmuseum Kröller-Müller

Poland
Kraków Muzeum Naradowe
Warsaw Muzeum Narodowe

Portugal
Lisbon Fundação Calouste Gulbenkian

Russia
Leningrad State Hermitage Museum
Moscow State Pushkin Museum of Fine Arts

Spain
Madrid Museo Arqueológico Nacional

Sudan
Khartum Sudan Museum

Sweden
Linköping Östergöttlands Museum
Lund Kulturhistoriska Museet
Stockholm Medelhavsmuseet
Uppsala Victoriamuseum

Switzerland
Basel Museum für Völkerkunde
Geneva Musée d'Art et d'Histoire
Lausanne Musée Cantonal d'Archéologie et d'Histoire,
Musée Cantonal des Beaux-Arts
Neuchâtel Musée d'Ethnographie
Riggisberg Abegg-Stiftung

United Kingdom
Birmingham Birmingham Museum and Art Gallery
Bolton Bolton Museum and Art Gallery
Bristol City Museum and Art Gallery
Cambridge Fitzwilliam Museum

Dundee Museum and Art Gallery
Durham Durham University Oriental Museum
Edinburgh Royal Museum of Scotland
Glasgow Art Gallery and Museum, Burrell Collection, Hunterian Museum
Leicester Museum and Art Gallery
Liverpool Museum of Archaeology, Classics and Oriental Studies
London British Museum, Horniman Museum, Petrie Museum of Egyptian Archaeology, Victoria and Albert Museum
Manchester Manchester Museum
Norwich Castle Museum
Oxford Ashmolean Museum of Art and Archaeology, Pitt Rivers Museum
Swansea Swansea Museum

United States of America
Baltimore (Md.) Walters Art Gallery
Berkeley (Ca.) Robert H. Lowie Museum of Anthropology
Boston (Mass.) Museum of Fine Arts
Brooklyn (N.Y.) Brooklyn Museum
Cambridge (Mass.) Fogg Art Museum, Harvard University, Semitic Museum, Harvard University
Chicago (Ill.) Field Museum of Natural History, Oriental Institute Museum
Cincinnati (Ohio) Art Museum
Cleveland (Ohio) Museum of Art
Denver (Col.) Art Museum
Detroit (Mich.) Detroit Institute of Arts
Kansas City (Miss.) William Rockhill Nelson Gallery of Art
Los Angeles (Ca.) County Museum of Art
Minneapolis (Minn.) Institute of Arts Museum
New Haven (Conn.) Yale University Art Gallery
New York Metropolitan Museum of Art
Palo Alto (Ca.) Stanford University Museum
Philadelphia (Pa.) Pennsylvania University Museum
Pittsburgh (Pa.) Museum of Art, Carnegie Institute
Princeton (N.J.) University Art Museum
Providence (R.I.) Rhode Island School of Design
Richmond (Va.) Museum of Fine Arts
St Louis (Miss.) Art Museum
San Diego (Ca.) Museum of Man
San Francisco (Ca.) M. H. De Young Memorial Museum
San José (Ca.) Rosicrucian Museum
Seattle (Wash.) Art Museum
Toledo (Ohio) Museum of Art
Washington D.C. Smithsonian Institution
Worcester (Mass.) Art Museum

from the *Atlas of Ancient Egypt* by John Baines and Jaromir Malek

Suggested Further Reading

Adams, B., *Egyptian Mummies* (Shire, 1984)

Allen, J.P. et al., *Religion and Philosophy in Ancient Egypt* (New Haven, 1989)

Andrews, C., *Egyptian Mummies* (British Museum Press, 1984)

Andrews, C., *Amulets of Ancient Egypt* (British Museum Press, 1994)

Baines, J. & **Malek,** J., *Atlas of Ancient Egypt* (Phaidon, 1984)

Bierbrier, M., *The Tomb Builders of the Pharaohs* (British Museum Press, 1982)

Bleeker, C.J., *Egyptian Festivals, Enactments of Religious Renewal* (Leiden, 1967)

Bleeker, C.J., *Hathor and Thoth* (Leiden, 1973)

Borghouts, J.F., *Ancient Egyptian Magical Texts* (E.J. Brill, 1978)

Bowman, A.K., *Egypt after the Pharaohs* (Guild, 1986)

David, A.R., *A Guide to Religious Ritual at Abydos* (Warminster, 1980)

David, R., *The Pyramid Builders of Ancient Egypt* (Routledge and Kegan Paul, 1986)

Dodson, A., *Egyptian Rock-cut Tombs* (Shire, 1991)

Englund, G. (ed.), *The Religion of the Ancient Egyptians: Cognitive Structures and Popular Expressions* (Uppsala, 1989)

Fairman, H.W., *The Triumph of Horus* (Batsford, 1974)

Faulkner, R.O., *The Ancient Egyptian Pyramid Texts* (Oxford University Press, 1969)

Faulkner, R.O., *The Ancient Egyptian Coffin Texts* (2 vols) (Aris and Phillips, 1973, 1977, 1987)

Faulkner, R.O., *The Ancient Egyptian Book of the Dead* (British Museum Press, 1989)

Foster, J.L., *Hymns, Prayers and Songs, An Anthology of Ancient Egyptian Lyric Poetry* (Scholars Press, Atlanta, Georgia, 1995)

Frankfort, H., *Kingship and the Gods, a study of Near Eastern Religion as the Integration of Society and Nature* (University of Chicago Press, 1948)

Ghalioungui, P., *Medicine and Magic in Ancient Egypt* (London, 1963)

Gwyn-Griffiths, J., *Plutarch's De Iside et Osiride* (University of Wales, 1970)

Hart, G., *Egyptian Myths* (British Museum Press, 1990)

Hart, G., *A Dictionary of Egyptian Gods and Goddesses* (Routledge & Kegan Paul, 1986)

Herodotus, *The Histories* (Penguin, 1972)

Hornung, E., *Conceptions of God in Ancient Egypt: The One and the Many* (Routledge & Kegan Paul, 1983)

Iversen, E., *The Myth of Egypt and its Hieroglyphs in European Tradition* (Copenhagen, 1961)

Janssen, R.& J., *Growing Up in Ancient Egypt* (Rubicon, 1990)

Kemp, B.J., *Ancient Egypt: Anatomy of a Civilisation* (Routledge, 1989, reprint 1991)

Lehner, M., *The Complete Pyramids* (Thames & Hudson, 1997)

Lichtheim, M., *Ancient Egyptian Literature Vol. I-III* (University of California, 1973-80)

Meeks, D. & **Favard-Meeks,** C., *Daily Life of the Egyptian Gods* (London, 1996)

Morenz, S., *Egyptian Religion* (Methuen, 1973)

Nunn, J.F., *Ancient Egyptian Medicine* (British Museum Press, 1997)

Pinch, G., *New Kingdom Votive Offerings to Hathor* (Oxford, 1993)

Pinch, G., *Magic in Ancient Egypt* (British Museum Press, 1994)

Quirke, S., *Who were the Pharaohs?* (British Museum Press, 1990)

Quirke, S., *Ancient Egyptian Religion* (British Museum Press, 1992)

Quirke, S., *Hieroglyphs and the Afterlife in Ancient Egypt* (British Museum Press, 1996)

Redford, D.B., *Akhenaten: The Heretic King* (Princeton, 1984)

Reeves, N., *The Complete Tutankhamun* (Thames and Hudson, 1990)

Reeves, N. & **Wilkinson,** R.H., *The Complete Valley of the Kings* (Thames and Hudson, 1996)

Robins, G., *Women in Ancient Egypt* (British Museum Press, 1993)

Romer, J., *Ancient Lives* (Henry Holt and Co., 1984)

Sadek, A.I., *Popular Religion in Egypt during the New Kingdom* (Hildesheim, 1987)

Sauneron, S., *The Priests of Ancient Egypt* (Grove, 1960)

Shafer, B.E., (ed.), *Religion in Ancient Egypt* (Cornell, 1991)

Shaw, I. & **Nicholson,** P., *British Museum Dictionary of Ancient Egypt* (British Museum Press, 1995)

Snape, S. *Egyptian Temples* (Shire, 1996)

Spencer, A.J., *Death in Ancient Egypt* (Penguin, 1982)

Taylor, J.H., *Death and the Afterlife in Ancient Egypt* (British Museum Press, 1999)

Velde, H. te, *Seth, God of Confusion* (2nd edn) (1977)

Watson, P., *Egyptian Pyramids and Mastaba Tombs* (Shire, 1987)

Wildung, D., *Egyptian Saints: Deification in Pharaonic Egypt* (New York University Press, 1977)

Wilkinson, R.H., *Reading Egyptian Art: A Hieroglyphic Guide to Ancient Egyptian Painting and Sculpture* (Thames and Hudson, 1992)

Acknowledgements

AKG Photographic
p7 top (Agyptisches Museum, Berlin), 12–13, 18 bottom (Egyptian Museum, Cairo), 19 left, p28 (Louvre, Paris), p29 bottom (Louvre, Paris), p32 top, p32 bottom (Luxor Museum), p39 (British Museum, London), p41 top (Kunthistorisches Museum, Vienna), p45 bottom, 46 left, p54 top, p66 (National Maritime Museum, Haifa), p77 bottom (Egyptian Museum, Cairo), p83 bottom (Kunthistorisches Museum, Vienna), p88–89, p92 top, p100–101, p114 right, p118, p121 (Roemer-Pelizaeus Museum, Hildesheim), p124 right (Louvre, Paris), p130 left (Egyptian Museum, Cairo), p138–139 (British Museum, London), p145 bottom (Aegyptisches Museum, Berlin), p165 (Aegyptisches Museum, Berlin), p168 top, p175 bottom, p176, p179 right (Louvre, Paris), p186 top and bottom, p195 top, p196, p197 Kunsthistorisches Museum, p212, p217 bottom, p224 bottom (Rijksmuseum van Oudheden), p230 top, p238 top, p241 (Louvre, Paris), p242

A M Dodson
p156 right, p208 top, p231 (Museum of Metropolitan Art, New York)

The Ancient Art & Architecture Collection
p8 bottom, p18 top, 36 bottom, 38 bottom, p58 top, p59 left, p64 left, p65 bottom, p67 top and bottom, p68, p71 right, p78 top, p102 top and bottom, p109, p110, p111 bottom, p112 bottom, p116 left, p119 top and bottom, p128 top, p131 right, p146, p148 bottom, p149, p161 left, p164 right, p169, p182 bottom, p204 top, p209, p213 left, p215 bottom, p218, p219 bottom, p220, p 229

The Ancient Egypt Picture Library
p19 right, p20, p30 top, 38 top (Egyptian Museum, Cairo), p43, 45 top, 47 top, p52 bottom, p56, p58 bottom, p62 bottom (Louvre, Paris), p64 right, p70 left, p80 bottom (British Museum, London), p84, p92 bottom, p94 bottom, p103 bottom, p105 top, p106, p108 bottom, p115 top, p120 right (British Museum, London), p122 bottom (British Museum, London), p133 top, p148 top, p156 left (British Museum, London), p168 bottom (British Museum, London), p175 top, p179 left, p184 bottom, p185 (Fitzwilliam Museum, University of Cambridge), p190, Egyptian Museum, Cairo), p193 top (Egyptian Museum, Cairo), p197 top, p200 left (Louvre, Paris), p204 bottom (Egyptian Museum, Cairo), p207 (Egyptian Museum, Cairo), p211 top, p219 top, p222 top (British Museum, London), p225 top (British Museum, London), p226 bottom (Louvre, Paris), p227 top and bottom, p230 bottom, p232 bottom, p233, p234, p243 top

The Art Archive
p6 bottom, p10 bottom, p21 right (Egyptian Museum, Cairo), p22 (Egyptian Museum, Cairo), p29 top (Egyptian Museum, Cairo), p31, p34 top, 37 top (Egyptian Museum, Cairo), p42 top, p70 right (Egyptian Museum, Cairo), p71 left (Louvre, Paris), p94 top (Egyptian Museum, Cairo), p113, p116 right (Egyptian Museum, Cairo), p120 left (Louvre, Paris), p143top right (Egyptian Museum, Cairo),

p145 top (British Museum, London), p150 top, p159 bottom (Louvre, Paris), p163 (Egyptian Museum, Cairo), p166 top (British Museum, London), p174 bottom, p181 top left (Egyptian Museum, Cairo), p184 top (Egyptian Museum, Turin), p187, p194 (Egyptian Museum, Cairo), p199 (British Museum, London), p205, top (Egyptian Museum, Cairo), p213 right (Louvre, Paris), p215 top (British Museum, London), p217 left (Louvre, Paris), p224 bottom (Egyptian Museum, Cairo), p226 top (British Museum, London), p228 (Egyptian Museum, Cairo), p236–237 (Luigi Mayer, 'Views in Egypt', 1801), p238 bottom (Antalya Museum), p240 top (British Museum), p243 bottom (Civic Museum, Turin)

The Bridgeman Art Library
p2 (British Museum, London), p9 left (The Louvre, Paris), p10 top (Ashmolean Museum, Oxford), p21 left (Louvre, Paris), p23 left (Freud Museum, London), p23 right (Ashmolean Museum, Oxford), p33 bottom (British Museum), p35 top (Louvre, Paris), p40 top (Sir John Soane Museum, London), p40 bottom (Louvre, Paris), p41 bottom (British Museum, London), p42 bottom (Louvre, Paris), p46 right, p51 bottom (British Museum, London), p 54 bottom (Fitzwilliam Museum, University of Cambridge), p57 (Stapleton Collection), p61 bottom (British Museum, London), p62 top (Freud Museum, London), p69 (Ashmolean Museum, Oxford), p74 top (Ashmolean Museum, Oxford), p74 bottom, p78 bottom (Giraudon), p80 top (British Museum, London), p82 (Fitzwilliam Museum, Cambridge), p85 bottom (Bode Museum, Berlin), p93, p95 bottom, p98, p99 top, 108 top, p114 left, p122 top (Louvre), p123 (Louvre, Paris), p130 right, p132 (Ashmolean Museum, Oxford), p140 bottom (Fitzwilliam Museum, Cambridge), p141 (Louvre, Paris), p147 top (British Museum, London, p147 bottom (Louvre, Paris), p 153 top (Louvre, Paris), p153 bottom (British Museum, London), p154 (Louvre, Paris), p155 right (Bonhams, London), p158 (Ashmolean Museum, Oxford), p159 top (British Museum, London), p164 left (British Museum, London), p166 bottom (Ashmolean Museum, Oxford), p167 right (Louvre, Paris), p167 left (Ashmolean Museum, Oxford), p170–171, p172 (Louvre, Paris), p181 bottom (Fitzwilliam Museum, University of Cambridge), p202 (Louvre, Paris), p211 bottom (Louvre, Paris), p222 bottom (Ashmolean Museum, Oxford), p224 top (Egyptian Museum, Turin), p232 top (Louvre, Paris), p239 (Museo Archeologico Prenestino, Palestrina), p244 top (The Illustrated London, News Picture Library, London)

C M Dixon
p27 right (National Museum, Florence)

Hulton Getty
p245 top and bottom

The Hutchinson Library
p177 top

Lucia Gahlin
p9 right, p30 bottom, 35 bottom, p50, p87 top, p99 bottom, p103 top, p111 top, p112 top, p128 bottom, p129, p177 bottom, p192, p208 bottom

Michael Holford
p27 left (British Museum, London), p27 middle (British Museum, London), p33 top, p198 left (British Museum, London), p203 top, p216 (British Museum, London), p223 (British Museum, London)

Peter Clayton
p37 bottom, p52 top, p63, p72 top and bottom, p81, p83 top, p115 bottom, p124 left

Robert Harding
p6 top, p36 top (Egyptian Museum, Cairo), p53, p85 top, p87 bottom, p95 top, p133 left, p182 top, p183 top and bottom (both Egyptian Museum, Cairo), p201

Sylvia Cordaiy Photo Library
p8 top, p104 top, p173 top (Guy Marks), p174 top, p178 (Johnathan Smith)

Travel Ink
p16–17, p55, p73, p79, p104 bottom

Veneta Bullen
p244 bottom (The Griffith Institure/Ashmolean Museum, Oxford)

Werner Forman Archive
p24 (Egyptian Museum, Cairo), p34 bottom (Egyptian Museum, Cairo), p47 bottom (Egyptian Museum, Cairo), p51 top (Schultz Collection, New York), p59 right (Egyptian Museum), p60, p61 top (courtesy L'Ibis, New York), p65 top, p75 (Archaelological Museum, Khartoum), p76 (E Strouhal), p77 top (Egyptian Museum, Cairo), p86, 105 bottom, p107 top and bottom, p117 (Louvre, Paris), p125 (Egyptian Museum, Cairo), p126–7 (Brooklyn Museum, New York), p131 left (Egyptian Museum, Cairo), p134–135, p140 top, p142 (Dr E Strouhal), p143 bottom left and right, p144 (Louvre, Paris), p150 bottom (E Strouhal), p151, p152 (Egyptian Museum, Cairo), p155 left (private collection), p157 (Egyptian Museum, Cairo), p160 (British Museum, London), p161 right (Egyptian Museum, Cairo), p162 left (Egyptian Museum, Cairo), p162 right (E Strouhal), p180 (Cheops Barque Museum), p181 top right, p188–189, p191 (Manchester Museum), p193 (Metropolitan Museum of Art, New York), p195 bottom (Graeco-Roman Museum, Alexandria), p198 right (Rijksmuseum van Oudeheden, Leiden), p200 right (Aegyptisches Museum, Berlin), p203 bottom (Fitzwilliam Museum, University of Cambridge), p205 (Sold at Christie's, London), p206 (British Museum, London), p210 (Egyptian Museum, Turin), p214, p221, p235, p240 bottom (Egyptian Museum, Cairo)

Index